A Jungian Analysis of Toxic Modern Society

Using evidence from anthropology, neuroscience, psychiatry, analytical psychology, and evolutionary biology, within this book Dr. Erik Goodwyn explores the current cultural psyche, and how elements of modern society are contributing to the current loneliness epidemic.

Despite tremendous advances in technology, developed countries are more anxious, depressed, suicidal, and addicted today than we were 100 years ago. Why? Research from many fields of study show that loneliness has become an epidemic in the industrialized world, causing very real medical consequences such as addiction, depression, anxiety, and suicide: all things which have been on the rise for decades. And yet, because of various historical, philosophical, and economic reasons, we do not nurture traditional cultural ways of satisfying these instincts. This book will explore the idea that stopping the rising misery will not only require socioeconomic changes, but will require a profound cultural change. Only then will we be able to stop the slow starvation of social belonging, archetypal narratives, rituals, spirituality, and images as vessels of meaning.

This will be an insightful read for depth psychologists and scholars of analytical psychology, as well as health care providers, therapists, sociologists, and those with an interest in cross-cultural studies.

Erik Goodwyn, MD, is Clinical Faculty with the Billings Clinic, part of the WWAMI University of Washington School of Medicine—Billings Montana affiliate, Department of Psychiatry and part of the adjunct faculty for both the University of Louisville and the University of Kentucky. He has authored numerous publications in the field of consciousness studies, Jungian psychology, neuroscience, mythology, philosophy, anthropology, and the psychology of religion. www.erikgoodwyn.com

'This evocative, informative and wide-ranging study of loneliness does not pretend to offer a cure but instead explores the rising tides of depression, addictions, suicides and anxiety disorders and the reasons behind them. Dr Goodwyn argues that the present emphasis on individual medication and individual psychotherapy tends to ignore the community and the influence of sociocultural factors and their effect in the decline of mental health, particularly in the US. He suggests that we look carefully at the debilitating nature of our modern infrastructures, their fast competitive, impersonal pace and their consummate consumerism. Such societal structures leave us hungry and desperate for deeper soul connections that might unify rather than separate us. Dr Goodwyn's multifaceted exploration into the feelings of loneliness that affect our mental health and wellbeing is a much-needed and heartfelt enquiry.'

Dr Elizabeth Brodersen, *Accredited Training Analyst and Supervisor, C.G. Jung Institute, Zürich, editor,* Jungian Dimensions of the Mourning Process, Burial Rituals and Access to the Land of the Dead: Intimations of Immorality, *(2023)*

'Erik Goodwyn M.D.'s latest book, *A Jungian Analysis of Toxic Modern Society: Fighting the Culture of Loneliness* is a timely commentary for our troubled times. Human beings thrive or perish in the soil of the culture. Each one of us has evolved survival, social and spiritual instincts for claiming our highest potential. Current culture is skewed towards a survival instinct misguided by the false gods of digitalization, materialism, narcissism and exploitation of environment and fellow human beings leading to a culture of isolation, addiction, and depression. We are in danger of losing several generations of our youth globally to this toxic culture. What stands out is the book's underlying message of hope: he provides not just a diagnosis but also a compelling roadmap for the restoration of our social and spiritual soil fed by the treasures of our depths and transcendence. The seeds of the soul that sprout in this soil blossom into flowers and fruits of meaning and purpose. This is a timely, relevant and an essential prescription for our times and a must read for seekers and scholars alike.'

Ashok Bedi, M.D., *Psychiatrist and Jungian analyst, author,* Path to the Soul *and other works at www.pathtotheosoul.com*

'Jungian psychiatrist Erik Goodwyn laments our current state of affairs where the human being has become objectified by biological science, fed medications like a lab rat, and stripped of the holistic commitments that make us uniquely relational and spiritual creatures. As people increasingly suffer in isolation and meaninglessness, the individual becomes sequestered to a lonely existence divorced from the greater communal life of the collective. Rethinking the machinations of Western medicine and capitalistic incentives that keep us enslaved in hegemonic power systems dominated by reductive ideologies, Goodwyn implores us to nurture the sociocultural dimensions of mental health aimed to remedy our malaise from the toxicity of our alienating environments. We have all but ignored our social craving for belonging eclipsed by digital realities and pseudo-cultural mass media that reinforce the pain of aloneness underlying our collective pathos. This book attempts to reorient us to actualize our craving for authentic relationality as social beings in search of soul. An important treatise on reintroducing the humanization of psychiatry in our age of the brain.'

Prof. Jon Mills, *University of Essex, author*, End of the World:
Civilization and Its Fate

A Jungian Analysis of Toxic Modern Society

Fighting the Culture of Loneliness

Erik Goodwyn

Routledge
Taylor & Francis Group

LONDON AND NEW YORK

Designed cover image: © Getty Images

First published 2025
by Routledge
4 Park Square, Milton Park, Abingdon, Oxon OX14 4RN

and by Routledge
605 Third Avenue, New York, NY 10158

Routledge is an imprint of the Taylor & Francis Group, an informa business

© 2025 Erik Goodwyn

The right of Erik Goodwyn to be identified as author of this work has been asserted in accordance with sections 77 and 78 of the Copyright, Designs and Patents Act 1988.

British Library Cataloguing-in-Publication Data
A catalogue record for this book is available from the British Library

ISBN: 978-1-032-72133-0 (hbk)
ISBN: 978-1-032-72136-1 (pbk)
ISBN: 978-1-032-72135-4 (ebk)

DOI: 10.4324/9781032721354

Typeset in Times New Roman
by Taylor & Francis Books

For Dad
You taught me how to think among the clouds
And seek the farthest horizon
Someday we will meet again

Contents

Chapter Abstracts

Chapter 1: Can Culture Be Toxic?

In this chapter I introduce the rationale for looking at the social contributors of mental illness and suffering, and how it is required by the bio-psycho-social model. I introduce the fictional world of "Miseria," which is imagined to be extremely toxic, asking the question of how we would ever alleviate the suffering of people living in Miseria if all we ever did was look at their brain chemistry and particular upbringing. This begs the question of whether some cultures might be more toxic than others, which leads us to whether our own culture—i.e., that of Western industrialized nations, particularly the US—might be toxic. Then I introduce the concept of the archetypal psyche, first proposed by Jung as his "the collective unconscious," and elaborated on by subsequent research in neurobiology, evolutionary psychology, and other fields. I explain how without this theoretical structure—however it may be conceptualized—we cannot really engage with the bio-psycho-social model in any substantive depth, which makes it necessary to define. I then go on to define it using the most up to date integrated efforts available, and describe how I think it engages with culture, which is itself an expression of the archetypal psyche but shaped by historical, economic, and other factors.

Chapter 2: The Social Instincts

Then, returning to answer the above question, I call attention to what I am labeling the Social Instincts: our natural human neurobiological systems that motivate us toward pro-social and cooperative behavior. By using well-known and established concepts in evolutionary biology and neuroscience, I review evidence that just like we have powerful instincts that guide us toward food and sex, and away from physical damage, we have just as powerful (if not more powerful) instincts that motivate us to seek social connection and avoid rejection or abandonment. These are divided into the individual (long-term mate seeking), interpersonal (family and friend-network seeking), and collective (community and tribe seeking) dimensions. These instincts, part of the archetypal psyche, however, are starving, as evidenced by the rising rates of depression, anxiety, addiction, and suicide over the last 100 years that coincide with cultural changes that appear to be implicated in these rising rates. Normally, such impulses are sated using traditional cultural means that Jungians are known for exploring in depth—myth, ritual, and symbol—i.e., with archetypal images and patterns. For various reasons, however, modern culture does not avail itself of these methods to an adequate degree, leading to the slow starvation of our Social Instincts. Why are these traditional methods not utilized? In the next few chapters I explore what I think the answers are.

Chapter 3: Hyper-Individualism

One way in which the social connections and archetypal expressions have slowly degraded and broken down over time is the increasing emphasis on individualism. Archetypal expressions of myth, ritual, and narrative are inherently social efforts requiring social contact and exchange to foster. The trend toward hyper-individualism, however, makes such expressions difficult to manage, and this trend toward hyper-individualism has been noted by anthropologists and sociologists for many years. In this chapter I examine the way in which our culture has slowly pulled us away from nurturing social connections at the expense of pursuing narcissistic self-absorbed pursuits instead. Various historical trends are behind this phenomenon, including widespread economic and technology changes, and many other complex factors. The end result is a negative impact on our social connections, particularly at the community level. I emphasize the complexity of the problem here, in that increasing emphasis on the individual over the community has caused and has been caused by a number of socioeconomic and technological changes in this country. These factors, I argue, will not be satisfied without viewing them through the lens of analytical psychology, as the means of addressing them will by necessity need to include a discussion of ritual and symbol in social interaction, as well as the value systems.

Chapter 4: Changes in Family Structure

Another factor impacting our Social Instincts is the slow disintegration of extended family and friend networks that were more common in the past and currently still exist in other cultures. Shrinking family structures and weakening of marriage bonds are implicated as partial causes of the oft-discussed loneliness epidemic plaguing many industrialized nations. Here I discuss possible reasons for this breakdown, as it relates to the hyper-individualism of the last chapter alongside other technological and social advances. The consequences of this are discussed in terms of the various kinds of "hunger" that is created when individuals are simply not present to resonate with the expectant archetypal image—i.e., the father and mother archetypes. Rather than considering these archetypes as airy abstractions or academic constructs, we find that the innate hunger for mothering and fathering that we are all born with plays out in very real ways with impacts on our mental and physical health.

Chapter 5: Spirituality

Another source of connection is that found in spirituality and religious traditions—an observation spoken of at length by Jung, but for various reasons not discussed perhaps as frequently as it should be otherwise. In this chapter I discuss how modern culture has seen a decline in spiritual and religious adherence, and what this might mean for mental health. Since non-fundamentalist religion and spirituality have been shown to correlate with greater mental health, their decline is likely to have consequences that may partially explain the worsening mental health discussed in previous chapters. The link between such traditions and social rules is discussed in terms of how such rules create and reinforce the kinds of communities that the Social Instincts target. Jung himself viewed one of the main problems for "modern man" as disordered, disengaged, and/or dissociated spirituality. With Jung, I argue that even those who reject all forms of spirituality find that this instinctive pressure that seeks greater meaning will simply operate unconsciously rather than consciously, projecting onto various "isms" or ideologies, but without any sort of counter-balance one might see in an established tradition.

Chapter 6: Nature Deficiency

In addition to the individual, interpersonal, and community aspects of the Social Instincts, I add a fourth dimension: the universal dimension, which seeks out connection with Nature. In this chapter I review the large body of evidence that shows how modern life, which commonly sees people living large portions of their lives in artificial environments, may be toxic for this reason. Evidence suggests that deprivation from natural environments may be harmful to mental health. Given the many cross-culturally appearing traditions that hold sacred beliefs of a connection between humankind and Nature, I add this to our Social Instincts as an additional dimension that is starving. Throughout world religious traditions, particularly those found in cultures with individuals who live in non-artificial environments most of their lives, Nature is seen as divine. Though this principle can be found in the more organized world religions, it is recognized even by specialists within those traditions that this principle is sometimes lost—much to our detriment. In the endless and increasingly desperate quest for meaning, the increasing amount of time modern culture spends in artificial environments, coupled with the evidence of nature deficiency, reveals this deeper need coming from the archetypal psyche. This psyche, which evolved for 99% of our existence in natural environments, comes to expect interaction with nature and inevitably will make Nature Herself a part of its pantheon.

Chapter 7: Education and Mass Media Effects

In this chapter I dive deeper into what I believe the causes are for the breakdown of social connections, looking at peculiarities of our education system and the insidious effects of mass media advertising on our Social Instincts. In depth psychology terms, much of this content is not coming from authentic sources within the psyche but rather is one-sided ego-driven content. Drawing from neuroscience studies of how we conceptualize ourselves, as well as multidisciplinary studies of culture and the mind, I explore the way our economics-driven and ubiquitous mass-media outlets likely contribute to hyper-individualism and thinning of our social resources. I also explore how and why sub-cultures form, ranging from cliques in middle school to wider counter-culture movements. These happen largely because the mass media creates what I call a "consumer pseudoculture" against which we feel the need to rebel because it is inauthentic and not based on flesh-and-blood human interaction.

Chapter 8: The Achievement-Based Value System

Alongside the other factors, I also draw from clinical experience to describe what I call an "achievement-based value system" that overemphasizes monetary and/or status gain over all else in self-assessment. This system, I believe, contributes further to the effects of our starving Social Instincts. Compounding the problem is worsening income inequality—a well-known correlate of culture-wide depression, which adds to and is caused by this toxic value system. From the perspective of depth psychology, furthermore, we can see how this value system is a major culprit in contributing to depression and anxiety by creating a tyrannical mythology that traps the ego.

Chapter 9: Modern Culture and Its Addictions

Under the current model, the many addictions I see clinically and their rise can also be connected to starving Social Instincts. The way I explain it is through the neuroscience of social connection. It is well known that attachment bonds form via the activity of the opiate systems in the brain (among others). Many addictions, furthermore, operate through this same set of neural systems, and so can be explained as halting attempts to satisfy starving Social Instincts through artificial stimulation. Things like drug addiction as well as gambling, pornography, binge eating, alcoholism, and shopping addiction operate similarly. Instead of looking at this behavior as simply triggering generic "pleasure centers," however, I ground the discussion in solid evolutionary theory and cultural awareness. This helps us to understand that addictions are actually maladaptive attempts to satisfy the Social Instincts. Early on, Jung recognized the importance of the spirit in defending oneself against addiction, which can be seen in his influence on the Alcoholics Anonymous movement. But rather than mere navel-gazing or airy abstraction, the kind of spirit needed for such effects needs to be flesh-and-blood to be effective at fending off addictions.

Chapter 10: Intimations of a Cure

I begin to bring the foregoing together in these last three chapters. I start in this one with a general review of the topics discussed so far and how they relate in so many complex ways. Overall, I look at the many causes for the breakdown of social connection (and connection with Nature) that has led to the rise of depression, anxiety, suicide, and addiction, and we can see how they are connected to our inborn and archetypal Social Instincts. As our culture has become dominated by hyper-individualism, our Social Instincts have slowly been starving over the last few generations more and more, and yet the effect has been so subtle it has been difficult to notice. From the perspective of depth psychology, furthermore, we can see how failing to attend to such instincts will often lead to neurotic suffering. Nevertheless, we can understand these symptoms as halting attempts to *heal* the starvation, which helps to orient and understand the current condition in a much more substantial way.

Chapter 11: Tribalism—The Dose Makes the Poison

In this chapter I look at one of the ways in which people maladaptively try to satisfy starving Social Instincts: by succumbing to tribalistic thinking, meaning behaviors typical of cults, extreme fundamentalists, and reactionary groups rife with hate and bigotry. I explain why these reactions to starving Social Instincts happen, and why they so commonly recruit paranoia and hatred as part of their connective fabric. Tribalism, we see, is a danger that we must be cognizant of when trying to heal our starving Social Instincts. As discussed in interdisciplinary work on social connection and psychology, in the climate of modern society, we are at risk for the emergence of such extremists due to the primordial, emotional nature of our Social Instincts. This chapter explains the causes of such extremism and suggests ways we can try to rebuild social connection and cautiously move away from hyper-individualism without catapulting into extreme overcorrection.

Chapter 12: The Meaning-Making Organ

In this chapter I explain that at the most fundamental level, the brain's primary function is in the construction of *meaning*. This is manifest in many different ways, in particular via the clinical observation of what Jung called the "transcendent function." This is a function of the human imagination, and it continues to seek deeper and wider meanings and connections in the chaotic swirl of everyday life. Its products are that of emotionally oriented self-narrative. These narratives moreover tend to be symbolic in nature, as symbol and metaphor are tools that allow us to condense and encapsulate the greatest expressions of meaning. As such, this natural, inborn element of the psyche is what clinicians use to promote health and well-being, but it is not a perfect process and it is often stymied by conflict, contradiction, and inadequate environmental nurturing. In this chapter I explore how the current worsening of mental health can be seen as largely an attempt of the individual mind to adapt to an inherently toxic/inadequate environment.

Chapter 13: The Quest for Sustenance

In the final chapter I recap the previous chapters, with an eye for the big picture. I warn that the situation we are in now will not be fixed easily or quickly, and there will be important balancing acts we will need to navigate to avoid making the situation worse. I review what appear to be the causes of toxic modern life and ways in which this knowledge suggests an antidote to it that will resonate with our human nature at the deep level, using tools perhaps well-known to indigenous cultures worldwide, but distant from modern, developed cultures around the world.

Chapter 1

Can Culture Be Toxic?

The Bio-Psycho-Social Model

Swiss psychiatrist Carl Jung argued that the way in which the individual interacts with culture is complex:

> We always find in the patient a conflict which at a certain point is connected with the great problems of society... [T]he apparently individual conflict of the patient is revealed as a universal conflict of his environment and epoch. Neurosis is thus nothing less than an individual attempt, however unsuccessful, to solve a universal problem.
>
> (Jung, CW7, §438, p. 265)

As a psychiatrist, I was taught to examine the biological, psychological, and social roots of mental illness, following the model first proposed by George Engel and John Romano in 1977. In this approach to diagnosis and treatment, illness and wellness are not defined as solely due to fluctuations in biomedical variables, but rather are argued to depend on a complex interplay between a person's biological status in the context of their human relationships, not only to other individuals but to the wider culture in which they are a part.

This means when looking at mental illness, we need to examine not only what the neurochemical and/or neuroanatomical contributors might be, but also how those biological states affect and are affected by a person's psychological state, social state, and (some add) their spiritual beliefs. All of these parts of our experience, the model argues, are important variables to examine. And in medical school and subsequent residency training, I was taught, and continue to teach, that when trying to understand a patient, one must consider all these domains of human experience and not simply focus on one.

And yet, despite this teaching philosophy being prevalent in US medical schools, I do not feel we have achieved the ideal set forth by Engel and Romano—not to the fullest it could be. Often (particularly in the popular discourse) we focus too much on psychopharmacology and not on interpersonal and sociocultural or psychospiritual contexts that might play a

DOI: 10.4324/9781032721354-1

significant part in their suffering. Part of this is (as we will discuss later) to do with our own culture being extremely focused on the individual rather than a person's community. Mental illness is seen as *your* problem with *your* brain chemicals, and *you* need to go see a doctor and "get it fixed." Family structures, social constructs and systems, spiritual values, community belonging, economic factors, and much else are all either given lip service or simply ignored in favor of our two primary modes of healing: individual medications and intensive individual psychotherapy. When a person suffers, it is assumed to be that person's problem, *not* the society's problem.

The main goal of this book is to argue that individual medications and therapy alone are not going to be enough to stem the tide of rising depression, addictions, suicide, and anxiety disorders that we are seeing and have been seeing over the last century. We need to think on a larger scale and take a long, hard look at the way we do things in the Western world, the US in particular, and ask some tough questions. Most of the book deals with identifying the problems and their most likely causes. It is therefore primarily a diagnosis, not a list of cures. I also recognize that many of my suggestions are likely to fall upon deaf ears because they involve major structural changes to our society as a whole, and those structures are the way they are because of whom they profit. Hence, they are not likely to change without resistance, nor are many going to be immediately applicable in a directly concrete way without further work. In other words, I'm diagnosing the problem and trying to root out the causes, but I don't have all the answers as to the cure, so don't expect that. I also think that what needs to change is not something anyone especially wants to change. Perhaps I'm wrong about that.

In any case, while huge amounts of work have been done in elucidating the neurobiological and individual psychological contributors to common mental illnesses like depression and anxiety, less work has been done on the *sociocultural* contributors to it. That is what this book is really about. And as I said, though society is not likely to change quickly or soon, I have found that a greater recognition of the social contributors to mental illness can be useful for health care providers, and for interested lay persons as well that might suffer from these ailments. The first step, however, is to examine what we really mean by "sociocultural contributors" to suffering and how it might relate to the other domains of experience. To do that I have created a fictional culture to illustrate what I am getting at throughout this book.

Miseria

Imagine for a moment that you and your family are instantly transported to a completely different world. Let's call it Miseria. In Miseria, life is difficult: to go anywhere, you have to walk through hundred degree tunnels covered with spiky metal rivets. Nobody has any shoes, and nobody knows how to make them. The air is constantly horrid smelling, and you never seem to get used to it. Meals are exactly the same every day, 365 days a year: a thin, pasty gruel that keeps you alive somehow. Everywhere you go, there are monitors of robots telling you that you need this and that, and you need to spend all your money on it, so much that it's hard to get the messages out of your head even when they stop, which is rare. In Miseria, music is not forbidden; it's just forgotten. Nobody knows any songs and whenever anyone starts to sing one, the robots chime in about how their song is terrible, outdated, stupid, and they should really stop all that nonsense. All other art forms are treated in the same fashion, as are any expressions of meaning beyond what is concretely right in front of you. No expressions of intangible values, no spiritual beliefs—none of that. Nobody knows any, and all efforts at creating them from the imagination are quickly muted.

Sleeping arrangements in Miseria are tiny, cramped steel boxes with no padding. Everything is a mazework of metal and rivets. The sun is never seen, nor the sky, nor anything else but robots and steel hallways. All work is mind-less repetitive tasks that are dangerous and mentally numbing. Everyone is separated constantly in their own private metal cubicles day after day, forever and ever, with no end in sight. Medical problems are addressed by injecting people with needles and subjecting them to tests all handled by the robots. Otherwise, every day is exactly the same as the next. No stories are told, and reproduction is handled in a sterile manner by machines and incubation chambers. Physical contact is impossible, and anyone caught looking at anyone else is "conditioned" by pain-inducing chips implanted in their eyes from birth. On the rare occasion where people wind up in the same area, they are so con-fused and disoriented they usually end up attacking each other viciously.

How might Miseria handle mental illness? Well, if they do it the way we do it, if any subject of Miseria complains that she or he is sad, they would be carted off to a doctor robot and "fixed." After all, your misery is *your* pro-blem. You need to adapt and adjust. Now you can see what I'm getting at.

A Thought Experiment

Clearly, Miseria is so awful it's a caricature. It's a deliberately extreme exam-ple, but I'm doing so for illustrative purposes. Obviously you or I wouldn't like Miseria very much; that's not the question I'm asking. The question I'm asking is whether or not some environments are healthier than others. As a physician, health is something I spend a lot of time thinking about. As a psychiatrist, I most often encounter the subject of health from a mental per-spective. On this question, I ask, what sorts of environments are mentally healthy. What ones aren't?

I think if any of us were whisked away to Miseria, we would rapidly dete-riorate and probably either waste away or commit suicide. But what if we were raised in Miseria? What if that was all we knew our entire life? Would we still be miserable? Couldn't we "adapt" to our surroundings? After all, aren't humans adaptable to changing cultural environments? We hear it all the time: we live in a rapidly changing world, and we can/should change along with it! It is often understood that we will. And, as environments and needs change, morals and values change, the rules change, we change, and on it goes. But the question remains: how far does this go? Just how much nastiness can *Homo sapiens* adapt to without seeing serious health repercussions, even in people raised in such an environment? I think *Homo sapiens* would not survive Miseria. Individuals that made it to adulthood (which would be few if any) would not resemble humans very much, even though they might share our basic DNA structure. In fact, I speculate that such an environment would probably destroy whatever semblance of a species there was—or that if through some miracle humans somehow mutated enough to survive it, it would become something other than human in the thousands of years it would take.

And that's really what we're talking about here: evolution. Humans evolved in a specific sort of environment. We evolved as cooperative, nomadic foraging primates that lived kind of like sophisticated wolves in warm climates. We lived in tribal bands in largely natural environments with very little in the way of artifice. This is the sort of environment *Homo sapiens* lived in for the vast majority of our time on this planet. Since humans have been around from roughly 200,000 years ago and the proto-humans from which we evolved lived in almost identical conditions going back to about 2 million years ago, we can safely say that humans are *adapted* to life in such an environment.

But clearly, given the great diversity of human cultures that live on the globe now, humanity can survive and indeed thrive in environments that deviate considerably from that. Lots of us live in high-rise buildings, in huge cities, surrounded by artifice. Through cultural adaptations, we have expanded our range to nearly the entire globe (at least in terms of land environments). Thus, it stands to reason that we are extremely adaptable beings. Perhaps there are no environments that we can't adapt to living in. Whereas fish simply *cannot* live outside of an aquatic environment, humans seem to have been able to "cheat" using cultural adaptations, technology, and what have you to get around such limitations. Right?

A Hidden Question

Ok, so let's assume we can "adapt" to all sorts of environments and survive in them. Being able to survive in an environment doesn't necessarily mean it's a *healthy* environment. That's a different question, isn't it? After all, surviving doesn't mean we are happy or healthy in it. What about Miseria? Sure, we might survive there (through brute force bio-engineering, maybe), but I have my doubts that we would be happy there, and I am pretty sure we would be riddled with health problems, especially of the mental variety. Thus, we can see that framing the question in terms of whether or not we can adapt hides a deeper question: are some environments *easier to adapt to than others*? Are some environments "noxious"—meaning they don't necessarily kill us, but we aren't very healthy in them? Are some perhaps even "toxic"? Sure, maybe Miseria is an extreme (admittedly contrived) example, but even in all the myriad environments where humans live now, if all we ask is "can we survive there" we miss the question of whether or not such a place is a healthy environment. Do we *thrive* there? Or do we simply exist? Are we miserable or happy there? Are we healthy there?

Plus there's another problem—normally when I say "toxic" one might assume I mean "poisonous"—i.e., that the environment biochemically interferes with our normal body functions and therefore it kills us. But that's not the only kind of toxicity. Even if our environment doesn't necessarily poison our basic biological functions, we still may have an environment that is so depressing that we consider or even commit suicide as a result. That's still toxic. And that's the kind of toxicity that I am asking about.

These questions lead me to the issue of mental health and our social environment. This is because our mental health—that is, whether or not we are depressed, sad, anxious, etc., can tell us whether or not the environment that we are in is a healthy one. As we will see, there are a lot of reasons to believe that while humans may not be universally happy in traditional foraging societies, they are considerably happier than we in modern industrialized nations are by a number of measures. But I'll get to that in the next chapter. For now, let me just say that I'm not looking for "the perfect human environment" (whatever that is). No, I'm just looking for a healthier one. The "perfect" environment may not exist; after all, even in foraging environments that closely match those we evolved in, there are health problems, wars, diseases, abuse, suffering, etc. Foragers still endure suffering and (occasionally) short and brutish lives, so there is no need to fetishize or romanticize them—not to mention they are quite diverse, so neither are they monolithic. My question is simply: is the modern life healthier, less healthy, or no different from what it used to be? Are we moving towards a healthier society or a sicker society?

This is not an impossible question to answer. If humans were infinitely adaptable to whatever new environment comes about, there should be no difference in the levels of anxiety and depression in those settings. Theoretically, in all environments (except perhaps Miseria), anxiety and depression should be about the same, since being raised in such a place should allow us to adapt, on the whole. Astute readers will no doubt be asking themselves "Ah, Dr. Goodwyn, but what do you mean by depression and anxiety? Aren't these things culturally defined?" I think the answer to that is "sort of," but with an important caveat—as we will see, even with such confounding issues as cross-cultural studies, language barriers, and all that taken into consideration, there is at the end of it still reason to believe that some societies are more miserable than others. Some environments produce greater levels of not only subjective sadness, anxiety, and suffering, but also objectively more suicide and addiction. Moreover, I have not consigned myself to the belief that anything can be "culturally defined" in just any arbitrary way. That applies even to things as subjective as our feelings. There is no need to employ such coy sophistry here—some cultures are genuinely happier overall than other cultures.

We should probably be grateful for this simple observation. Why? Because, the alternative—the idea that any and all environments can be adapted to infinitely—is actually a terrifying notion, even if only from our own limited perspective. If we believed the human condition could adapt infinitely to any environmental change, then any cultural environment, no matter how brutal, exploitative, or cruel, would be argued to be potentially just as healthy as an environment of egalitarian hope, joy, and love—it's just a matter of we weary humans adapting to the new environment. Even if we believed that all moral valuations are "culturally constructed" (which by necessity must include such assertions themselves), we have to deal with the immoral idea that we can subject human beings to environments as bad as Miseria and it's OK because they'll adapt to it eventually with enough "cultural conditioning." I'm not very comfortable with that idea. Are you?

In any case, another problem with not asking ourselves if some socio-cultural environments are more toxic than others is that in the absence of any known difference, we might continue to carry on thinking we just need to try harder to adapt to whatever new setting we find ourselves in. In our case, that means *more* neurochemicals and *more* people enrolled in intensive psychotherapy. In fact, the problem might not just be our unwillingness to adapt—it could be the increasingly toxic environment we've been put in. Put another way, it could be our *inability* to adapt.

I think that while *Homo sapiens* is without a doubt a highly adaptable species, we are not infinitely so. There are limits to what sorts of cultural environments we do well in vs. environments we struggle with. Stated most tentatively, I think theoretically some social environments must be mentally healthier than others, which means some cultural environments are generally more toxic to the human mental condition than others. Is there a large array of such environments in which *Homo sapiens* can live at some optimal level of peace and happiness? Yes, probably. And of course we humans are highly adaptable—up to a point. But outside a certain boundary, which has yet to be clearly defined, environments will inevitably begin to become gradually more and more inhuman and unlivable. This book seeks to begin the discussion about exactly what that boundary might be, and moreover, I intend to show that we are, in fact, likely already outside the boundary of what is healthy for the human soul in Western developed countries. And it is not getting any better. Rather, I intend to show that even though we have made great strides in many areas, such advances have not apparently translated into greater human happiness. Instead, we have still been steadily heating up like frogs in a pot for at least the last 50 or more years (probably more like over a hundred), only it has come on so insidiously it has been difficult to notice.

The Archetypal Psyche

I began this book with a quote from early psychoanalyst C.G. Jung because, In addition to evolutionary psychology, epidemiology, and other fields, I believe clinical depth psychology has an additional and essential part to play in the present analysis. Psychoanalytic perspectives on this subject could be argued to have started in 1923, when Sigmund Freud published *Civilization and its Discontents*. In that book, Freud proposed a theory that despite civilization being developed over the generations to bring us happiness, it has paradoxically made us more unhappy. But was Freud right? Perhaps he was— as we will see, over the last several decades, research in social science, cross-cultural studies, epidemiology, and mental health sciences has indeed uncovered a disturbing finding: over the last century, or perhaps more, the rates of mental illness, addiction, suicide, and anxiety disorders have increased dramatically. In short: it's actually worse than Freud imagined.

Freud's thought evolved, however, into a theory which went beyond this simplified view of his approach. In his mature psychology, he recognized the importance of *social and communal drives* as equally important to the individual's instinctive desires and civilization's tendency to oppress them. Thus, I believe the situation is much more complicated than a simple "individual vs. culture" dichotomy. The early psychoanalysts recognized that our instincts go far beyond simple urges for sex and violence, but include an incredibly strong desire for social connection. Jung's contribution to this discourse was an emphasis on the importance of mythology, spirituality, ritual, and art—all universal human activities (though to varying degrees) as modes of expression for the pro-Social Instincts.

I have discussed my own elaboration on Jung's hypothesis of a universal core of the human psyche in books such as my 2012 *The Neurobiology of the Gods*, as well as essays which I have published since in academic journals. Without going beyond the scope of this book, suffice it to say that a number of fields since Jung's death in 1961 agree in a general way with many of his theories on innate human instincts. These instincts, based on our biological inheritance as *Homo sapiens*, and evolving over countless generations of hunter-gatherers long before the innovations of modern culture, seek expression and connection in our cultural environment—often identified as archetypal roles, images, and stories. When such expected archetypes are not found in our cultural environment, however, we struggle just as a fish might in the wrong kind of water.

It would, therefore, be wrong to propose that the solution to the above quandary would be to make peace between the oppressions of society and the base instincts of humankind. That is not why there is so much suffering. Rather, I contend that the reason we are so much more anxious, depressed, suicidal, and addicted today than we were 100 years ago is because our culture has not only become more anemic in terms of contents for such social archetypes to attach themselves to, but actually toxic, and in subtle ways. We have actually become not so much fish out of water, but more like fish swimming in a poisoned ocean—but it has happened over several generations, so it's all we have ever known and so we don't know we're being poisoned. But the problem isn't that individuals are not free enough. Indeed, many have quite a bit of freedom and are still miserable. It is that modern culture does not nourish the psyche as it should. Rather, for various historical, economic, and political reasons, many aspects of modern culture have become corrosive to the very things humans crave perhaps most of all: strong, long-lasting bonds of social connection, partly expressed in non-verbal (i.e., mythic or archetypal) ways. Rather than merely a nuisance or "cultural construct," however, I argue that the human need for connection is ingrained in the human condition and is part of the archetypal psyche we all share—our quintessentially core psychic human nature.

Using evidence from anthropology, neuroscience, psychiatry, analytical psychology, and evolutionary biology, I will argue throughout this book that *Homo sapiens* is perhaps the most social animal that has yet evolved on Earth, and that this is no accident—it is biologically embedded in our evolutionary history and written into the genome because it has helped us survive. Thus, much like a starving person feels pangs of hunger when her needs are not met, we are slowly starving to death because our culture has disintegrated so many of our means of human connection and mythic expression that we cannot help but crave deep down in our bones.

As we will see, rather than exploring the cultural contributors to mental illness, we continue to consider only the biological or psychological origins, thereby missing a full bio-psycho-social formulation of the problem. By ignoring the social component of the cause, we continue to swim in a toxic sea. By failing to nurture traditional cultural ways of satisfying these instincts—i.e., through not only certain social structures but the pursuit of archetypal narratives, rituals, spirituality, and images as vessels of meaning—we continue to worsen along many different health outcomes.

Chapter 2

The Social Instincts

Like Carl Jung, Albert Einstein once speculated on the challenge between the individual and culture:

> [Man's] position in society is such that the egotistical drives of his make-up are constantly being accentuated, while his social drives, which are by nature weaker, progressively deteriorate. All human beings, whatever their position in society, are suffering from this process of deterioration. Unknowingly prisoners of their own egotism, they feel insecure, lonely, and deprived of the naïve, simple and unsophisticated enjoyment of life. Man can find meaning in life, short and perilous as it is, only through devoting himself to society. The economic anarchy of capitalist society as it exists today is, in my opinion, the real source of evil.
>
> (Einstein, 1949, p. 10)

While I don't entirely agree with Einstein here (I don't think Social Instincts are weaker), I think he is onto something. I think we have Social Instincts that, when neglected, wreak havoc on our mental health. The opening quote by Jung (Einstein's contemporary) reveals his opinion that cultural problems of the current age can manifest within the individual; I think Jung is spot on here, and moreover I believe we can say quite a bit about what the cultural problem is, and in what precise way it is making us individuals suffer. And as I will attempt to show in this book, some societies are better equipped to satisfy our Social Instincts than others. Humans were not meant to live isolated and alone—and by that I simply mean we did not evolve to be comfortable when we perceive that we are alone. Much like pain, which evolved to protect us from harmful and damaging environments, we evolved Social Instincts which cause us *emotional* pain when we are in a potentially harmful and damaging *social* environment, and a lot of this centers around the concept of *belonging*.

DOI: 10.4324/9781032721354-2

Belonging and Not Belonging

Analytical psychology has concerned itself with the innate and instinctive elements of the mind long after Jung. Such researchers as Roger Brook, in his 1991 *Jung and Phenomenology*, Anthony Stevens, in his 2003 *Archetype Revisited*, or John Haule's (2010) book *Jung in the 21st Century* attest to the truth of Jung's statement in *The Structure and Dynamics of the Psyche* that "Nervous disorders consist of primarily an alienation from one's instincts" (Jung, CW8, para 808). These authors, along with myself and many others, have drawn upon a large array of cross-disciplinary study to show the truth of this simple assertion about suffering being largely an alienation from our various instincts.

Here I am focusing on our Social Instincts. As social animals, we tend to be unsettled when we don't feel we belong. In addition to food insecurity, we have *attachment insecurity*. Every day I encounter people who describe loneliness and feeling like they don't belong, which they often translate into "I don't know who I am," or "I don't feel accepted/loved/cared for/etc." It might seem like this is a minor thing to complain about, but it can be lethal—though I don't think it is very well recognized, which is a large part of what this book is attempting to illuminate. But I am serious when I say it can be lethal, and the way that it can kill us is via suicide and addiction. Nearly everyone who is suicidal has this feeling behind it in some measure. In any case, this pervasive dread of not belonging can be miserable to experience and contributes to anxiety and depression. I will explain the evidence for this statement later, but for now, let's just think about whether or not it's plausible that we might have instincts that guide our emotions to avoid feeling like we don't belong. Why might that be? Why might we have inborn emotional motivations to find a secure group to be a part of? I believe Nature has instilled these instincts into us at a very deep level, so that we would be driven to cooperate with one another for the benefit of shared survival.

Consider us at the species level. Across the animal kingdom, animals employ many means of survival. Some, like tigers, are solitary creatures. They do not roam the forests in packs or tribes. They live their lives in solitude except for brief sexual encounters. But tigers can get away with this because they are *tigers*. They can take care of themselves and need no others. We, however, are not tigers. In the ancestral environment, solitary humans roaming the wilderness had a low survival rate (much like lone wolves do). We don't have the immense strength, sharp claws, highly honed predatory agility, or huge fangs of the tiger. Compared to other mammals in our size range, we're slow, weak, and take forever to reach maturity. Not even the greatest heavyweight champion stands a chance against a tiger in a one-on-one fight. And yet as a species, we are thriving to the point that we are driving other species to extinction—ironically one of these is the tiger. This is because not only do we tend to cooperate for mutual survival in the moment, we do it across generations, and our ability to communicate complex information so accurately (major news media outlets aside) gives us even more of a survival advantage.

Thus, while one human is not much of a threat, dozens or even hundreds of humans all working together is a tremendous threat. Evolutionarily, we put nearly all of our eggs in one basket: cooperative survival efforts. This investment has paid large dividends, since we are extremely good at it. So good, in fact, that we have managed to unfortunately almost wipe out the tiger by comparison. So, one might think that's all great—but like everything else in Nature, it does not come for free. It has been a very long journey to get here, because the level of extreme cooperativity observed in humans requires a very complex set of biological pre-existing conditions. It requires complex communicative capacity and the underlying substrate to support it, which means large brains, communicative capacity, long adolescence (to facilitate huge amounts of learning), and many other adaptations. But these alone still would not produce the needed behavior of coordinated cooperative survival effort. Merely having the physical and cognitive capability will not be enough without the *motivational* instincts to drive the behavior. This is the cost we pay for this incredible survival benefit as a species: we have had to inherit a set of emotional predispositions to motivate this behavior, and such motivations can be very harsh taskmasters. The level of human cooperativity that is required to ensure survival would never work if there were no emotional motivations for it. Just like we would never deliberately avoid sticking our hands in fire if it didn't hurt like hell, or reproduce if it didn't feel good, we would never bother with cooperating with one another without an emotional stick (the incredible agony of loneliness) and carrot (the sheer joy of camaraderie) to drive the behavior.

Consider that the only serious threat to our existence comes from bacteria and viruses that prey upon our very Social Instincts—the recent Covid-19 pandemic has thrown this into sharp relief. We don't *like* social distancing. We don't *like* avoiding gatherings. We don't *like* being unable to see each other's faces. And since these restrictions have been put into place (which, again, would not work if we didn't have instincts to conform to group standards), it has increased our suffering and loneliness.

In any case, these inborn tendencies are written in the genome and will be present in all cultures. Where the cultural adaptations to environments come in is in *how* a culture (being a set of values or lack thereof) handles this fact and either amplifies it or suppresses it. Culture does not create emotional predispositions, biology does—however culture can heavily modify how our emotional predispositions are expressed. In this case, we are talking about the instinct to belong. It is very powerful and can lead to misery when this hunger is not fed. Unfortunately, it is becoming increasingly evident that the current culture of the United States (and other similar cultures) is growing increasingly neglectful of these instincts. Modern American life values individualism to the extreme. We valorize the rebel and the "unique" genius who stands out to be praised far and wide for "going their own way" and "breaking all the rules." As such we are hyper-individualists (which I will explore in greater depth later) who are skeptical of rules and dismiss their value. We tend to expect "acceptance" and non-judgment without really paying for it via the usual tradeoffs that are required. The exception to this are pockets of hyper-rigid cults where conformity is enforced with draconian fervor—and this exception proves the rule I'm talking about. Every social group has norms and rules, but these do not need to be rigid, nor are they evil in themselves.

The Social Instincts

But, you might say, shouldn't people just love and accept each other without judgment, and everyone should just live and let live? I would argue that yes, that would be ideal. I would never deny that such a world would indeed be beautiful in theory. Indeed, we should let people just be themselves without any judgment whatsoever. Trouble is, we *don't*. And we are not going to because it would require us to somehow eliminate a deep emotional need that exists to *belong*. This need has been etched into our genome through millennia of hominin Natural Selection. What this means is that *even in such an above world*, we would still have people feeling like they were outcasts, oddballs, "black sheep," unloved, etc. Many would still feel a lack of belonging. Why? Because the potential to feel a lack of belonging is an instinctive reality. It is innate and part of the human condition. It is human nature, shared by all. So saying we "should" be happy with one another and accept any and all behaviors without judgment is sort of like saying if we are starving we should just simply "stop being hungry."

Let us therefore call what I am describing the Social Instincts and capitalize them for distinction. These instincts, like all instincts, wound up on the genome because they motivate behaviors that lead to selection advantage in the long haul. Just like sexual desire, the desire to play and explore, the desire for food, the desire to avoid painful stimuli, etc., the Social Instincts are inborn. In this case, the Social Instincts ask, "ok, so all things being equal, who is my tribe? Where are they? How do I know?" It feels good to have a clear idea of what one's tribe is, and it feels miserable to feel like you are not part of one. The instinct is effective because all those humans who occupied themselves with this question tended to have a better chance at survival because they were more willing to cooperate—our primary human survival mechanism. If we were tigers, we would not have Social Instincts. Tigers don't give a damn about social belonging. But we do.

If I am right, then the Social Instincts should be responsive to environmental variables. In more dangerous situations, it should be more active, whereas in times of relative peace and plenty, it should be more quiescent. I believe there is evidence that this is the case historically when one looks at how the political landscape has changed over the course of the last century. The 1950s were marked by a period of reactionary socio-political landscape. This was in the context of the end of World War II, and the beginnings of the Cold War and the threat of nuclear annihilation and rise of the USSR. The Social Instincts kicked in on a large scale. Once that era passed, however, and the following generation of "baby boomers" grew into adulthood, the perception of threat lessened, and the previous mechanisms that had arisen in response to the need for attachment security (i.e., the rigid social mores of that era), were no longer necessary. Suddenly the rules were held to be oppressive and tyrannical, and all of them needed to be torn down. The Social Instincts became quiet, leaving many free to question why we had any need for "arbitrary" cultural rules that only stifled authentic individual expression. Yet, even relatively quiet, the Social Instincts operate. Cross-culturally, it is commonly observed that tribes and cultures that are surrounded by enemies and are very warlike have cultural practices that serve to produce tough defenders. In those cases, the in-group identity needs to be strong to ensure a deep emotional investment in coalitional violence against "them" so as to protect "us." And in fact, the more warlike and conflict-heavy a given culture is, the more brutal and painful such rites are likely to be, and hence the more solid and resilient the self-identity will be. In such cases, the Social Instincts will be well satisfied and serving their evolved functions: to motivate cooperation and the physical reinforcement of the boundaries of collective identity.

Loneliness and the Social Instincts

Let us explore the evidence for what I'm talking about here. The analogy between the pain of loneliness and physical pain is more than a mere literary flourish. According to a 2005 chapter of *The Social Outcast* by neuroscientists Eisenberger and Lieberman, there is a lot of neurocognitive overlap in the two systems, which suggests that physical pain, which is present in all mammals as a motivator to avoid dangerous stimuli, was co-opted by evolution and expanded to include certain social environments for humans (and no doubt other social animals like wolves, gorillas, and cetaceans). Eisenberger and Lieberman argue that the pain of social separation rivals physical pain and may indeed be even worse subjectively as well as neurologically. They point to the fact that social isolation has been used across the ages as among the worst forms of punishment rivaling the death penalty, as well as cross-culturally appearing language that equates the two, along with their neurological evidence.

They argue that the state of being sensitive to social rejection, moreover, does not merely derive from associating caregiver faces with the satisfaction of basic drives like hunger or warmth. This was the theory of social cognition that was popular in the early part of the 20th century. Rather, they point to mounting evidence in the latter half of the last century that social connection is an independent biologically derived autonomous need on par with the need for food, warmth, and safety:

> along with the evolution of mammals, a species unique in their need for early nurturance and care, came a corresponding lifelong need for social connection... so essential to survival that social separation, like other unmet needs, is experienced as painful.

(p. 110)

These authors describe social pain as arising from perceived social distance, perceptions of rejection, exclusion, non-inclusion, or cues that signify being distant from or not valued by important others, either individually or as a group. This suggests that we are biologically predisposed to be concerned with our social standing, in no small measure because being rejected or dismissed by others *hurts* almost as much as, if not more than, physical tissue damage hurts.

The work of cognitive scientists Cacioppo et al. is supportive, as evidenced by a 2014 paper that reviews the evidence that loneliness has a significant heritable component, which further supports the idea that loneliness is a significant part of our proposed Social Instincts and is *biological* in origin. Cacioppo et al. review a large body of evidence that loneliness has non-additive genetic influence (meaning it was likely selected for in our evolutionary past). This biological predisposition is, naturally, sensitive to a number of specific environmental conditions. A number of such environmental conditions appear to *worsen* the subjective feeling of loneliness, including leaving home for college, being unmarried, having few to no siblings, lower education and income, living alone, having infrequent contact with friends and family, chronic work stress, and poor quality of social contacts. Thus, it appears that (like physical pain), learning and early experience can have profound influences on how the Social Instincts function. These authors also note that across other social animal species the effects of social isolation are similar to those noted in humans: worsening cardiac health, obesity, diabetes, shortened life span, worsening immune function, and poor inflammatory control. That social isolation causes these effects in both humans and social animals again strongly implicates these feelings as instinctual in nature and biological in origin. They are therefore only going to be influenced by culture in the manner of expression. They are not, however, *created* by culture to begin with. Biology creates them. These facts therefore link the predisposition, manifestation, and sensitivity to social environment to our biological inheritance as an innate part of our human nature—i.e., the Social Instincts are a part of the archetypal psyche. The above evidence also suggests that the Social Instincts will have certain environmental expectations and innate responses that the culture of our upbringing will either satisfy or not satisfy. Not every culture will be exactly equal in its ability to meet these inborn needs. As we will see, all of the above factors that predict loneliness and so many other socially responsive health problems tend to be *worse* in modern life than in the past, suggesting a causal connection to the worsening and pervasive loneliness problem. As we will see, many of these observations about loneliness make sense given the socioeconomic changes of the last century.

Interestingly, Cacioppo et al. review evidence that the *quality* rather than the *quantity* of social contacts is the dominant force in protecting against feelings of loneliness. They attribute this to the fact that since we can be duplicitous and allegiance-changing in general as a species, it makes sense that our Social Instincts will be fairly discriminating. And in fact, it takes a significant amount of reassurance to convince our Social Instincts that a given social contact is reliable and stable. Thus, this finding is in line with the idea that humans have inborn Social Instincts that value, seek out, and reward high-quality dependable social contacts, and that furthermore this instinct punishes those who do not have any such contacts by deep-seated subjective feelings of lack and misery.

Cacioppo et al. review also several studies that argue that cooperation and the evolutionary mechanisms that drive it (i.e., loneliness) have a straightforward evolutionary explanation: groups that conduct warfare such as ancient hunter-gatherers as well as non-human primates such as gorillas and chimpanzees do so in an organized and coordinated manner because it is more effective. That is, it provides a selective reproductive advantage. This, in combination with the evolution of long-term pair bonding (seen in early hominins as well as gorillas, if not in chimpanzees) contributes to lower sexual competition among males for mates (leading to less in-fighting), and increased paternity certainty, which leads to increased paternal investment in offspring and shared parenting efforts. These changes further sent us down the track of desiring a collective identity, within which the nuclear family was fully integrated. Interestingly enough, the collective identity seems to have evolved *first*, then the nuclear family identity within it—a situation that seems exactly the opposite of what is emphasized in modern American culture. More on this phenomenon later when we explore family structures.

So, one might ask, if it's such an advantage, why don't tigers do it? Why don't all animals band together and form armies? In 2013, famous evolutionary biologist E. O. Wilson asked a similar question in his book *The Social Conquest of Earth*. He points out that even though highly complex cooperative behavior does indeed come with significant advantages, it takes a very specific evolutionary trajectory that most animals do not achieve in order to get to it. It requires a massive evolutionary investment in brain size, learning capacity, communication abilities, and so forth. Most species never have a need to evolve the many precursors that are required in order to achieve this level of cooperative behavior and so it is rarely seen in the animal kingdom. Humans have achieved arguably the highest levels of this capability thus far, followed by other primates, some mammals such as wolves that are pack hunters, and cetaceans (whales, dolphins, etc.), and some species of insects that build complex hives (though they don't have huge brains, they make up for it in other ways, as Wilson explains in his book). In humans, this power-trade came with a great cost: the vulnerability to the abyssal misery of loneliness. This is why tigers don't engage in this behavior, nor do they likely care a whit about what other tigers think about them (except for early moments of mother-cub interactions).

In any case, Cacioppo et al. conclude that "the capacity for feeling loneliness, when viewed from an evolutionary perspective as an adaptive biological capacity, is not so much about a dysfunctional property of humankind that produces personal misery as it is about promoting an individual's genetic legacy. We have argued that loneliness may have deleterious consequences for an individual in industrialized societies..." (p. 13). These findings help us to define the idea that humans are born with a set of Social Instincts that seek out affiliation and belonging within a social group, that this capacity is innate, and that subjective feelings of pleasure and pain motivate this behavior.

A 2005 article by Hawkley et al. shows that there is some sophisticated complexity to this inborn capacity by reviewing studies that show that the human self does not develop or exist in a vacuum but is inextricably linked with *social relationships and social identity*. They report that loneliness can be influenced not only by our individual connectedness to a long-term partner (i. e. married or unmarried), but also our interpersonal connectedness (i.e., friends and extended family) and our *collective* connectedness (community, group, ethnicity, etc.). Whereas earlier studies of the self (unsurprisingly) focused on one's personal sense of uniqueness differentiated from everyone else, newer research of the last few decades in social neuroscience added that interpersonal and collective elements of the self are equally important to maintenance of the self, and all three "layers" of interconnectedness are required to fend off loneliness. These three levels include the **individual**, the **interpersonal**, and the **collective**. We will return to these three dimensions throughout this book because of the evidence that shows if any of these are lacking, dysphoria can result. The individual level represents intense one-on-one connection to a life partner as is found in marriage (an absolute human universal found in every culture on Earth). The interpersonal level represents one's sense of worth in dyadic relationships—for example, having a number of close friends and relatives to speak with at least every two weeks. The collective level represents a need for identity and belonging as group membership, such as affiliations, tribal identity, ethnic identity, religious identity, social organization identity (much more on all these later). These three levels, according to Hawkley et al., are distinct from one another in terms of whether or not their needs are filled, and so may be useful to describe elements of the internal structure of the Social Instincts. That is, the Social Instincts consist of individual, relational, and collective dimensions. As we look forward toward what a healthy culture might look like—one that is better aligned with who we are as a species—we need to be aware of the cost/benefit tradeoffs of different social arrangements so we can make a better decision. As it stands now, we will see how the current trends in our society exemplify the blind spot we have for the Social Instincts and how we don't have any respect for them. In Jungian terms, our culture creates the "neurosis" of loneliness because we are constantly pulled away from and alienated from our Social Instincts. We emphasize individualism to such a high degree that long-term partner, inter-relational, and collective identity all get lost in the discussion. This attitude will not be productive moving forward and we will see how this blind spot may be causing us grave harm, not only in rising levels of dysphoria, but in subsequent health problems. But don't just take my word for it. Let's look even more closely at the evidence.

The Evidence

Without some good evidence that modern social changes have resulted in worsening moods and lower happiness, all of this book may be for naught. As such, I will spend considerable time examining the evidence that we have. If modernity is associated with a more toxic culture, which is toxic because it neglects the Social Instincts, then not only must I show that our level of dysphoria and stress has gotten worse, but I also must show that this is largely in part due to neglect of our Social Instincts, as Einstein and Jung suggested. In all cases, when I refer to a study, you will be able to find it in the References section via the name and year of publication. I encourage every reader to check these sources for accuracy—honestly, I'd like to be proven wrong. I'd like to believe everything is awesome.

I don't think it is.

If it is true that our cultural environment (which includes typical behaviors that are either encouraged or condoned within it) is becoming more toxic, it should be reflected in increasing rates of depression and anxiety. If not, then levels of various health problems, including mental illness, should not change over time, or if they have, it will not be because of anything to do with social arrangements. Problem is, they have changed, and not for the better, and it seems we are not on the road to happiness. Furthermore, a significant contributor to this is cultural in origin.

Let's explore the data. Depression is an illness defined by persistently low mood, feelings of hopelessness, feelings of helplessness, worthlessness, suicidal or morbid thoughts, low energy, and disturbed sleep patterns. It has been recognized as a major health problem for centuries, and in the United States it has become more and more of a problem over the past century according to a variety of studies in the last few decades.

According to the World Health Organization report on depression, in 2021, depression was noted as a leading cause of disability worldwide and is a major contributor to the overall global burden of disease. This fact is well known, but it is unclear as to why there is so much depression. Modern, wealthy nations such as ours have much to be thankful for: improved medical care, greater wealth overall (despite income disparities—more on that later), improvements in equality and human rights compared to earlier centuries— but despite that, we are sadder, more anxious, more suicidal, and more addicted than before. In the United States we have had a progressive increase in material wealth but a corresponding drop in overall mental health. It seems we have made a deal with the Devil. For example, in a large-scale (over 85,000 respondents) retrospective study of studies such as that of R.C. Kessler et al. in 2007, we see a successively increasing lifetime risk for depression and major depressive disorder (MDD) with each generation over the past century. That is, every generation is more depressed than the last. One possible objection to this result, however, is that these are retrospective studies. Perhaps people are casting the past in a rosy light. But the problem is that the downward trend can be observed over shorter periods of time in prospective cohorts. For example, longitudinal surveys such as that of Compton et al. in 2006 show that the one-year prevalence of MDD increased from 3.33% to 7.06% even just between 1991 and 2002. That's almost double. Klerman and Weissman, as early as 1989, reported worsening depression between 1960 and 1975. Studies like these cast doubt that the retrospective survey results are solely due to hindsight bias. There is more. In a 2015 report by Case and Deaton, both depression and suicide have increased over time adding suicide to the list of worsening mental health outcomes. Yu et al. in 2020 found that between 2005 and 2016, there was an increasing trend in severe depression, especially in the elderly, although Weinberger et al. in 2018, using a different statistical method, reported that the worsening trend was among youth. Either way, Yu et al. attributed the increasing depression to worsening loneliness, demoralization, and worsening income disparity (which triggers feelings of injustice, resentment, and inferiority). Weinberger et al. reported that their findings of increased depression agreed with that of the older studies.

Suicide in particular appears to be highly sensitive to social isolation. In a 2019 review article by Calati et al., it was found that social isolation is one of the strongest predictors of suicide, suicidal ideation, or self-harm behaviors. Feelings of alienation, loneliness, living alone, and social isolation were all predictive of suicide, whereas feelings of belonging, being married, and feeling connected were all protective factors. The result was found cross-culturally. This group therefore suggested targeting social isolation for suicide prevention. That is one of the major purposes behind this book, in fact.

This and other evidence reviewed by Hidaka in 2012 prompted the alarming statement that we are in the midst of an *epidemic of depression*. Hidaka and other reviewers show that the prevalence of depression, substance abuse, and anxiety disorders have all increased substantially since the early 20th century, and this can be seen in the United States and other developed nations despite rising material wealth and supposed standards of living improvements. In 2020, Twenge and Cooper found an overall decline in happiness from 1970 to 2018.

Still other social scientists and psychologists have noted the same thing, piling on even more evidence of the apparently slowly increasing toxicity of modern society. Raison et al. in 2010, for example, compiled a large body of studies that have been gathering over the previous 20 years or so. These studies show that the rates of depression have been increasing in the United States and worldwide. Further studies show that when individuals come to the United States from other cultures, they had rates of depression that typically match their parent cultures, but their descendants born here have the higher rates of depression associated with the US. Thus, Raison et al. state in a 2010 article: "it is American life itself, and not acculturation shock, that accounts for the increase" (p. 3). As we continue, I will bring attention to further studies.

But Is It Really "Toxic Culture" Causing Any of It?

The study by Raison et al. raises an interesting question: how do we know it is our *sociocultural environment* that is getting worse and causing this slow rise of mental illness? Maybe the problem is individual families and it has little to do with the overall cultural environment. According to scores of cross-fostering twin studies in behavior genetics that have been conducted over the past several decades, it is well known that personality variables including neuroticism and anxiety-proneness have a strong genetic component. In fact, about 40–45% of the variance in anxiety-proneness and neuroticism can be accounted for by genetics. The reason we are suspicious that it may be the overall culture that is contributing to the increase in mental illness is that only 5–10% of the variance in these personality variables can be accounted for by immediate family environment. That leaves about 45–50% unaccounted for, and it is likely a significant part of this variance is down to the influence of the surrounding cultural environment as a whole. When looking at a broad class of studies into personality, anxiety, and depression variations across individuals, researcher R. J. Twenge points out in her 2000 review that researchers often have assumed that the only factors that influence anxiety and personality variables are individual genetics and immediate family environment. Twenge points out that only *now* are we looking at cultural environment as another source of the mysterious other 45–50%.

Twenge traced neuroticism and anxiety-proneness in different birth cohorts. This was done because neuroticism has been found to be the strongest predictor of life satisfaction, happiness, and negative emotion according to a 1998 study by DeNeve and Cooper, which was repeated by Gale et al. in 2013. What Twenge in 2000 found was that overall anxiety-proneness *increased* between 1952 and 1993. Moreover, these increases could be firmly linked to changes in social connectedness, as the number of people who live alone has increased from 11% in 1950 to 25% in 1997, and Americans are less likely to join community organizations and visit friends than they used to. Recall that interpersonal and community identity were both aspects of our Social Instincts and appeared to independently contribute to worsening subjective feelings when their needs were not met. I don't feel it is too much of a stretch to connect the misery of loneliness to feelings of depression and anxiety, as all such feelings are natural responses (and sometimes *over*-responses) to situations that have (in deep time) been perilous for a variety of reasons.

In any case, we will get much more into this business of social connectedness later. For now, note that the increase in anxiety over the last 50+ years is not a small increase: the prevalence of anxiety disorders has increased nearly one standard deviation from the 1950s to the 1990s. This was reported by Twenge in 2000. A similar increase in overall lifetime risk for developing an anxiety disorder was found in most developed countries surveyed by Kessler et al. in 2007. The upshot of Twenge's (2000) meta-analytical study was that in both college students and school children there were significant increases in anxiety and neuroticism between 1952 and 1993—for those not versed in statistics, a standard deviation is a *huge* increase, and Twenge was able to methodologically eliminate retrospective bias and a few other confounders. This change was able to account for a full 20% of the variance in the population anxiety—far higher than is accounted for by the 5% contributed to by family environment. In other words, our culture seems to have become more toxic in *at least* the last 50+ years if not more. This change in anxiety is so large, in fact, that by the 1980s, "normal" children were reporting more anxiety than child psychiatric patients in the 1950s were. Furthermore, this evidence (along with a lot of other evidence) tells us we need to stop looking at individual family differences (only 5–10% of variance) and start looking at cultural factors contributing to anxiety and other mental illness.

A follow-up 2010 report by Twenge et al. used strong meta-analytic methods that eliminated retrospective reporting, selective reporting based on the stigma of mental illness, and the time-lag problems associated with cross-sectional studies. This follow-up report found a dramatic rise in psychopathology from the 1930s to 2010—it should also be noted that a large number of the later respondents were probably on antidepressants, which means the rise in mental illness is probably *worse* than that found by these investigators, because the mental illness increased *despite* the explosion of antidepressant availability.

I feel it is important to state here that we shouldn't take these results to mean that *all* the changes in our culture over the last century were "bad." Things like efforts to improve equal opportunity for women and minorities, along with tremendous advances in dental care and antibiotics for example, are unlikely to be the cause of *worsening* anxiety. In fact, figuring out the *causes* of the worsening anxiety is actually a separate issue from identifying if we are, in fact, more anxious. That said, it seems as though we are, and this is *despite* the technological, medical, and human rights advances that have been made. Tragic irony at its finest. In any case, the more likely targets of the cause are cultural changes that have to do with less material and tangible effects than we have been looking at so far, and—if I'm right—more to do with cultural changes that have impeded our ability to satisfy our Social Instincts.

Cross-Cultural Comparisons

That said, how do we know that worsening anxiety/depression in the Western countries studied in the above research has anything to do with modernization or modern lifestyles? How do we know that it is because our culture is becoming more toxic rather than simply a huge global increase in depression and anxiety? Can we say that it is fairly unique to our culture or cultures like it? Are there factors of modern lifestyle that are toxic as compared to, say, foraging societies, that might be causing a worsening of mental health overall? The evidence we have seems to suggest: yes, there are. Researcher H. Hidaka's (2012) in-depth review notes a number of factors that connect the lifestyle of modern developed countries to these counter-intuitive *increases* in depression, anxiety, and substance disorders. This conclusion is pointed to by cross-cultural studies, though this data is limited due to the difficulty of conducting such surveys. In any case, what data we do have from anthropological reports suggests that depression is rare among hunter-gatherer societies that are relatively unperturbed by the interference of developed countries. This is a *very* important distinction—it is well known that indigenous populations that have been historically oppressed and/or repeatedly attacked, like persons living on federal reservations, have very high rates of mental illness, suicide, and substance abuse problems. This fact is an exception that proves the rule we are developing.

In any case, the low rates of depression among unperturbed foragers comes from the work of a 1986 report from Schieffelin on the Kaluli of New Guinea, the 1986 report of Keyes on the Thai-Lao of Thailand and the 1994 and 1996 reports of Hollan and Wellenkamp of the Toraja of Indonesia. Not only do such foraging societies have apparently low rates of depression, but the modernization of hunter-gatherers very commonly corresponds to a huge *increase* in depression and suicide rates—sometimes tripling in a single decade as reported by Shephard and Rode in 1996 while reporting on the Ik of Uganda. Such results are saddening to say the least. It is hard to see how such changes could reasonably be labeled "progress."

Other evidence gathered by Hidaka includes a correlation between various cultural activities such as hunting, gathering, belief in magic, agriculture, and technological simplicity—all indices of so-called "primitive" cultures—and lower depression rates. For example, when rural and urban Nigerians were compared to rural and urban Canadian and American women along these "modernization" scales, they found that the *degree of modernization correlated with depression rates in a dose dependent manner.* In other words, the more modernized they were, the more depressed they were. Still more evidence that modernization correlates with increased depression, suicide, and anxiety comes from studies of Mexicans adopting an American lifestyle and the Chinese before and after the massive cultural changes that occurred in the early 20th century, and even comparing rural and urban populations in the same country. The link between a feeling of meaningfulness in life and subjective happiness is well known, and this too appears to have been hit by "progress": an overall goal of meaningfulness in life has furthermore declined between the 1960s and 2006, also according to Pryor et al., when reported in 2007.

Trust in others is another area that seems to have declined. Overall trust in others dropped in the decades before the 1990s according to an article by Smith written in 1997. According to this comparison, in 1975, 34.5% of high school students agreed that you can usually trust people, as opposed to 18.3% in 1992. I bet this percentage has continued to drop since then, but a follow-up study would be useful for comparison.

Any one of these observations alone would not necessarily be impressive. What is impressive, and also highly concerning, is the sheer number of them, and how they all point to the same conclusion: that the modern Western, increasingly urbanized lifestyle is mentally toxic, and associated with increased anxiety, depression, addictions, and suicide.

Hidaka finishes his review by making some fascinating and concerning observations:

> More money does not lead to more happiness. By appealing to evolutionary proclivities, like a desire for energy-dense food and status competition, the economic and marketing forces of modern society have engineered an environment promoting decisions that maximize consumption at the long-term cost of well-being. In effect, humans have dragged a body with a long hominid history into an overfed, malnourished, sedentary, sunlight-deficient, sleep-deprived, competitive, inequitable, and socially-isolating environment with dire consequences.
>
> (p. 10)

The effect of culture on mental illness has been studied even in schizophrenia. A 2009 multicenter study by Karagianis et al. found that patients living in less "developed" countries often had a more favorable course of illness, including less medication, less hospitalization, and a number of other outcome measures. Identified as protective factors here: extended family structures, more social inclusion, and higher rates of employment. Thus even schizophrenia, commonly considered to be more "biological" than depression and anxiety, can be significantly affected by social structure and connection.

What all this evidence points to is that, in addition to other unhealthy aspects of modern American culture that are toxic, such as overdependence on processed foods in excess, and out-of-balance work-life demands, modern life does not satisfy our Social Instincts, and this may be the worst offender of the bunch in terms of rising depression and anxiety.

What About Our Better Angels?

In a widely commented-on 2011 book *The Better Angels of Our Nature: Why Violence Has Declined*, along with his follow up 2019 *Enlightenment Now: The Case for Reason, Science, Humanism, and Progress*, cognitive scientist Steven Pinker presents evidence that despite proclamations of doom and gloom (among which he might likely put this book) the changes associated with modernity, including large nation-states, technological globalization, increasing emphasis on feminism, rising cosmopolitanism, and an emphasis on rational solutions to problems are all associated with an improvement in the human condition. There are numerous criticisms of these works, and a full analysis of them goes beyond the scope of this book, but I felt it prudent to include them here and make a few comments.

Throughout my career I have always found Pinker's work thought-provoking even when I am skeptical of his conclusions. To be fair, Pinker repeatedly denies implying that we are headed for any utopian future free from all suffering—only that the above sociological advancements have in the main improved the lot of members of such societies. But I feel there is certainly more complexity to the issue of comparing ancient and modern cultures in terms of violence, suffering, oppression, etc. Foraging societies, for example, are typically associated with relatively egalitarian social structures as compared to later early empires, which were associated with widespread atrocities, expansion, war, and the deplorable exploitation of women. Thus, rather than emerging from a dark age, brutish and short, into a post-Enlightenment state of continued progress, I think it more likely that humanity has tried many different styles of culture, each associated with many changing variables, some more and some less associated with suffering and anxiety.

In any case, I am not really attempting to tackle so huge a subject as Pinker has in his works. My focus is far narrower, and I ask: are the social changes associated with increasingly "modern" (and mostly American-focused) society associated with improving or worsening levels of mental suffering? Needless to say, along with other scholars, I am not so optimistic as Pinker, and while I certainly can recognize that technological and sociological advances have given us all better dental care and material possessions, it simply does not seem to translate into a happier society. The very things Pinker sometimes advocates for—large, impersonal centralized government bodies—definitely seem to have some major advantages in some respects, but I am not convinced it was a gain without tradeoffs or costs. The evidence reviewed throughout this book is data to the contrary.

Diagnosis

It appears from the foregoing that despite the considerable technological and sociostructural advances we have enjoyed over the last century, it may be the case that none of this has purchased us any greater happiness—in fact the opposite may very well be the case because of the breakdowns in social structures that satisfy our Social Instincts (among other problems of modernity). Naturally, this conclusion could be mistaken and everything could be just fine. But if it isn't, and we really are getting more anxious, depressed, addicted, and suicidal, we need to look at why this is. In the following chapters we will continue to examine evidence that our mental health is worsening, and moreover, what evidence suggests may be the cause of it, not only an alienation of our proposed Social Instincts, as Jung might suggest, but in many other ways.

Chapter 3

Hyper-Individualism

MACBETH: Canst thou not minister to a mind diseas'd,

Pluck from the memory a rooted sorrow,
Raze out the written troubles of the brain,
And with some sweet oblivious antidote
Cleanse the stuff'd bosom of that perilous stuff
Which weighs upon the heart?

DOCTOR: Therein the patient

Must minister to himself.

MACBETH: Throw physic to the dogs, I'll none of it.

(Macbeth, Act 5, scene 3, 40–47)

Hyper-Individualism, Narcissism, and Limitless Freedom

In America, we worship freedom. Freedom at all costs. In fact, it is very safe to say that in general very few people feel there is such a thing as too much freedom or too many possibilities. Advertisers, being master psychologists, of course know this, encourage it, and capitalize on it: in the last few decades, there has been an exponential explosion of choices, not just in terms of things we can buy, but even how we can choose to *be*. Traditional constraints have steadily been broken down, particularly from the 1960s on. Traditional roles, morals, and values have been and continue to be viewed with suspicion as tyrannical, oppressive, and limiting. It goes without saying that in some cases such systems definitely *were* tyrannical, oppressive, and limiting. I am not necessarily advocating for any kind of ill-advised "return" to the way things were done, particularly since we have yet to determine *what* exactly about the "old days" seemed to support greater levels of well-being and happiness. I seriously doubt that the social structures that excluded women or tolerated

DOI: 10.4324/9781032721354-3

hate and violence against LGBTQIA+ persons contributed to a greater sense of well-being overall. But even though those things have changed and move toward a more ethically favorable state, and I think efforts to continue to improve those things are laudable, it does not explain why we are sadder and more anxious despite them. In fact, I think it is likely that such sociopolitical changes have little to do with the worsening mental health state, and are desirable on independent ethical grounds.

I realize this is dangerous ground to tread without triggering someone-or-another's pet sociopolitical belief system. But I think the characteristics of social structures can be studied for whether or not they contribute to human happiness in a way that is reasonably objective and ethical. The social impact on mental well-being is a scientifically answerable enterprise, after all. In any case, we have to start somewhere, and the ever-increasing choices available to the typical American is as good a place as any. Psychologist Barry Schwartz (2000), in a fascinating article in the *American Psychologist*, tackled this subject. Schwartz observes that psychology is often focused on empowering patients to unlock their own self-actualization and open up more and more possibilities and opportunities. Depression has typically been seen in psychology as a situation of learned helplessness in the face of harmful constricting environments, and the balm is the removal of all barriers to freedom. Why should anyone be subjected to arbitrary cultural constraints—who gets to decide what's right and wrong? What I should or should not do? I should be free to create my own values and my own universe of meaning.

Sounds nice, doesn't it?

And yet, strangely enough there seems to be a point at which the removal of all constraints and the opening up of limitless possibilities has a paradoxical effect on the human psyche. Schwartz uses the example of language: a language is an example of a system which is allowed tremendous flexibility in meaning, but only *because* there are certain constraints. The rules of grammar, of diction, and of syntax are all understood by everyone and *that* gives it such a tremendous power to convey meaning. If we were to strip away all those "arbitrary rules," viewing them as tyrannical and oppressive, we would wind up in a society in which everyone was free to babble incoherently in their own language, with no one understanding anything. Each speaker, free to invent her own string of noises, might be content that she is not beholden to anyone's rules, but it's an empty freedom, because none of it means anything, since *meaning is generated through the context of other people.* Human beings are inexorably tied to one another, whether we like it or not, and this situation is analogous to value systems in modern life where traditional value systems become dismantled and deconstructed in the name of unlimited self-determination. And while it is true that some value systems (like ones which denigrate minorities) *should* be dismantled, some kind of new value systems will be needed (more on that later). Schwartz asks:

Modern Americans refuse to have their behavior governed by tradition, and market driven affluence frees most of us from the dictates of necessity. As a result, everything is a matter of choice. This is the best of all possible worlds. Or is it?

(p. 85)

I'm skeptical, but one might fairly ask: is there any evidence that unlimited choice is really all that upsetting to anyone? In fact, it seems there is. Some of it we have already described—in this case, the rising rates of depression and anxiety which correlates with the explosion of choices offered in our lives. Over the decades, personal, religious, ethnic, racial, class, geographic, and gender norms continue to disappear. Naturally that is not necessarily bad in itself, particularly if such constraints were extreme and unfair. Nor is there ever any excuse for bigotry or violence against those who are exploring or expanding those norms. I would strongly recommend advocating for those who find themselves in marginalized categories. We are only asking if there is a point at which such stripping down of social norms finally becomes more harmful than beneficial. Mobility has skyrocketed, consumer options have exploded, and yet we are more mentally ill. But, we must ask ourselves, is there any reason to think *increased choices* are the cause of this increase? Is this a true cause, or merely a correlation?

That is tough to answer definitively. But consider that in general, when we are offered more choices, we tend naturally to increase our *expectation* of control. Thus, the more choices we have, the more we expect out of life. This sounds good on the surface, but it means a gradually diminishing return of satisfaction with whatever choice we finally wind up making. With limitless choice, we may become paralyzed with fear of regret over making the "wrong" choice, and once we decide, we fret over having possibly missed out on something better. We expect perfection and cannot accept imperfection, and when things go wrong, it's because we didn't choose well, so everything becomes our fault. Furthermore, excessive emphasis on individual autonomy, choice, and control as the paragon of all value ultimately comes at a cost: community, commitment, and belonging. We cannot pursue limitless individual self-actualization without chafing against what others want from us. The typical American answer to this dilemma, of course, is to shout, fists to the sky, that we are free to live our lives our way! Don't tell me what to do! Stop oppressing me!

Casting off all troublesome expectations others have of you and breaking any and all obligations you have to others may be liberating if they were suffocating and you were overextending yourself to please everyone else. But taken to the extreme, it gives us exactly what we wished for: a life where no one needs you or wants anything from you. This I hear from patients almost daily: nobody cares about me. Nobody cares if I die tomorrow. *Part* of this problem can be traced to the value of what I am calling "hyper-individualism": as we will see in later sections, over the last 80 years or so, Americans have increasingly traded values of affiliation, competence, extended family, and interpersonal connection for values of narcissistic aggrandizement, material possessions, and physical appearance. Freedom from any and all obligation and constraint continues to be pursued with reckless abandon, and no thought to the natural tradeoff that must occur: as Schwartz puts it:

> there is a dark side to all this freedom from constraint, to all this emphasis on individuals as the makers of their own worlds, their own destinies. It leaves people indecisive about what to do and why... just on the other side of liberation sits chaos and paralysis.
>
> (Schwartz, 2000, p. 87)

I have heard it put this way: when everything is ok, it really means *nothing* is ok—in other words, if *all* judgments are eliminated and nothing is "wrong," well then nothing is "right" either. We have to have some kind of foundational base from which to build our lives. For the vast majority of human existence, this foundation has come from our surrounding communities, religious institutions, and family traditions. But modern life, with its hyper-individualistic focus, global capitalistic consumerism, vastly increased and technologically enhanced ability to choose, combined with a steady cultural impetus to throw the baby out with the bathwater, seems to want us to tear down any and all of the old cultural constraints as biased, outdated, and to be cast aside. I will get into why this has likely happened later, but for now this situation seems to be leaving many people in a state of paralytic angst. This poison runs deep, as we will see when we discuss the identity problem in a later section.

In her 2010 article about the huge increase in anxiety culture-wide, Twenge et al. echo Schwartz's concern that the increasing individualism and freedom of American society may have as an unintended consequence rising levels of anxiety, as it is so isolating—hyper-individualism is isolating by definition, after all. In Twenge et al.'s (2010) study, they found, using MMPI scales, that depression, anxiety, narcissism, anti-sociality, and other indicators of mental illness rose dramatically from the 1930s to the 2000s:

> These results suggest that as American culture has increasingly valued extrinsic and self-centered goals such as money and status, while increasingly devaluing community, affiliation, and finding meaning in life, the mental health of American youth has suffered... interventions must work against current American cultural values such as materialism, but the benefit may be improved youth mental health.
>
> (p. 153)

Twenge et al.'s (2010) analysis furthermore investigated what the sociocultural factors that influenced the generational increase in depression and anxiety might be. As we can see, some of it involves the Social Instincts. Their evidence draws from a number of studies that show that people who pursue extrinsic goals like money, looks, and status tend to be more anxious and depressed as compared to those who pursue intrinsic goals such as competence, affiliation (i.e. belonging to a social group), and stable interpersonal connection. Coinciding with this, surveys have shown that young Americans have continued to choose increasingly extrinsic goals since they were first studied in the 1970s. Further supporting this shift is the sharp decline in community involvement since the 1960s (where before it had increased from the 1930s). Twenge et al. were able to eliminate other possible explanations such as economic causes of depression and reporting bias in favor of the cultural explanation. Thus, in other words, we are more depressed and anxious possibly because our culture has become increasingly narcissistic (separately found to have increased also, as we will see), consumer-driven, and uninterested in affiliation and participation in favor of increasing individualism, materialism, and superficial self-aggrandizement.

What was the price for this increase in preoccupation with material gain? It may have been an overall goal of meaningfulness in life, which declined between the 1960s and 2006, according to Pryor et al. reporting in 2007. Twenge et al. point out that along with the rising rates of depression and anxiety, we also have seen a cultural shift in emphasis from encouraging young people to seek out community building, competence, and stable social reputation above other values to seeking money, power, and physical beauty above other values. Correlation is not causation, but it is further data to support the hypothesis.

Narcissism

In the previous section, it began to look like what we were talking about was an overall increase in generally narcissistic traits in people on average. This very subject has been studied as well and appears to be a part of the overall problem contributing to worsening mental health caused by cultural shifts emphasizing self-aggrandizement over social connection. In a target article from 2014 by Joel Paris, the changing appearance of narcissistic traits was discussed. Paris noted that cultural elements appeared to be correlating with the rising prevalence of narcissistic traits found in studied populations in the US. For example, narcissistic themes in song lyrics have increased particularly after 2000, drawing on research from the 2010 study by Twenge et al. referred to earlier that suggested changing parenting practices influenced the levels of narcissism—including increased permissiveness, over-indulgence, and promotion of self-esteem independent of accomplishment.

In a 2001 study by Durvasula et al., samples from the US, New Zealand, India, and China were compared for their rate of concern over personal appearance and achievements, and they found the US and New Zealand scored higher, which agrees with the finding by Foster et al. in 2003 that there are more narcissistic traits found in the US than in Asia or the Middle East. Paris argues that modernity (i.e., post-industrialism and associated cultural changes from traditional societies) is associated with a greater focus on individual feelings at the expense of focus on conforming to external expectations. This tradeoff results in a weakening of family and community roots, which is accelerated by increased economic and geographic mobility. This tradeoff allows for greater freedom to focus on individual wants and desires at the cost of a reduced "buffer" against family and life stressors, as the weakened/thinned family and community buffer is less able to provide for basic human needs for connection, belonging, and meaning, things traditional societies seem to be better equipped with and more able to provide. Price asks the question of whether the surge in individualism may eventually shade into narcissism, and that is what we are seeing as a result.

Price puts it this way: "Narcissism is hardly a new historical phenomenon. No purely collectivist traditional society has ever been described; in every historical period, ambitious people have indulged in self-display and sought fame and attention... What is unique about modern societies is that they promote values that encourage narcissism in everyone, not just in an elite" (Paris, 2014, p. 223).

Price argues that the turning point in our society seems to have started around 1900 and has accelerated since then, resulting in overall mores that encourage seeking fame, celebrity, and money as opposed to duty, honor, and service. Political philosopher Amitzai Etzioni in 1993 saw modern Western culture as inherently atomizing the individual and dismissing the natural human need for social connection and belonging. Again, we see the point made that our social inclinations—our Social Instincts—are neglected, with suffering being the result, no matter how we may wish to explain it away or ignore it. Thus, we are seeing here that the changing cultural landscapes that have fostered such an increase in individualism have come with higher levels of narcissism, and this has come in turn with worsening depression and anxiety.

Individualism and Digital Media Use

Hyper-individualism unsurprisingly leads to loneliness. I say "unsurprisingly" because that is exactly what one would predict if we have, as I believe, Social Instincts. The drive to power spoken of so eloquently by Alfred Adler over a century ago is no doubt a part of the drive toward narcissism, but what has yet to be recognized is that it clashes with the Social Instincts that long for secure, reliable social connection, and the lack thereof which causes such pain. Loneliness, depression, and self-harm have increased sharply since the early 2010s according to a 2021 meta-analysis by Twenge et al. which reviewed research from various sources across 37 countries. Twenge et al. note that 2012 marked a critical period when smartphone use increased dramatically and has become very widespread ever since. They review several studies which show that adolescents began to spend less time with each other in person and more time using digital media. Drawing from research from Sherman et al. in 2013 which appears to demonstrate that digital media does not produce as much emotional closeness as in-person interaction, Twenge et al. conclude that the dramatic rise in smartphone use may be a contributor to the sharp increases in loneliness and self-harm among adolescents (who are now entering adulthood as of this writing).

Twenge et al., in 2021, found that school loneliness increased with greater student access to smartphones and when they used the internet more per weekday, even when controlling for environmental factors like unemployment, family size, and income inequality, as these factors tend to affect adults more than adolescents (and is this necessarily a good thing? I don't think so). But is this causation or merely correlation? Twenge et al. suggest it is causal, drawing from research that demonstrates social interaction is often disrupted by smartphone use, and social media creates exclusionary cultures (especially among girls) that may contribute directly to loneliness. Twenge also draws from her earlier research on individuals that well-being appears to be ideal when technology is used a small amount that is neither non-use nor excessive use. More on social media and other forms of media later, but for now it seems that the hyper-individualistic values that led to the widespread use of smartphone technology has been an accelerating factor in the already increasing isolation that was going on prior to their invention.

Individualism, Egalitarianism, and the Desire for Autonomy

But is hyper-individualism really all that bad? Not in principle. After all, behind the rallying cry for "Equality!" lies a longing for egalitarianism and equity—noble goals. Behind the rallying cry for autonomy lies the longing for self-governance and a longing to pursue one's own interests. And perhaps behind the continual rebellion we see (at least in lip service) lies a disquietude with "unnatural" social bureaucracy, stratification, forced conflict resolution, division of labor, wealth stratification, and slavery. These are all honorable goals. Not only that, I believe that to the essentially Paleolithic human heart, all of these things are reasonably achievable in a Paleolithic world. But we don't live in a Paleolithic world. Our archetypal evolutionary proclivities—i.e., our emotions and instincts—are largely biological in nature and have not had a chance to "catch up" with so much change in the modern world. What we are rebelling against are late additions to our environments and are self-created. Hunter-gatherer societies, after all, do not have extensive power hierarchies and tend to be more egalitarian than, say, agricultural societies. Such structures are therefore reasonably seen as depressing, oppressive, and not aligning with our Paleolithic emotionality and Social Instincts. It is for this reason that I do not think returning to the "good old days" of, say, the 1950s or even the 1890s is really going to help anything. Recognizing that we are more miserable now than we were in the 1950s does not mean the 1950s were a human paradise. But it does mean that whatever we were doing wrong then has either been replaced with other things even worse, or what has changed from then has not really improved our sense of well-being and happiness.

Therefore, it is understandable that, given the wealth and opportunity to do so (as many first world nations do), we would—all things being equal—continue to push the boundaries of individual freedom and constantly be fighting off the chains of oppression. What appears to have happened is that the pursuit of autonomy and freedom from all social constraint has forgotten about and/or continues to selectively ignore the Social Instincts, which has led to us feeling miserable in return. And yet, rather than recognize this, we continue to explain it away by claiming that all we need is more freedom and disconnection to pursue our own special individual destinies and only *then* will we be more content, rather than work on forging communities capable of satisfying our need for belonging in a non-tyrannical way. We do not seem to do well in the *absence* of social contacts, however limiting they may be. And our mental health seems to rebel against limitless individualism, only it has become so ingrained in our cultural narratives we don't seem to be noticing it on a widespread scale.

But what if we could change it—what would we change it to? What is the "sweet spot" where we have enough social contact to fend off bitter, suicide-inducing loneliness on one hand, and oppressive micromanagement by ginormous faceless bureaucracies or tyrannical cult leaders?

Perhaps a historical perspective might help. The invention of agriculture roughly 10,000 years ago gave previously foraging cultures the ability to create sprawling sedentary empires in a relatively short time. With the increased ability to produce food, the population density in such cultures could expand far beyond the capacity of foraging subsistence methods. One consequence of that change is that the size of social networks could expand exponentially. As I hope will become clearer as we go, a common thread that runs through much of this material is that so long as we have *known* human contacts and kin networks, a lot of social constraints and expectations can be tolerated without them feeling so tyrannical, mainly because they are people we *know*. Since social expectations and constraints are part of every society, it seems we can tolerate it because it is reasonably similar to our deeply tribalistic Paleolithic sensibilities—i.e., the Social Instincts. But as societies continue to explode in size and become more anonymous, it seems rules and constraints begin to be enforced more and more by complete strangers and faceless institutions. I believe *this* is, in part, what the human heart rebels against when we shout our rallying cries for equality and autonomy. Therefore it is understandable. It is not, however, nor *should* it be a rallying cry to destroy any and all social structures no matter what—I don't believe that will work either. That will lead us to Miseria.

Notably, I do not think widespread calls for "positivity" and emphasis on "happiness" for its own sake will help either. Happiness does not seem to be a useful end in itself. Just telling people to "be happy" isn't going to work unless we know what *makes* us happy. Moreover, we do not seem to be very good judges of such things, given that with all the improvements we have achieved in terms of technology and health, we are more miserable. To a degree it seems we don't really know what we want from life, and we must study what factors correlate with people reporting that they are happy. Thus far, it appears that happiness is a *consequence* of the above factors that have changed—i.e., a meaningful life associated with affiliation, stable reputation, service to community, with a downplaying of personal aggrandizement and material-seeking. These things are number one suspects on our list of things that *actually* make people happy because these are cultural elements that have changed along with reported happiness and/or rates of depression/anxiety/suicide/substance use. Therefore, a persistent focus on trying to force happiness may do more harm than good to those who are stressed. There is some evidence that this is the case. Bastian et al., in 2015, for example, found that environments brimming with expectations of happiness had the opposite effect on people—that is, they found evidence that constant social pressure to "be happy" and conversely that being sad indicated "something was wrong" tended to just make people more depressed. The effect of social media comes to mind here, with many young people spending hours on it daily—in some contexts the pressure to present yourself as blissfully happy, stunningly beautiful, and infinitely prosperous is likely to have a damaging effect in the long term.

The Social Instincts and Social Rules: Proof-in-Action

What the presence of hyper-individualism seems to push toward is a removal of all social rules and constraints. As I said before, this can be a good thing if not overdone. But the fact is humans tend to look for rules and constraints whether we admit it or not. That is because our Social Instincts cannot be fooled by empty sentiments, ideas, and talk. Remember, it appears the Social Instincts are picky and demanding to a degree at the deepest levels. In an environment of relative prosperity and peace (such as we have now), I think it is possible to relax the rules quite a bit without too dire of consequences. That is because the Social Instincts, like any instincts, will not really be activated to their maximal intensity unless circumstances become more dangerous. But they never quite go away because that would be detrimental, too, on an evolutionary scale. There is no guarantee that a given environment will always be propitious—therefore it pays to have been installed with Social Instincts that are always active—even if mostly unconsciously—and on the lookout for cooperative, affiliative bonds, whether it be close family, spiritual or religious path, "found family," celebrating one's ethnicity or cultural tradition, or what have you, on the off-chance that things begin to get more dangerous again. If they are not satisfied, the Social Instincts will generate feelings of uneasiness, loneliness, and worry, and often it will be inchoate, subtle, and difficult to identify.

This is why the Social Instincts, and the despair and pain they can cause in response to the perception that one has no tribe, is never satisfied with "deeply held convictions" or "sincere belief." It is not satisfied by assertions that "we are all human" and "we are all one," and so forth. The Social Instincts were forged by blood and conflict. They are only satisfied by *action*. That is why rules are always a part of collective identity because without them it feels unsatisfyingly empty, despite our attempts to calm it with sincerely felt expressions. Yet that is how we often try to calm it when it is engaged. When we feel alone, unaccepted, uncared for, etc., our cultural script for this is to try to convince the person that they are valued through talk, verbal reassurance, or emotional expression. But vehement emotional expression will only go so far.

I'll provide an example: hazing rituals. If you've ever wondered what the point of them is, it's this demand for proof-in-action, rather than just verbal sentiment. Hazing rituals will always be a part of fraternal and sororal organizations to one degree or another. They ensure commitment to the collective, because of the way such rituals are always structured. They are deliberately made unpleasant so that anyone going through it will therefore be able to refer to it as a painful/embarrassing experience that they would not otherwise have chosen to endure *save* for their desire to be a member of the collective. Proof-in-action. The Social Instincts are also why, when early 20th century anthropologists working on ethnography would ask their host culture why they did certain rituals, the answer was frequently "oh we have always done this!" For anthropologists raised and trained in hyper-individualistic Western nations, this answer was often frustrating. They wanted the ritual to have some kind of linguistically precise "meaning." But they completely missed the meaning which was right in front of them. By participating in a ritual that "we have always done," it solidifies you as a member of a tribe—a tribe that spans generations, now, because "we have always done this." No hyper-verbal "explanation" of the ritual is really needed at the level of the Social Instincts here, because the enactment of the ritual achieves the result needed to satisfy the instinct. The proof is generated through the action.

As we will get into later, communities, families, and traditions have all become gradually eroded over the course of the last century. If there were no Social Instincts, and the previous ways of life were merely extant because arbitrary cultural rules were only generated to fuel the "status quo" of a given power dynamic, then the disintegration of such cultural rules should be a relief. I'm not saying power-jockeying wasn't a part of cultural rule-enforcing. I'm certain it was. But anyone seeking power will use what works, and manipulating people through their social desires and emotions works. But my question is: why does it work? My point is if social rules were *only* perpetuated due to mindless repetition of cultural scripts, we should be much happier now that we are less unjustly constrained by the oppressive rules demanded by the previous generation's collective entities. And this indeed would be the case if we had no deep-seated need to feel like we belonged in a collective of some kind. But we do, and this is why, despite the breaking down of so many structures, oppressive and otherwise, we seem to be more miserable than ever, because what was removed was never replaced with something that the Social Instincts found substantial enough.

Does this mean I think it was a "mistake" to break down the cultural institutions of the previous generations? No. At the turn of the 20th century, our American world was rife with racism and sexism. The completely normal variants of LGBTQIA+ sexual and gender expression were excluded and unfairly treated along a number of measures to put it mildly. Much social effort has gone into dismantling such structures. The trouble is, I believe, these well-meaning social movements underestimated the Social Instincts. We have been so focused on removing the rules, but little effort has been made to feeding the needs of the Social Instincts that were previously, however imperfectly, being met before so many social changes happened. The old structures were not replaced by anything but narcissism and consumerism due to the dominant economic forces that have operated in the US since then. And hyper-individualism and runaway consumerism does not satisfy the Social Instincts.

In therapy, when faced with patients who have starving Social Instincts, this aspect of proof-in-action has come to light many times. Patients with borderline personality disorder, for example, are paradigmatic in a way because they have terribly hungry Social Instincts, and part of what is so troublesome about their lives is that they are constantly *seeking* proof-in-action in a world where verbal sentiment and talk is expected to satisfy them. In other words, such individuals have great difficulty forming stable, supportive attachments, usually because of childhood trauma or neglect. Nevertheless, being humans, they still crave them despite their learned fear of them. This puts them in a double-bind wherein they feel horrible loneliness without attachments, but are also terrified of trusting anyone. What they wind up frequently doing is "testing" their attachments, and/or looking for "proof" that the other person is not trustworthy. Thus, they are seeking proof-in-action to satisfy their Social Instincts.

From the perspective of analytical psychology and other kinds of depth psychology, often the only recourse I have—since I cannot change the hyper-individualistic nature of our culture which feeds into this condition—is to stay alert to the spontaneous imagery of dreams and reverie in such patients. In the case of a particularly powerful dream or spontaneous fantasy image, we obtain powerful symbolic material to work with that helps to concretize this proof-in-action need. This can emerge in the form of a quasi-religious figure (a personification of their desires for meaningful contact free of egoic defenses), or an animal that is representative of their unmet emotional needs, or the very common "inner child" image so often reported in patients undergoing psychodynamic psychotherapy, which we can then translate into concrete artistic works the patient can choose to share, or at least keep hold of. This practice can be very effective, primarily because symbols, as defined by Jung in the context of psychotherapy, are not mere verbal allegories or arbitrary abstract signs. Rather, they are spontaneous metaphorical and embodied constructions of one's unconscious mind. In his words: "a symbol is the best possible expression for an unconscious content whose nature can only be guessed, because it is still unknown" (*The Archetypes and the Collective Unconscious*, para 7). Such archetypal expressions can be useful in therapy because not only are they spontaneously from one's own unconscious mind (and body), they have a certain tangibility to them not easily dismissed as arbitrary or empty.

Is this technique as effective as concrete signifiers of attachment might be to alleviate such a patient's psychic pain? Possibly not, but generally, we have a woefully poor recognition for the Social Instincts in the US even in the best cases, and even in psychology. We have precious few interventions we can implement at the *cultural* level. Instead, our culture valorizes the "rebel"—the guy or gal who "bucks tradition," "goes their own way," "forges their own path," and is a "rugged individualist." We admire those who "don't care about fitting in," but "try to stand out from the crowd." We carry on *ad nauseum* about how "the masses" are "sheep," and we denigrate those who "can't think for themselves" and need a "crutch to feel like you belong," etc. We almost *expect* adolescents to rebel, which of course gives them the perfect excuse to do so. Ask a member of a culture which has a more strongly developed collective identity if adolescents are "always rebellious." Cultures like parts of China and India, Pakistan, Nigeria, Thailand, Japan, South Korea—they will tell you that it is very rare and considered "disrespectful." By contrast, being disrespectful is frequently used as a badge of station for American youths. Again, I'm not trying to sound like a curmudgeon complaining about "kids these days" (that, too, has a long tradition spanning thousands of years—elders complaining about new generations). I am focusing only on the fact that cultural structures, rules, boundaries, etc. have benefits, and abandoning them has drawbacks. One of the reinforcing entities that has traditionally provided such structures and rules as opportunities for proof-in-action is the family, and that has changed too, as we will see in the next chapter.

Chapter 4

Changes in Family Structure

The previous chapter we looked at the cultural value system of hyper-individualism and how it appears to motivate continued separation and isolation not only from one another, but exchanges things that actually make us happier (connection, affiliation, meaning, etc.) for things that *we think will* make us happier (money, personal aggrandizement, narcissistic expression, etc.) but don't. But hyper-individualism didn't arise in a vacuum. It is a response to cultural and historical changes. Not only does it contribute to many situations, it is also itself caused by other cultural elements.

For simplicity, we are talking about the factors in our culture that contribute to worsening mental health and suffering, using what data we have to make causal inferences. That is how we will best be able to diagnose the relative toxicity of our culture. Hyper-individualism seems to be one factor. But we need to look at many other contenders. And as we do this, we also need to remember that any one given factor is not likely to be completely unrelated to the others. In this chapter we will start with some nuclear family changes that may further contribute to worsening mental health levels or lowering happiness. But let's remember that such changes in family structure are likely to influence the level of individualism we tend to share, and vice versa.

Changes in Family Structure

In 2003, the American Academy of Pediatrics put together a "Task Force on the Family" for the purpose of identifying common problems encountered in medical practice related to the changing family structures in America. A number of changes in family structure have co-occurred with the rising rates of depression and suffering in America, and these were felt to be directly linked to worsening rates of mental illness.

For example, in the 30 years between 1970 and 2000, children in two-parent families decreased from 85% to 69%, and 26% of all children lived with a single parent (usually the mother). These statistics coincide with a rise in births outside marriage from 5.3% in 1960 to 33.2% in 2000, which had continued to rise to 37% when the AAP report was updated in 2011. The

DOI: 10.4324/9781032721354-4

rates of children living in single-parent families went from roughly 12% in 1970 to over 30% in 2000. For African-Americans, the change went from roughly 35% to over 80%. The divorce rate, at nearly 50%, has decreased a little since its peak in the 1990s, but at present it is still double what it was in the 1950s. Single-parent families led by the mother (female-headed households) have increased by 146% between 1970 and 2000, and the number of children living in poverty is five times greater for such children than it is for married-couple families. This is the well-known "feminization of poverty" effect that has been discussed for some time in sociology. Associated with this is the fact that 84% of children in single-parent families are led by the mother. In 2005, this situation had not changed, and 63% of all mothers with preschool-aged children worked, which is double that measured in 1970, and 50% of all female-led single-parent households lived below the poverty line in 2004.

Poverty, of course, is a large detractor from children's health, both mental and physical, and according to the 2011 updated AAP report, the number of children living in poverty continues to rise in the US. Do these social and economic changes, however, correlate with declining mental health? The 2003 AAP report states: "Unequivocally, children do best when they are living with 2 mutually committed and loving parents who respect and support one another, who have adequate social and financial resources, and are actively engaged in the upbringing of their children" (p. 1542). Children raised in single-parent families can, of course, do well, but nevertheless they are at significantly higher risk for emotional problems, poverty, poor family support, dependence upon poor-quality childcare, and less parent–child time.

Marriage rates do not exactly equate with "two committed, loving parents, etc.," as it is always possible to have such supportive bonds outside the cultural constraints of traditional marriage vows. Nevertheless, changes in marriage rates may hint at other contributors to worsening mental health. It does appear that having a stable marriage is beneficial for a number of reasons, suggesting the greater disruption of it may contribute to worsening mental health. Married men and women are healthier mentally and physically, and live longer (especially married men). Married couples are also approximately twice as wealthy as unmarried couples. Interestingly enough, despite the widely accepted idea that cohabitation before marriage gives couples a chance to "try out" living together, there has never been any evidence in this country that cohabitation improves the likelihood of staying together, and what little evidence exists suggests, in fact, that the opposite is true: that cohabitation *reduces* the likelihood of staying together. The reasons for this remain obscure to me—I wonder if the social reinforcement of marriage, even in the current state it is in, may still impact mental health to such a degree that one doesn't see the benefits until one "makes it official." Considering the impact that rituals like marriage can have on mental state (a subject I tackle in much greater detail in Goodwyn, 2016), I consider this to be likely.

In any case, marriage has changed over the decades, and a stable divorce rate may mask the fact that fewer people are bothering with marriage in the first place, despite its apparent benefits. Births to unmarried parents have increased steadily since the 1940s to about one-third of all children. This proportion has stabilized since the 1990s. In many cases this corresponds to children growing up with absent fathers, and father absence does appear to contribute to children's worsening mental health. Multiple studies show that father absence can result in lifelong increased risks for health problems, school attendance, poor achievement, emotional problems, substance abuse, poverty, and unemployment. According to the AAP, "when fathers stay involved, the adverse effects of divorce are substantially reduced" (p. 1548). I might clarify this by pointing out that according to this research "divorce" itself does not appear to be the largest factor—father absence is (in this case). We will get more into the stabilizing effect of marriage a little later, however.

Though there are likely many cases in which children are better off when parents get divorced, particularly when abusive treatment is involved, in general children of divorced parents appear to have a greater risk of emotional problems. Children of divorced parents are more likely to suffer from depression, poor school performance, poor self-esteem, social problems, poor parent–child relationships, and poverty (probably because children usually live with their mothers, who subsequently suffer a substantial worsening of economic status due to sexist social structures). Girls and boys both suffer from divorce, but the externalizing behavior of girls in female-led households can be mitigated somewhat with a high-quality mother–child relationship. Boys, however, are more prone to depression regardless of the quality of this bond, and require active and involved fathers to reduce the risk. Note that same-sex marriages were not considered in this research.

Healthy families are critical in producing healthy people. But families don't exist in a vacuum. They self-organize in the context of the larger cultural surround which either supports their existence or puts strains on it. Notably, in the US (as opposed to other developed countries), there is no clear set of policies that supports the family, and it seems that family support structures are worsening. The AAP states: "The rising incidence of behavior problems among children attests to families' inability to cope with the increasing stresses they are experiencing and their need for assistance" (p. 1543).

A stable family furthermore is unlikely to benefit children if (due to economic pressures), there is not enough family *time* to engage its supportive influence. Again, we see here a decline in the ability of families to provide support because of our modern lifestyle that is hyper-focused on work—a situation made continually worse by the ever-widening gap between average income and housing costs. Family time has diminished in the past several decades, and a substantial number of children are taken care of by persons who are not parents or extended family members, and/or they are unsupervised. This may be caused by the continuing increase in either a single working parent or both parents working, and for roughly one-third of these families, parents must work evenings, nights, split/rotating shifts, and what have you, which further disrupts family time. Thus, whereas the stabilizing effects of a strong and supportive family on a child are well known, what is less well known are the sociocultural effects that *destabilize* families—I suspect this is another way in which modern culture indirectly worsens mental health. Modern society has more and stronger centrifugal forces acting on families than before (increased work pressure, reduced time, less sleep, etc.) making family disintegration more likely, which leads to hyper-individualism as a defense.

Families need the support of their surrounding community. This is impossible when families constantly move: 18% of children move every year—this number has stayed constant over the last 30 years, but there is a strong relationship between residential stability and child well-being. Frequent moving has been linked to dropping out of high school, delinquency, depression, early sexual activity, disruption of health care, and non-marital teen births. According to Zlotnick in 2007, and the Ninety-Seventh American Assembly in 2000, residential mobility continues to fractionate extended families. This phenomenon isolates parents and

> prevents the intergenerational transmission of cultural and community-specific advice and support... Longer hours away from their children, disconnection from close extended family support, and disintegration of traditional community interdependence all reduce the time, energy, and external supports available for rearing healthy children.
>
> (AAP, 2011, p. 1681)

Marriage Effects

It is well known in the psychiatric world that being married is linked to greater happiness. Earlier, we identified the reinforcement of long-term partner connections as one of the three main Social Instincts—the individual level, with the other two being interpersonal and the collective. One recent study in 2019 by Grover and Helliwell shows that this is still the case. So just how stabilizing is marriage in itself? Many children are born into settings where the parents are cohabitating rather than married. While far more common now than in the 1970s, say, and supported by some cultural narratives that it doesn't matter, cohabitation rather than marriage appears to correlate with greater family instability. It seems to matter, after all. In the two decades before 2015, most of the increase in non-marital childbearing was the result of cohabitating parents rather than a single mother. This would be fine, if not for the fact that non-married parents seem to be less stable, leading some researchers, such as McLanahan and Sawhill in 2015, to call them "fragile families"—half of whom will split before the child is five, who then go on to form new partners and children.

This instability affects children's mental health in a variety of ways—meaning that children of married parents fare better than those of non-married parents, though it's not exactly clear why. For our purposes, the problem is that since marriage is on the decline overall, it means this change in marital patterns may be one of the contributors to the worsening mental illness we are seeing.

In any case, the decline of marriage appears to be—at present—correlative to the decline in mental health, possibly through a number of channels. This naturally does not mean that the so-called "nuclear family" model is the ideal one. There are many ways of forming families that have been explored through the various cultures of the world—what we are lacking is detailed data on which one is the "best" one—or at least which one fares better under what circumstances. For now all we know is that the typical marriage which began before childbirth and stayed stable throughout the child's life seems to, on average, provide the highest likelihood for supporting resilience. Research presented by McLanahan and Sawhill (2015) in the 2015 journal *The Future of Children* by Princeton Brookings outlines many of the reasons why marriage, including gay marriage, seems to have a privileged position in terms of providing the best mental health support for children. Unsurprisingly, many of them are economic, but there does appear to be an effect marriage has on child well-being that goes beyond the sum of its parts.

And since it is on the decline, which may be a cause and/or an effect of worsening economic conditions along with many other variables, this may be one of the contributing factors we are looking for. In any case, it should be pointed out that when children grow up in a *stable* cohabiting family, they gain the benefits that are *equivalent* to what stable married parents provide. It's just that unmarried cohabitation *itself* is correlated with far greater instability. This may seem like a quibble, but it's important not to judge non-married cohabiting parents on this scale negatively, simply because they are not married. That's not the point of exploring this data. In other words, it appears likely that *stability* is the key feature, and that such people tend to get married more often than they simply cohabitate. In other words, inherently more stable couples self-select to marry. It's a sign of stability, not necessarily the cause. This may be why marriage has the privileged position in the data. But let us not forget that marriage, as a social rule and ritual, is one of the proof-in-action signifiers we have been talking about thus far, so it could be self-reinforcing. By that I mean, inherently stable couples are more likely to go through the process of marriage, which may then reinforce their stability.

It's also important to note that the benefits of marriage also were shown to apply to same-sex couples or couples with trans parents—that is, though such couples measure as less stable overall on average (which may be due to increased bias against such couples socially), when they are stable, they provide benefits equal to stable married couples. It is the *stability* that seems to make the difference.

Social Structures

All of this hand-wringing about disintegrating family structures, however, might not matter much if there were other social structures available that could conceivably fill the need that increasingly pressured and fractionating families cannot. If our culture had some way of satisfying the individual and interpersonal levels of the Social Instinct, it would not contribute to worsening depression and anxiety as it seems to have done in our country. And it seems that other cultures have indeed invented ways that appear to work. Scott Atran and Douglas Medin note, for example, in their 2010 cross-cultural work, that in the Maya Itza' society, a Mesoamerican tribe, there are no "orphans." Households invariably adopt parentless children whether they are relatives or not—in this case we can see that even when children are saddled with parental *death*, some cultural practices can exist to account for the lost social contact. At one point such village-raising-a-child behavior was seen as the exception, but as M. Konner in 2010 reviews, more up-to-date information on foraging societies shows that the *opposite* is true: the Western ideal of an isolated nuclear family fending for itself, with the poor mother often getting sole blame and responsibility for the attachment behaviors of her children, is by far the exception. Tight-knit small communities where nearly all adults co-parent children that meander throughout the community in continuous social contact even as toddlers is the true norm, and likely representative of the social environment in which *Homo sapiens* evolved. This group parenting even includes suckling toddlers that are not one's own.

Psychologist Gilda Morelli, in 2015 points out that researchers in attachment theory—a very prominent theory of well-being based on our Social Instincts—have been biased by (yet again), Western hyper-individualistic attitudes about the importance of autonomy and separate functioning from family and friend networks. In classical attachment theory, healthy attachments are characterized by those that emphasize autonomy in a child and the ability to explore without social contact. But Morelli points out that cross-culturally this value system does not hold in the majority of cases. Equally important, she argues, are social settings often found in non-Western contexts, in which *harmonious* functioning is emphasized instead. In such settings, "healthy attachments" are not merely oriented around the development of autonomy, but instead oriented around responsiveness to social cues, coordinating one's own and others' needs, and compliance with group norms. Quite a bit different from the West. Though emphasizing conformity and compliance in children is likely to cause Westerners to gasp in horror, one wonders if the track record for mental illness might be usable as a measuring stick for determining which mode of cultural expression is more in line with human happiness. Even our theories about what "good attachments" are, argues Morelli, were derived historically from households split into smaller and smaller units into so-called nuclear families, when this is actually not the most likely social situation in which we evolved.

Unfortunately, we have no data on mental illness among the Itza' as far as I'm aware, but we can at least say that the presence of increasingly disconnected and strained family relations in America *could* perhaps be compensated for by other kinds of social contacts. If so, then we would have to mark disintegrating family structures off our list of potential causes of the mental health decline because of compensating social structures. Only the problem here is that we *don't seem to have any compensating structures.* In fact, general social contacts seem to be deteriorating in general.

An earlier 2000 report by Twenge, for example, shows an increase in rates of anxiety coinciding with reduced social connectedness. There seemed to be two factors contributing to this result. One was an overall increase in threat, as measured by rising crime rates and violence, but the other was the changing landscape of overall social connectedness. Notably, these changes *preceded* the changes in personality measures and anxiety-proneness, which suggests a causal connection. As Twenge puts it:

> contrary to views that children have nothing to worry about except bullies and Oedipal dynamics, these findings indicate that children's anxiety strongly reflects what is happening in the society at large… children live in the society as a whole rather than in a narrow, circumscribed world.
>
> (p. 1017)

Moreover, an alarming 2006 study by McPherson et al. finds that, using the General Social Survey, the modal number of close confidants reported by American participants went from three in 1985 to zero in 2004! Cross-cultural research shows us how unusual this is. For example, Hidaka in 2012 noted that, citing several anthropological reports, the amount of time spent completely alone in modern life is very different from that of traditional foraging societies. But so what? So people are more lonely—is that really a problem? Does it correlate to worsening mental health? Not only does Hidaka note that it does, citing various sources, many others have as well. Just one example is a review study by Cacioppo et al. in 2009, who noted that isolation and loneliness correspond strongly with a tremendous increase in the risk of physical and mental disorders including anxiety and chronic inflammatory diseases. Thus, the disconnection of hyper-individualized culture has not only mental but physical effects.

The Roseto Effect

A small town in Pennsylvania, Roseto, provides an interesting illustration of all the factors we have been discussing up to now. Roseto had been largely settled by immigrants from a town in southern Italy in 1882, and by the 1950s, it still had a high level of ethnic and social cohesion, homogeneity, close family connections, and tight community relationships. It became the subject of scientific inquiry beginning in 1962 because of the extremely low rates of death from myocardial infarction compared to four nearby communities. In 1992, Egolf et al. reported on the results of what ended up being a 50-year study of Roseto and the nearby communities.

Despite the nearby towns being served by the same water supply, same doctors, and same hospital facilities, Roseto continued to have much lower rates of heart attacks for many years into the study, and the investigators came to the conclusion that the most important differences between the communities were cultural and social. Roseto, as opposed to the other communities studied, had a stable social structure which emphasized family cohesion and a supportive community. By the early 1960s, however, social changes swept into Roseto, and many of the young people of that time were reporting that they were going to abandon their own community ways in favor of more "typically American" behavior characteristic of the nearby communities, which meant a significant loosening of family ties and community cohesion.

By the late 1960s and early 1970s, the protective social factors on the inhabitants of Roseto had been lost, and mortality rates increased to comparable rates with the surrounding, less traditional communities. Participant observers in Roseto noted that the largest changes in social behaviors included:

- Family centered life
- Absence of ostentation even among the wealthy
- Near exclusive use of local business
- Predominance of intra-ethnic marriages
- Three-generation households
- Strong commitments to ethnic religion, traditional values, and practices

The communities in Roseto were therefore deeply connected, and notably, quite a bit more similar in basic structure to a "tribal" culture than a modern one, at least in terms of social connections, economic displays, family ties, and so on. Once these values changed to the more typical and less cohesive and materialistic "Americanized" norm, cardiac mortality rose to the higher, more typical levels of the surrounding communities, and this so-called "Roseto Effect" was afterward cited in various studies as evidence for the positive health benefits of strong social cohesion, shared values, and social support in a community.

But were the worsening rates of cardiac disease really due to social changes? In 1992, Egolf et al. investigated whether or not the increased mortality was really due to social factors and attempted to control for a variety of other confounders. According to the research, the sharp rise in mortality between 1965 and 1974 was strongly associated with major changes in social cohesion, but no differences in other cardiac risk factors were found. This result then supported the Roseto Effect as a real phenomenon related to cultural variables.

It's important to note here that mental illnesses and physical illnesses can often go hand in hand. Anxiety, for instance, has been linked to a number of ailments including asthma, heart disease, irritable bowel syndrome, ulcers, and inflammatory bowel disease (for a thorough review, see Richard Kradin's 2008 book *The Placebo Response and the Power of Unconscious Healing*). Thus, though it was not discussed, it is possible that depression and anxiety levels in Roseto increased as well.

Consequences of Shrinking Family Structures

So why might shrinking family sizes make such a big difference? Overall, it appears that the slow disintegration of family structures and social connections are factors contributing to the worsening of mental health. But why have they shrunk? Has there been some kind of social movement to cause this change deliberately? I doubt it. It seems the reasons for why families have shrunk are economic in origin. For example, greater mobility, widening income disparity, greater pressure for working families to take on more and longer hours, the increasing need for both parents to work, all have contributed to disrupted home life and family time that might be leading to greater levels of isolation and loneliness, which then would naturally lead to higher levels of anxiety and depression.

Have these changes been absolutely necessary, though? One might argue, "no," and that families do not necessarily *require* two working parents, for example. But all of the factors we have been discussing so far feed into each other. When we have a cultural value system that emphasizes personal aggrandizement, wealth, status, and looks, advertisers will capitalize on these factors (pun intended) and use their considerable talents to convince us that we need more and "better" stuff, which means we need to bring in more money, which means we need to work more. When combined with higher costs of living (themselves culturally defined, and so suspect), and the reduced buying power of the typical American, that is a recipe for the above situation.

For now, though, let's look at whether or not this explanation really makes sense. Advertisers could not capitalize on such values if they were not already there to a degree. Moreover, they could not do it if there was not sufficient media exposure to get out their message. To argue that we should just "do with less" is easy to argue in theory (especially when one is rich, looking down their nose at everyone else), but seriously underestimates the cultural pressure we feel to "get more." This would be bad enough even *if* our economics had been stable and what a typical family could live on had not changed. But since the late 1960s, income disparity has skyrocketed and the buying power of most Americans has plummeted. Yet despite this, practically everyone since 2012 now has a smartphone—no small feat of advertising savvy. In any case, all the things various media outlets are telling us we need to be happy don't seem to be actually making us happy. More on media effects later.

For the time being, we already know that family time is diminishing, which likely means the interpersonal dimension of our Social Instincts is being underfed. Compounding this has been a continual thinning of extended families, resulting in the mid-20th century with a near-fetishizing of the nuclear family, which has nevertheless continued to fragment itself despite politicians claiming to be so "pro-family." Whereas in many traditional cultures, constant contact with large extended family is the norm rather than the exception, modern American culture in the last 100 years has continually shrunk in terms not only of children but the number of adults in a given child's life in positions of parental or near-parental importance. Thus, despite pontificating *ad nauseum* about the importance of family, very little is really done in this country to encourage or support its fully flourishing. Demands to work and consume continue to increase, buying power diminishes, and endless advertising that feeds into our proclivities to pursue narcissistic ends wildly outbalance any message that encourages the reinforcement of connection. I suspect this is because the former has a far greater profit potential than the latter—though social media companies have found a way to monetize our Social Instincts. But as mentioned earlier, the manner in which this has been administered seems to have done only more harm. Thus we still see families drifting apart from all the centrifugal forces acting on them from our culture.

So what? Why does it matter? Consider that in a more traditional setting, or even just a culture that has a greater emphasis on interpersonal (family/friends) and collective (ethnic) identity, the enormous physical and emotional needs of a given child might be distributed among many people (mom, dad, uncle, older cousin, grandparent, etc.) who are part of that closer knit group. By contrast, in our culture, all those needs are focused on two or even one person who barely has the time due to work and other demands. There is no doubt that many American parents make heroic attempts to juggle all of this, but this is not the setting in which *Homo sapiens* evolved. Supermoms and Superdads were never needed in ancestral conditions because the culture had mechanisms in place to "pick up the slack." We do not have such mechanisms to a significant degree. Thus, when the usual sources of care children need inevitably fail, we have no "plan B." Now, when parents are unable to meet these needs, generally the outcome is resentment from the children and further parental alienation. This is compounded, unfortunately, by cultural narratives even within the psychiatric and psychotherapy world that constantly want to blame mental health issues on parents. This in turn has been caused by a too-narrow focus on the individual and her/his psychology and family upbringing, while giving no thought to cultural impacts on psychology. This is *not* how the bio-psycho-social model is supposed to operate! It may be time for us to be asking ourselves two questions: 1) how much should we expect parents to accomplish given so many cultural forces pulling them away from their children? And 2) when children are suffering, what are the significant effects of toxic culture being exerted on that child, even from a young age?

Final thoughts on this subject emerge from the context of clinical depth psychology. Often analytical psychologists refer to the archetypal needs that arise in family relationships—the Mother and Father archetype, and the Child archetype, for example, have not only been elaborated on as innate and essential to our human experience, but also in terms of their ever-changing nature in the face of life changes. Roger Brooke, an analytical psychologist, in his 2015 *Jung and Phenomenology* explores how such anchoring and universal embodied experiences can influence our entire lived world, in a way that can present itself in dreams and visions as archetypal images. He gives the example of an old man's helping hand, which can embody several meanings surrounding the core of relatedness, ranging from the resentment one might feel at being treated like a child to an acceptance of one's vulnerability, to an expression of one's relationship with God (p. 156). These images, in the absence of cultural material to work with (which, of course, derive from the same archetypal source within the human soul), must in modern therapy *become* the proof-in-action concrete signifiers our Social Instincts demand. Part of such a therapy involves opening a patient's eyes to the fact that helping hands embody all of these meanings and emotions, so that one may experience them in a new and nourishing light wherever they may occur. In the absence of family presence, along with an absence of ritual and ceremony—a subject I explore in depth in my book *Healing Symbols in Psychotherapy*—therapists can only "reinvent the wheel" with patients on an individual basis. We cannot create a nurturing culture in a vacuum. In any case, the point I'm trying to make here is that for decades and likely centuries, modern industrialized nations have dissolved such *cultural* nutrients for our Social Instincts for various reasons, and without any sort of replacement, it falls upon individual therapists and psychopharmacologists to tackle the starving Social Instincts which have resulted. Such efforts, while admirable, may not be up to the task on their own, as the above evidence on worsening mental health shows.

Differences in Modern Culture and Contemporary Hunter-Gatherer Family Structures

In late 2023, Chaudhary et al. published a fascinating study that compared typical child caretaking practices observed in several contemporary hunter-gatherer cultures such as the Mbendjele, the Aka, the Efe, and the Kung, and those found in Western, Educated, Industrialized, Rich, and Democratic cultures (the ironically chosen acronym "WEIRD") to see what we might infer about our Social Instincts. While careful not to consider such societies as "living fossils" but rather every bit as contemporary as any Western nation, hunter-gatherer societies can still provide us clues as to what our ancient lifestyle was like during the period in which we spent over 95% of our existence on this planet (far more if you count the very similar hominins which preceded us).

How do the child-rearing practices of hunter-gatherer societies differ from our nuclear-family-based model in the West? For one thing, non-maternal caregiving or "alloparenting" is found in such cultures to a very high degree, and it has been observed that this style of parenting was normative through-out most of human evolutionary history (Chaudhary et al., 2023, p. 2). Whereas historically Western psychology has focused far too much on the mother–infant dyad alone (not surprising considering our obsession with hyper-individualism), now we are seeing that caretaking *networks* are much more important than previously thought. Multiple caregivers is a core human adaptation and typical in hunter-gatherer societies, hence it is logical to assume that children are born expecting such an environment and may struggle when it is not there. In other words, we are evolutionarily primed for a hunter-gatherer style environment and not a WEIRD environment. It is my contention that this fact may be yet another causal factor behind the wor-sening suffering reviewed earlier.

What Chaudhary et al. found was that in the Mbendjele and other hunter-gatherers observed, alloparenting was quite high, amounting to roughly 40–50% of total caregiving. Moreover, responsiveness to crying or distress is swift and sensitive (as opposed to scolding or controlling) from a multitude of caretakers, with hardly anyone advocating for letting children "cry it out" or spend time crying alone. In fact, children in such social environments are virtually *never* alone at any time, given the communal, non-hierarchical style of life that hunter-gatherers employ. Chaudhary et al. argue that aloneness is so unlikely to have been encountered in ancestral settings that "spending substantial amounts of time without cues of caregiver presence is likely an evolutionarily novel situation; this may explain why infants can find separa-tion so distressing" (p. 12). Considering that hunter-gatherer lifestyle is quite a bit more dangerous than the WEIRD lifestyle, it is not surprising that alo-neness would be strongly repellent to *Homo sapiens*.

Levels of close physical contact is also different in hunter-gatherer cultures as compared to WEIRD cultures—ranging from five to seven *hours* per day, as opposed to the 30 minutes or less found in WEIRD cultures studied (in this instance, Canada and Holland). Hunter-gatherer cultures studied uni-versally showed highly sensitive, responsive, and proximal caregiving—which implies that the lack of such things may come at a cost in terms of vulner-ability to disordered attachment, anxiety, mood dysregulation, and so on. Another consequence of this research likely impacts *parents* just as much as children. The sheer scope of alloparenting found in hunter-gatherer cultures is not matched by WEIRD cultures. And yet, the former context is the one in which our Social Instincts evolved. Children have seemingly boundless needs, yet it is possible to meet these in the communal, egalitarian (if dangerous) hunter-gatherer context. WEIRD parents, however, wed to the nuclear family or single-parent situation, will face children with biologically derived expec-tations of multiple caregivers. Yet these children will have no recourse but to pursue the only caretakers around for their attention needs, a situation that leads to the high prevalence of parental exhaustion in the West (Chaudhary et al., 2023, p. 13). Moreover, formal childcare systems that exist in WEIRD cultures merely exist in order to allow parents the ability to fill up the time with more work, so they do not provide the same benefit seen in the high alloparenting contexts of hunter-gatherer societies.

In the hunter-gatherer cultures studied, children had access to an average of 14–20 caregivers *per child* (with a core of 3–4 high-intensity caretakers flanked by less commonly interacting caretakers). A significant number of these also provided close physical contact. These are not only parents and grandparents but siblings and family friends. It is well known that in many indigenous cultures even the language of family relations reflects this sort of caretaking, such as in cultures where all adult females are "aunt" or "mother" and all adult males are "uncle" and "father," regardless of the precise family relation.

One cannot help but wonder if children in such communal, high caretaker to child ratios do not develop more quickly in the skills of theory of mind and emotional intelligence given so much constant interaction and opportunities to learn varying interaction styles. By contrast, in Western psychology we lay all such skill development at the feet of the parents or parent (usually the poor mother). We did not evolve in such contexts, and so the absence of so much constant social interaction may reflect that WEIRD settings are *socially impoverished*. Social, empathic, and emotional intelligence skills, in such settings, will give insufficient material to work with, and so result in WEIRD children who are relatively stunted by comparison. To my knowledge direct assessments of emotional intelligence have not been conducted between these two groups, and as such this must remain purely a hypothesis. But it is certainly worth testing.

In any case, the above data may imply that WEIRD parents are being asked to do the impossible: stand in for 3–4 main caretakers and 10–17 peripheral ones. Is it any wonder, then, that 30–40% of WEIRD children wind up with disordered attachments (The Sutton Trust, 2014). Disordered attachments are, again, another possible contributor to the rising rates of mental illnesses discussed earlier. Note, too, the difference between caretaker to child ratios seen in hunter-gatherer contexts: in Chaudhary et al.'s (2023) study, the *smallest* ratio was 6:1 (p. 14). Some were significantly larger. Contrast this to WEIRD childcare environments where the ratio is typically *inverted* to a significant degree! (i.e., one caregiver to multiple children). Thus the sheer amount of personal attention given to each child in the ancestral hunter-gatherer environment was likely much higher and this fact likely fine-tuned our evolutionary instincts to *expect* it. This means when such expectations are not met, there is likelihood that we become more vulnerable to mental illness or stunted/impoverished development. One aspect of hunter-gatherer cultures that likely makes such high caregiver to child ratios possible is that they have no qualms about sub-adults providing care, on down to children in single digits of age. Such caregivers tend to be well-known people who are frequently encountered on a daily basis (even though genetic relatedness in such settings tends to be low), rather than the "strangers" employed in WEIRD settings. In summary, Chaudhary et al. conclude that:

> parenting manuals that expect babies to spend extended periods of time playing alone or devoid of physical contact may be at odds with children's psycho-biological expectations... it is essential not to place caring responsibilities solely on the mother... [this would be] very much at odds with the highly collaborative childrearing systems which have been so crucial in our species' evolution.
>
> (p. 15–16)

Despite this data, however, child rearing in the West tends to be much lonelier well past childhood, and places undue strain on the few caretakers around.

Chapter 5

Spirituality

Jung felt spirituality was very important for mental health:

> About a third of my cases are not suffering from any clinically definable neurosis, but from the senselessness and aimlessness of their lives. I should not object if this were called the general neurosis of our age.
>
> (Carl G. Jung, 1954, CW16, para 83)

As we widen our search for the causes of the mental health decline, one quickly notices that the changing religious landscape of the last century (and before) may have a part in this story as well, as others have hinted at in their review studies. Spirituality, meaning-based communities, and traditional religions have been a means through which we have connected with one another on a community level since time immemorial. Humans are inherently spiritual creatures—what is the relationship between the religious shifts of the last hundred years and the worsening mental health, if any?

Spirituality and Mental Health

We will start off with a 2010 study by E. Childs, the latest of many such studies that show religious service attendance is linked to greater happiness. But is this merely because of the social connection? Or is there an independent factor spirituality provides? Perhaps it provided meaning/purpose, or a coherent narrative that explains life's mysteries, including ones that celebrate life's mysteries. To determine this, Harold Koenig and David Larson of Duke University reviewed the question of the relationship between religion and mental health in 2001, looking at a total of 850 studies in all. Their results were fascinating. First, interestingly enough, early studies of the 1950s and 1960s were initially very negative in terms of the relationship between religious belief and/or participation and levels of anxiety, poor sleep, worry, perfectionism, "conformism," and a number of other variables. Simply labeling "conformism" as a negative variable out of hand is already somewhat suspicious for hyper-individualism, but let's continue. These early studies were

DOI: 10.4324/9781032721354-5

unfortunately plagued with methodological problems including lack of controls, focus on adolescents or college students, and overdependence on cross-sectional designs that were unable to identify causality—after all, it's common knowledge that when people are stressed they often turn to religious faith/practice to help them through tough times. But that's not really what we want to measure, unless we can show that religion *actually helped or hurt* those people.

In fact, later and better designed studies from the 1970s and on showed a much more positive association between religion and mental health. For example, Koenig and Larson report that 79 of 100 studies found religious belief/practice to be consistently related to life satisfaction, happiness, and higher morale; 10 of 12 prospective cohort studies correlated religiosity with greater well-being, and the magnitude of these associations were equal to or greater than correlations between social support, marital status, and income with well-being; 12 of 14 studies reviewed showed religiosity correlated with hope, optimism, purpose, and meaning, and none of the religious subjects had less hope or optimism than the non-religious ones in these studies.

Correlations, however, do not mean causation. It could very well be that people who are hopeful, optimistic, and feel purpose and meaning for other reasons are simply more likely to attend or profess religious belief and/or engage in religious practice. Naturally researchers already know this, and so have gone to some lengths to have a clearer picture of whether or not religious belief/practice is actually a causal factor in mental health, rather than not.

The three late 1990s studies with the best scientific methodology reviewed by Koenig and Larson in 2001 showed religious subjects were more hopeful and optimistic—both qualities which themselves correlate strongly with overall physical and mental health and longevity (as reported in 2011 by Vahia et al. in a meta-analysis of 83 studies of health protective factors). In 60 of 93 studies examined by Koenig and Larson, greater religiosity correlated with less depressive disorders and fewer depressive symptoms. Of these, 22 were prospective cohort studies of high quality—these would presumably better show the causal connection that we are looking for. Of those 22 prospective studies, 15 showed greater religiosity predicted less depression over time. Two of these studies picked depressed subjects and followed them over time and both found that more religious subjects had a quicker resolution of their depression. This result extended into the outcome of suicide also: 57 of 68 studies found lower rates of suicide among the religious, and 4 of 5 prospective cohort studies found that baseline religiosity predicted less anxiety over time. The protective effect of religion extended to substance abuse disorders as well: 76 of 86 studies in Koenig and Larson's review found lower alcohol use/abuse among the more religious, and 8 of 9 prospective cohort studies found baseline religiousness predicted less alcohol use/abuse on follow-up.

How does this work? Why does religion appear to have all these protective correlations? Koenig and Larson explore the relevant studies behind that question as well. One possible factor is social support: 19 of 20 studies reviewed showed that religiosity correlated with greater social support, and 35 of 38 studies showed that greater religiosity or similarity in religious background predicted greater marital happiness and stability, suggesting religion protects against mental illness via its stabilizing effects on marriage, discussed in the previous chapter. In all, religious involvement appears to correlate positively with greater well-being, less anxiety and depression, better social support, and less substance abuse.

In 2014, Weber and Pargament published another, more up-to-date review of the association between religion and mental health. These authors found continued evidence that religion improves mental health, increases overall well-being and quality of life, and is associated with lower rates of suicide, substance abuse, fewer posttraumatic stress symptoms, fewer eating disorder symptoms, fewer schizophrenic symptoms, less personality disorder symptoms, improved coping abilities, better social support, and less depression and anxiety, with certainty and conviction correlating with better mental health.

But Weber and Pargament also show that religion can also have *negative* effects as well that need to be recognized when the subject is looked at more closely. Specific kinds of religious belief are associated with better or worse mental health. For example, those who report using religion for personal gain also report lower well-being. Psychotic patients who incorporate religious themes into their delusions have worse symptoms. Negative coping or "spiritual struggle," where spiritual struggle is defined as either anger with God, negative encounters with other believers, or internal religious guilt and doubt. Each of these is associated with different kinds of worse functioning. Furthermore, belief in a punitive God is associated with more paranoia, obsession, compulsion, depression, and anxiety.

In 2012, Weber et al. conducted a review of research articles on non-believers—a subject that receives relatively little attention in the research community. Of the relatively low number of 14 articles surveyed, the authors found that degree of inner conviction—atheist or religious—was associated with greater well-being. No doubt atheists would object to being labeled as having "atheist belief," but nevertheless it correlated with improved well-being if there was conviction behind it. That said, non-believers were measured to have greater anger at and non-forgiveness of God—aspects of "religious struggle" above. The results of overall depression, anxiety, and fear of death were mixed when comparing believers to non-believers in this review, but one consistent finding was that doubt and uncertainty about religion was correlated with worsening well-being along several scales. Atheists, however, experienced more distress due to negative social views of them and they had unique struggles compared to believers, such as finding meaning and awe in life.

It should be noted that belief does not always equate with participation in a religious community. Examples abound of non-believing Jews, Christians, or Neopagans who feel that participating in the community and services does not have to coincide with sincerely held belief. But it does appear that having non-fundamentalist spiritual belief is correlated with greater health and wellness along a number of scales.

An intuition of this relationship may have prompted early Swiss psychoanalyst Carl Jung to write in 1933:

> Among all my patients in the second half of life… there has not been one whose problem in the last resort was not that of finding a religious outlook on life. It is safe to say that every one of them felt ill because he had lost that which the living religions of every age have given to their followers, and none of them has been really healed who did not regain his religious outlook.
>
> (Jung, 1933, 229)

In my 2016 book, *Healing Symbols in Psychotherapy*, I explore how ritual scholarship bears on the subject of depth psychology and the many ways in which rituals of all kinds (especially ones with spiritual themes) appear to impact mental health via their ability to resolve ambiguities in life. One of the benefits of religious adherence may be due to these effects, and may account for Jung's intuition. In any case, outside of empirical studies, it is well known within many depth psychology traditions that finding a spirituality that is consistent with one's own personal intuitions can bring about feelings of "coming home," i.e., *belonging*. What is challenging for us in Westernized nations, however, is the sheer multiplicity of choices available along these lines. While this can be a good thing, of course, it imports all the difficulties involved in the explosion of choice and the many anxieties it produces.

Just as we have atomized interpersonal connections, we have also atomized religious affiliation. Anyone can attach themselves to whatever affiliation they like, making it like a giant salad bar. This raises the inevitable question in my patients: how do I know I have chosen the right one? And for those who simply choose what's been called "Shielaism" (essentially making up one's own religion via an eclectic admixture of many sources), an insidious conflict emerges within the psyche: am I just "making this all up"? Or can I rely upon this system as an anchor of meaning in my life? Robert Bellah and others, in their 1985 book *Habits of the Heart*, define the explosion of Shielaisms since colonial times in America as yet another example of increased disconnection from community, and harshly criticize it as self-absorbed. Whether one agrees with that or not, my concern is that such a spirituality may be much less protective against mental illness since it is enucleated of the social nutrients that normally complement it.

In any case, if non-fundamentalist religious belief correlates with protection against mental illness, might that play a part in the aforementioned rise in mental health problems? Has there been a decline in spirituality over the time scale in which we have seen mental well-being decline?

The Great Decline

Jung argued that the archetypal symbols employed by religions have been in decline for centuries, and he felt that this has contributed to the worsening mental health state of human beings in Westernized cultures. For Jung, religions were not merely socially constructed and arbitrary expressions of control, but arose from deeply human unconscious sources:

> At all events experience shows that religions are in no sense conscious constructions, but that they arise from the natural life of the unconscious psyche and somehow give adequate expression to it. This explains their universal distribution and their enormous influence on humanity throughout history, which would be incomprehensible if religious symbols were not at the very least truths of man's psychological nature.
>
> (Jung, CW8, para 805)

If Jung was right here, then that means a gradual and/or sudden dissolution of such symbols may leave us wanting for meaning and connection on this deep level. But has that actually happened in the US?

J. Tobin Grant, a Professor of Political Science at Southern Illinois University and Assistant Editor for the *Journal for the Scientific Study of Religion* (as of this writing), has put together an Aggregate Religiosity Index (ARI) to measure the overall "religiosity" of the US. Using a variety of statistical methods that he validated in multiple ways, Grant (2014) shows that religiosity in the US has, with a brief upsurge in the late 1950s, steadily declined since the early 1960s. Numerically, his ARI is a unitless scale (much like IQ scores)—the reasons for using such a score he describes in his work, but overall it is an aggregate of the results of sources such as the Gallup Poll, the General Sociological Survey, and the National Election Study poll among others.

The ARI includes overall church membership, reported feelings of closeness to God, religious identification, attendance at services, reported religious identification and experience, frequency of prayer, and felt salience of religion among other reports. Using this validated scale, Grant (2014) shows that by 2013, overall religiosity in the US hit an all-time low since the earliest data was available in 1952, going from a relative value of 80 in 1962 to below 70 in 2013—which is a substantial drop statistically speaking, and it appears to be accelerating. In statistical terms, for example, the ARI dropped roughly 1.5 standard deviations between the 1960s and 1980s, but between the late 1990s and 2013 it dropped 3 standard deviations. This is such a huge drop that he calls the last 50 years the "Great Decline." Feeding into the ARI are numbers such as changes noted even from just 1994 and 2013:

- Religious identity dropped from 94% to about 85%.
- Church attendance "more than seldom/never" dropped from 62% to 53%.
- Reported membership in a church dropped from 69% to 59%.
- Reported importance of religion (a way to ask about spirituality that isn't "organized religion") dropped from 88% to 78%.
- Reported feeling that religion is "relevant for today" dropped from 80% to 70%.

Given the aforementioned protective effects that non-fundamentalist religious belief, participation, or affiliation appears to have, then, the fact that such belief and affiliation has declined perhaps reveals another causal factor for worsening mental health. This data suggests that declining religiosity may play a part. As for what has caused *that* phenomenon, however... that is difficult to say.

There are a number of possibilities in my mind, given what we have discussed so far. In fact, most of the apparent contributors to the decline in mental health that we are seeing are likely to be all related to one another in some way. Religious affiliation, for example, is more difficult when families shrink and/or lose contact with one another and communities dissolve over time. Longer work hours makes going to services more difficult. Increasing hyper-individuality makes acceptance of religious customs, rules, and rituals more difficult—rather than seeing them as a tradeoff wherein one gains affiliation, group belonging, and a shared cultural meaning in exchange for conformity to a set of mores and customs of dress and behavior, it is seen as the tyrannical oppression of the authentic human expression of the individual.

The reality, however, is that viewing it in this manner, which is so common in hyper-individual value systems, we think of throwing off the chains of community oppression as an unmitigated gain for the individual—a triumph of the unique, the individual, and the self over "conformity." No thought is put into why it is often so emotionally difficult for people to do so, no matter how many times they might be encouraged to do so from (unfortunately all-too-often) uninvested observers with no skin in the game. But why would it be difficult for people to break away from a religious tradition if it was nothing but an oppressive regime?

Because it's more complex than that. And pushing people to break away from a family, religion, group, etc., simply because we idolize the "non-conformist" dismisses a very real human need for belonging. Bullying such people for being "weak" simply because they struggle with such things is not helpful. Rather, it pushes people toward extremist groups. There is a reason why cults are so seductive—more on this later.

Summary

Recall that one dimension of the Social Instincts relates to collective identity—i.e., an identity related to a larger group, whether it be sociopolitical, ethnic, communitarian, or spiritual in nature. The above discussion suggests that this tool for satisfying that dimension of the Social Instincts is also diminishing for whatever reason in the US. But spirituality is naturally not the only way to satisfy this human need.

Clinically, I have found evidence of Jung's intuitions regarding the inborn need for "higher" meaning and purpose, though many times much of this is found through simple attachment and affiliation. We can often find meaning in each other. But even beyond that, it seems that most individuals I have encountered have a more or less vaguely defined overarching narrative of meaning lurking somewhere in their heads, and that exploring and helping to define it often can lead to a great deal of clarity and counterbalancing of anxiety and low mood. Anxiety, after all, can be seen as worry over what life means, whereas depression may well be a reflection of a belief system that there is no meaning. In any case, in the absence of such a system that one can affiliate oneself to with more than lip service, there appears to be evidence that merely *spending time in natural environments* can help protect against mental illness to a degree. As we will see, this may be usefully seen as an extension of our Social Instincts, which is the subject of the next chapter.

Chapter 6

Nature Deficiency

Another causal factor that has been noted by researchers from a variety of different fields has to do with our contact with natural environments. That is, some feel that we are more anxious and depressed simply because we spend too much time in artificial environments and not enough time in "nature." Let's explore the evidence.

Worsening Food, Sleep, and Exercise in the World of Artificial Environments

The past century has seen more than just changes in a few social variables. There have also been widespread food, sleep, exercise, and lifestyle changes that are likely partial contributors to worsening anxiety and depression that are contributing to our worsening mental state directly or indirectly in conjunction with Social Instinct mechanisms. First is the well-known correlation between modernized living and obesity. Obesity correlates very closely with depression, as reported in a systematic review of prospective studies by Luppino et al. in 2010—so closely that the link can be identified as cause-effect. The diet that often leads to obesity (high sugar, high fat, low protein, etc.) has itself been linked to depression independently of obesity as reported by Sánchez-Villegas et al. in a 2009 study. Other factors linked to depression and modern living include reduced direct sunlight associated with working and living constantly indoors as well as overall reduced activity level. Reduced overall sleep is another factor that has been uncovered as a contributor to depression that has worsened since the mid-20th century. The typical American gets over an hour less sleep on average now as compared to the 1960s, as reported by the National Sleep Foundation in 2009.

Modern life, then, appears to be associated with diet and behavioral patterns that themselves are strongly linked to depression. Put another way, the modern lifestyle, with its indoor work pattern and high calorie dense, high sugar/low nutrient content foods, high obesity, and inadequate sleep all may contribute to increased rates of depression and other mental illnesses.

DOI: 10.4324/9781032721354-6

Nature Deficiency

Perhaps in addition to the individual, interpersonal, and collective dimensions of the Social Instinct that we have yet to explore fully so far is a dimension involving our identity as a part of the natural tapestry of environments, flora, and fauna of the natural world itself. Let us define this as the "nature" dimension of the Social Instinct. Like the other dimensions, alienation from this dimension may cause anomie, loneliness, and existential angst that can be quite serious because these things can lead to suicidal ideation—I have seen this clinically time and again. That is, I am suggesting that separation from the natural world may be a part of the starving Social Instincts, too. Is this some kind of adaptation that encourages us not to linger too long in completely artificial environments? Maybe—another explanation is that it is a side-effect of the other adaptations toward feeling connected and engaged with the world in which we originally evolved over hundreds of thousands of years. I include this in our discussion of the Social Instincts because there is evidence that we suffer subtly but significantly when we are separated from natural environments.

In a 2010 article in the Archives of General Psychiatry, for example, Charles Raison, MD, et al. show that there is good evidence for the notion that during evolution, *Homo sapiens* was exposed to a number of microorganisms that were not pathological but nonetheless ubiquitous in the environment. These microorganisms are referred to as "Old Friends" because we co-evolved with them and depend on them to fine-tune our immune system during our lifetime. Raison shows that when we are separated from these microorganisms, such as is the case in the modern, relatively sterile environments of indoor workplaces, houses, and urban environments, our out-of-tune immune systems malfunction. This happens because the Old Friends stimulate regulatory cells in our immune systems that tell it when to launch an attack and when something is harmless—pretty important functions.

Without this regulatory exposure to the Old Friends (such as *Bacteroides, Mycobacterium vaccae, Lactobacilli*, and *Bifidobacteria* among many other harmless organisms), our immune systems overreact to environmental stressors. This lands us with a much higher incidence of inflammatory diseases such as asthma, allergies, gastro-intestinal diseases, and—most importantly for our discussion—*depression*. In fact, a very large body of evidence has gathered in recent years pointing to depression as (in part) an inflammatory disease. Raison shows how mounting evidence suggests a significant contributor to the rising depression rates, therefore, is a lack of exposure to natural environments that our ancient ancestors spent most of their lives in. Perhaps counter-intuitively, exposure to such things as animals, dirt, even fecal matter, therefore, are not the enemy, but (in limited amounts) probably very beneficial to our immune systems. Modern life, however, does not typically include much time in the natural environment that has the Old Friends. Thus we wind up cut off from Nature in a very concrete and tangible way.

Note that it is of course possible to point to human-created environments and call them "natural." After all, humans naturally build structures to live in—what could be more "natural." This move appears to call into question the very definition of what "natural" means. But such sophistry is too clever by half. We don't need to split hairs here—we're just talking about environments constructed independently of human intervention. Whether we call that "natural" or not is immaterial—we are measuring the effects of too much or too little time in artificially constructed environments, as opposed to spontaneously emergent ones that are devoid of human influence. For our purposes we will call the latter such environments "natural."

In any case, it seems the human genome, accustomed to having the Old Friends everywhere in the environment, wound up using these organisms to train the immune system so that it didn't have to code for structures to do the job itself. This is a very common phenomenon in evolution—wherever possible, organisms will use what is already there in the environment to do what needs to be done. In our case, it was dirt and crud!

Although in its infancy, there is early evidence that spending time in natural environments improves self-reported mental well-being. In a meta-analysis of 12 trials reviewed by Coon et al. in 2011, a majority of participants reported greater feelings of revitalization, enjoyment, satisfaction, and positive engagement, with reduced tension, confusion, anger, and depression and increased energy following exercise in the natural environment vs. an indoor environment. Despite these results, the studies suffered from overall poor quality of data collection and reporting, so the results are not definitive and the investigators called for more, higher quality research on this subject.

In his 2012 book *The Nature Principle*, researcher Richard Louv musters a huge amount of evidence to support his hypothesis that humankind has an innate need to spend time in natural environments. Louv argues passionately that humans originally evolved not in a surrounding "non-human" environment, but in natural environments that were more accurately described as "more-than-human." Louv argues that this connectedness can be cut off by excessive time in artificial environments. The research looking into the effects of natural environments began with psychiatrist Harold Searles in the early 20th century, but it was mostly ignored until the 1980s, at which point new interest gathered in it.

The argument goes that "Nature"—meaning non-artificial environments—is of primary importance to the psyche, as it is a simple matter of evolution selecting for brains and bodies primed and ready to interact with natural environments. If we had evolved over the last 100,000 years spending all our time in shopping malls, for example, our bodies would be selected for by such environments. But humans have not had enough time in *urban* environments let alone anything so specific. Rather, we evolved in savannahs and rainforests for the large majority of our time on Earth as recognizably modern *Homo sapiens*. The emergence of sprawling artificial environments one could spend their entire life in, however, have not existed for nearly long enough to make profound changes to our inherently human constitution. This simple fact may have wide-ranging consequences, of course, including the idea that our minds are geared to spend time in such natural environments.

The matrix in which the species evolved over geological time was for most of our existence on Earth a matrix of non-human elements. Unsurprisingly, poets and sages throughout history and in countless indigenous tribes world-wide have recognized the profound impact natural environments can have on the emotions and thoughts, and of course even in urban environments, one can typically find gardens and parks that are recognized as places of restoration, recreation, etc.

Louv reviews many so-called ecopsychologists who view the modern urban-industrial environments as contributing to grief, despair, and anxiety due to the estrangement of our deep human ecological instincts and expectations, and these sentiments are strongly reflected in analytical psychology literature as well. These researchers and clinicians propose that the state of the environment is strongly connected to the psyche, and suggest the human mind/body operates in different modes and rhythms while in natural settings. This includes gardening and small-scale farming, hunting, or any outdoor activity as a way to redirect energy that may have no other easily obtainable outlet. The natural environment, so it is argued, brings us into the present through engagement of our human instincts, slowing us down to help provide us with context in the wider universe, whereas artificial environments typically operate to isolate us from them and things outside of us, to our detriment.

Though not thoroughly characterized at the biomolecular level, these statements have a reasonable basis when one studies the ecology and behavior of non-human animals. All animals have mechanisms that attune them with day/night, weather, other creatures, etc., and to assume humans are somehow exempt from this characteristic seems quite unrealistic.

In some of the therapies discussed by Louv, patients are encouraged to engage with a "not-talking cure" that involves spending time in a natural environment, and it is argued that this engagement moves us away from overly interiorizing sensations and body-self sense, and reconnects our psyche and body to our immediate surroundings in a profoundly healing way. This activity encourages "present-ification," or grounding, which is recognized as beneficial from a number of theoretical backgrounds, even outside of ecopsychology.

Louv reviews case studies on traumatized war-veterans participating in this sort of therapy, for example, and finds that they often report an *acceptance that is somehow not infantilizing* about nature, and they find this deeply satisfying. It seems to constitute a proof-by-action enacted by Nature Herself that one is an accepted part of the greatest community of all—the natural world. Rather than meeting a setting where you are expected to do this and that, Nature meets you and engages with you on whatever level you are presently—while at the same time, it does not ignore you. Spending time immersing oneself in a natural setting for a time, whether with others or in solitude, appears to link the psyche to something much greater than itself on a visceral, unconscious level, and this seems to promote natural healing processes within the mind. Note that there is a difference between *loneliness* and *solitude*, however—solitude is when one goes alone *into* a natural setting, not to be confused with going alone into a small, disconnected artificial environment. That would be solitary *confinement*—not healthy!

Rather, perhaps oddly enough, solitude can be healing, because it still connects you to something outside yourself, which appears to be the most important function of the Social Instincts that are so highly sensitive in humans. Human connection can be vexing and overwhelming, and yet we still desperately need to connect. Solitude in nature can help by reconnecting on a deeper, more anchoring and grounded level, and perhaps paradoxically alleviate the terrible isolation of trauma or perceived social rejection. Whoever you are, no matter what you have been through, Mother Nature sees you and accepts you, while at the same time silently demands that you look out for yourself as well. Nature mothers but does not mollycoddle.

If Louv and other ecopsychologists are right about all this, of course, the fact that so many of us in modern Western society spend so much less time in natural environments may clue us into yet another causal factor behind the decline in mental health overall. We are part of the tribe of the natural world as well, and yet we cut ourselves off from that too! Spending day after day almost entirely in indoor environments, through likely near countless, subtle, and difficult to measure interactions, may be partly behind the influence of modern consumer culture's effects on our mental well-being by not feeding the needs of this dimension of the Social Instincts.

Impoverished Interactions with Nature

This effect is probably multigenerational, meaning that cultures in transition must adapt and readjust to a given environment (natural or otherwise) to return to a state more attuned to the Social Instincts. In Scott Atran and Douglas Medin's 2010 *The Native Mind and the Cultural Construction of Nature*, compelling evidence is given to strongly suggest that individuals in modern developed countries have had an increasingly impoverished knowledge and understanding of nature since the Industrial Revolution. That may not be much of a surprise, but Atran and Medin (2010) have demonstrated it with some clever experiments, showing how individuals from small subsistence cultures often have a far greater knowledge of their surrounding flora and fauna than the average American has of her or his own.

The reason for this impoverishment is, at its base, rather simple—hunter-gatherers and small-scale horticulturalists simply spend a great deal of time in natural environments rather than artificial ones. Using a variety of cross-cultural experiments of unprecedented sophistication, Atran and Medin demonstrate that:

> despite Western science's historical take-off from universal principles of folkbiology found across cultures, in globally mobile, technologically oriented societies there is a marked deterioration in commonsense understanding of the everyday world... on an individual and cultural level, knowledge about living kinds is diminishing.
>
> (pp. 36–37)

This they refer to as their "devolution" hypothesis—the idea that modern Americans know relatively *less* about the natural world than they did 100 years ago, and quite a bit less than a number of Native American traditional societies. Atran and Medin's research shows that knowledge of trees and tree species, for example, has declined to a level that is poorer than at any other time in the history of the English language (p. 44), and several potential confounders were eliminated through their methodology.

Ecological Mindedness

The level of *interconnectedness* with nature can be measured as well. Atran and Medin conducted a number of cross-cultural experiments that have yielded some fascinating results with respect to the level at which a particular culture feels they are 'interconnected' with nature or not. To understand this phenomenon, Atran and Medin studied three different Mesoamerican tribes in the Guatemalan El Petén area: the native Itza' Maya, the Spanish-speaking immigrant ladinos, and the immigrant Q'eqchi' Maya, all of whom lived in the same general area, but had different belief systems and histories with respect to each other and life in the semi-tropical quasi-rainforest. To briefly summarize Atran and Medin's richly detailed work, the Itza' are a tribe that have lived in the Petén forest for millennia, whereas the Ladino immigrated from a variety of areas (including refugee populations) to coalesce into a more or less unified social group that had begun to live in the forest much more recently. The Q'eqchi' Maya are related to the Itza' in terms of language but not location of origin—they migrated from the mountain regions further north due to various political issues.

As one might imagine, the Itza' were the most knowledgeable about the flora and fauna of the region, their folk taxonomies most sophisticated. In fact, their classification system agreed the most with scientific taxonomies despite the fact that the Itza' had no knowledge of Western classification methods. Interestingly, the Itza' also showed the greatest level of ecological mindedness of all three groups, meaning that they recognized the inter-relatedness of the flora and fauna of their homeland, and were more likely to say that humans were part of nature rather than separate from it and that every species had a part to play. To see if they could generalize these results, Atran and Medin did the same experiments on Wisconsin majority-culture outdoorsmen as compared to the Menominee tribe—a tribe of Native Americans that had lived in the area for millennia—as well as urban Americans, and they found the Menominee the most knowledgeable and ecologically minded. Such ecologically minded groups tended to think of all nature as alive and interconnected, and these lessons were taught to children from very early on, whereas American children (as demonstrated by looking at a number of textbooks) are taught very little ecology and tend to emphasize nature as an externality to be exploited, cared for, learned about (i.e., from a distance), etc., rather than teaching that humans are a part of nature.

Ok, but so what? It's almost a cliché that such cultures tend to view humans as part of nature rather that separate, and that "everything is interconnected." All too often in America these sorts of beliefs get dismissed as just so much "tree-hugging." In other words, all Atran and Medin have showed with the above experiments is that those groups who have lived in the same environment long enough tend to, over probably very long times, develop extensive and sophisticated knowledge of that environment, and they furthermore tend to view all living things as interconnected and inclusive of humans. But do such beliefs amount to only so much empty sentiment? Or do they translate into anything tangible about how the environment actually fares with such human presence?

To test this, Atran and Medin actually compared the three Mesoamerican tribal activities with a number of ecological measurements. Accordingly, they discovered that in terms of soil quality, plant and animal biodiversity, and canopy cover, the local environment fared better among the Itza', the most ecologically minded of the three groups, followed by the Ladino, who often mimicked Itza' practices, and then finally the Qéqchi' Maya, who were the least ecologically minded and most destructive. In other words, the cultural mindset and beliefs correlated strongly with actual physical measurements of ecological well-being and overall health. This was despite the fact that the Itza' were essentially spending a great deal of time and energy preserving a forest that other groups were actively exploiting—a fact which puzzled Atran and Medin:

> Only Itza' seem to have a positive vision of the role of plants, animals, and humans in helping the forest survive that is based on species reciprocity... [perhaps] Itza', and perhaps other native peoples with a long history of ecological maintenance, might not treat resources as... objects of a payoff matrix... Instead some people treat resources, such as species, as intentional, relational entities, like friends or enemies.
>
> (pp. 195–196)

To test this theory, the three groups were asked about their belief in spirits or God to see if perhaps these beliefs shaped such behavior. They found that the

Itza' showed awareness of ecological intricacy and reciprocity between animals, plants, and people that the Q'eqchi' had little understanding of. Without being able to attribute causality to correlation, they noted that it was remarkable the great extent that knowledge and ecological values mutually reinforced beliefs about forest spirits. Such beliefs appear to contribute significantly to the superior sustainability practices of the Itza'. This finding was also replicated in the studies of Wisconsin fishermen and Menominee tribespeople, who also had superior sustainability coinciding with belief in nature spirits. Such beliefs are, in Atran and Medino's words "a different way people have of going about their business, and their environments may be the better for it" (p. 208).

Nature Spirits

What is interesting is the relative lack of such beliefs and sustainability among the immigrant Q'eqchi', who were otherwise highly similar to the Itza'. The difference was the lack of generation-spanning contact with the forest. However, the Ladino tribe also lacked this contact, but because they tended to absorb ideas avidly from the Itza', including spiritual values, they also fared better on sustainability practices apparently. This idea, that the degree of exposure to an environment, whether shallow and recent (as found in immigrant populations) versus deep and transgenerational, can significantly shape cultural beliefs and sustainability practices, was replicated in the Wisconsin studies of the Menominee and the surrounding majority-culture. Atran and Medin noted that the parallels among the Itza' and the Menominee were striking, both in terms of their superior sustainability practices and their firm belief in nature spirits that condemned greedy or wasteful treatment of the land.

According to the Menominee, animals are our cousins, and we are descended from the Great Bear. The land is therefore not a commodity but a relational entity like a grandmother. Such beliefs might be considered quaint fodder for children's books among many Americans, but consider what anthropologists Atran and Medin had to say on that subject:

> Overall, it appears that lack of intimate contact with plants and animals may be responsible for the anthropocentric bias observed with urban Americans, but cross-culturally, however, anthropocentrism in reasoning about the environment is the *exception* rather than the rule.
>
> (pp. 129–132)

Atran and Medin note that Americans in practice and education generally regard nature as an externality, whereas native cultures with a long history in a particular environ differ sharply, viewing themselves as an integral part of the ecology in which they live. Furthermore, such native groups have spiritual values that simply cannot be translated into liquid asset calculations that smear everything along a single cash number line. Furthermore, Atran and Medin show that these values are not simply posturing or empty sentiment:

> Not only do Itza' say that the ramón tree is protected by spirits, but also when we do tree counts on their forested plots, we find a greater number of ramón trees than in adjacent plots managed by Q'eqchi' Maya and Ladinos.
>
> (p. 264)

This suggests that different analyses are needed when the resource is considered a participant. The ground-truthing of such spiritual values forces us to take such things seriously. These studies show the importance and value of proof-in-action when it comes to considering archetypal ideas such as nature spirits. Such an approach is not merely a New Age woo-woo affectation, but a natural consequence of simply spending time and getting to know the flora and fauna of an area.

Atran and Medin found that Itza' believed they would be punished if they crossed the forest spirits, and these fears translated into real behavior patterns whose consequences could be traced back a thousand years (p. 269). The Menominee shared such beliefs about their homeland in Wisconsin. When we consider the above evidence that interconnection with nature appears to correlate with greater levels of well-being, less depression, and less anxiety, and improved ecological variables, it seems reasonable to suppose that taking such beliefs seriously, however alien to modern Westerners, might be beneficial to mental health—a theme often defended in analytical psychology literature, which has traditionally valued cross-cultural, and particularly indigenous belief systems.

Does this mean we should all start "believing in forest spirits"? Not necessarily. To my mind, based on the extensive research I did for *Healing Symbols in Psychotherapy* (2016), a strict *belief* is probably nowhere near as important as treating such natural environments and entities *as if* such things were true when it comes to action. Proof-in-action applies both ways—meaning not only does it convince others, it convinces oneself. In other words, I am less concerned with the veracity of a belief that is nearly impossible to verify, so much as I am concerned with what holding such a belief might *do*. Faced with the knowledge that acting *as if* such things are true may have beneficial effects on myself and my environment, I can behave in such a manner for that reason and help myself and my surrounding natural environment. That said, in a 2021 article for the philosophy journal *Synthese*, I review how philosophers of mind have been unable to definitively rule out that plants and environments may have some sort of consciousness. Therefore, I would argue that it might be prudent not to rule it out in practice.

Finally, I believe that the practice of treating elements of natural environments *as if* they were conscious beings is one proof-in-action way that one shows one's affiliation with the natural environment that may recruit the other dimension of the Social Instincts. It is a curious effect that such activities lead to greater levels of conservation, but then again, why should this be so unexpected? Mutualistic and symbiotic relationships are also well known in the biological world, and this may simply represent an element of the Social Instincts that orient us toward such a state under ideal conditions. That said, modern Americans have precious few opportunities to explore such possibilities, as interactions with the natural world, both as children in school and as adults, have become increasingly drowned out by mass-media projects—the subject of the next chapter.

Chapter 7

Education and Mass Media Effects

When looking at what elements of culture may be toxic, we cannot overlook the extreme influence of mass media and the education it provides us all from early childhood onward. As we will see, all the above factors that have occupied the previous chapters can be seen enacted by culture in no small part by the mass media.

Hyper-Individualism, Lack of Identity, and the Media

In 1991, Markus and Kitayama showed how the concept of "the self" is highly culture specific. How the self is defined in relation to others is one of the key differences cross-culturally. Americans, of course, regard the self as a very independent entity, with thick boundaries between it and all others. Independence, autonomy, self-actualization, and self-determination are prized above all else. This construct of the self, however, is not the norm, though many Americans probably think it is. Rather, many other cultures (even developed countries like Japan) have an altogether different construct of self that includes a large number of other people, usually one's family and other long-standing close affiliations. In such settings, it is the collective goals and values of the group that concerns the self, less so the individual.

Kitayama and Park, in their 2010 article on the emerging field of cultural neuroscience, review how subjects from Western cultures including the US are heavily influenced by the value system of independence vs. the interdependence seen in other societies such as that of China, India, or Japan, where family and cultural identity produce stronger affiliations. To clarify, people with *independent* value systems value their personal self and keep it in the forefront of their minds, and this schema of a firmly separated, independent self influences social perception and even non-social attentional biases. Furthermore, their emotional life is rooted in personal goals, desires, and needs, and their motivations are heavily influenced by such needs. By contrast, *interdependent* cultural value systems foster individuals who value their social self more than their personal self, and use this schema to color their social perception and attention. Moreover, their goals, agendas, and concerns

DOI: 10.4324/9781032721354-7

are grounded more in their identity not as a highly separated self removed from social context, but as a self that is *defined* by its surrounding social context. Such individuals guide their emotions and motivations based more on group goals rather than individual goals. Kitayama and Park show how recent neuroscience demonstrates that independent vs. inter-dependent self-representations vary systematically across cultures at the level of brain representations. For example, Zhu et al., in 2007, reported that brain regions used exclusively when the self is thought about among Westerns are also recruited by Chinese subjects when told to think about one's mother, suggesting that Chinese include their mothers as part of their own self representation in the brain.

Kitayama and Park show in their 2010 review that studies on the cultural variation in cognition show that as opposed to cultures that foster an inter-dependent self-construction, Western culture fosters an independent self-construction. This means Western culture (as we have in the US) appears to coax us into biasing toward ignoring contextual information in social and non-social domains. Instead, we become biased toward experiencing more and stronger *socially disengaging emotions* such as pride, superiority, anger, and frustration. What it distances us from are *socially engaging emotions* such as friendliness, respect, guilt, shame (both of which motivate us toward caring about what others think about us), and a tendency to value social harmony as causing happiness. Western culture, then, seems to nudge us away from collective-mindedness and toward individualism right down to our biological makeup, brain activity, and even gene expression. Put to rest is the old "nature vs. nurture" debate, and in its place is a view of the brain as biologically prepared for culture, which in turn is heavily modified by culture through continuous active participation *in* the cultural environment. But this does not mean our brains and sense of self simply "adapts" infi-nitely to whatever culture dishes us. No, it means that with any given cul-ture, our brains will respond by *trying* to adapt as best it can. Given a culture which is hyper-individualistic and continually reinforces the "follow your dreams and to hell with everyone else!" narrative, while at the same time advocating for equality, I think what we wind up with is a tendency in the Western world toward primarily being concerned only about ourselves, pushing back against others' opinions of what we should be doing, and doing our best to leave everyone else alone. I am not arguing that this is "evil" or "wrong." I am only arguing that this state of affairs may leave a part of our souls starving for collective identity, and that this situation is possibly behind the pervasive loneliness problem that we have. It turns out there is a significant cost for infinite freedom and limitless individual expression, and the better we understand it, the better we might be able to build a culture that satisfies those collective needs without sacrificing too much equality and freedom.

Mass Media Consumer Pseudoculture

How are such cultural effects on our brains and sense of self caused? I think part of it is through mass media, in particular that is brought to us by advertisers. Bent on giving people what they want, advertisers produce greater and greater opportunities to encourage self-serving goals via its obedience to a mass-market economy bottom-line approach. There is nothing necessarily "wrong" with doing this, after all, advertisers are simply trying to sell a product. But I think widespread exposure to advertising may have some unforeseen, subtle, but powerful effects. I think there is something deeper going on here. As mentioned before, social connections are reinforced through mores, constraints, and rules—for better or for worse. The Social Instincts demand proof-in-action, and as children grow up, we often non-verbally and/or unconsciously absorb such rules, simply as a matter of the Social Instincts operating the way they always have. And this process has itself been explored in great depth in a 2008 book by Professor of Religion Adam Seligman, anthropologist Robert Weller, historian Michael Puett and psychoanalyst and psychiatrist Bennett Simon called *Ritual and Its Consequences: An Essay on the Limits of Sincerity*. There, Seligman et al. explain that family and collective identity (two dimensions of our Social Instincts) are usually non-verbally enacted and absorbed by children via ritualistic behaviors, unconsciously adopted behavioral constraints, taboos, and attitudes. Children are especially adept at picking up on these rules—unsurprisingly, given such rules are hungered after by the Social Instincts that demand we have proof that we are securely within the fold of some kind of collective entity.

As Seligman et al. observe, in the Western World, hyper-individualism has "deconstructed" such typical social interactions to such a high degree that everything becomes subject to verbal debate and endless elaboration, and this loses the proof-in-action quality that is needed to satisfy the Social Instincts. Seligman et al. argue that this situation leads to conditions all too favorable for extremist beliefs to emerge, as well as causing widespread anomie. Given our discussion about the Social Instincts and how their neglect can lead us to such misery, we can see in greater detail why their observations might hold.

But how did we get to this place? Why would such structures, typically reinforced and renewed via standard upbringing practices, break down? Consider: it is often thought that media outlets simply regurgitate whatever cultural value system is extant within the culture. I think that is an oversimplification. Economic factors play into this because of the subtle but ubiquitous influence of advertising. That is, whatever value system you might employ within your family and/or community (if one exists), the steady pipeline of advertising that is pumped in via television, cable, internet, smartphone, etc., can run counter to it, and the dynamics of this interaction seem to be perfectly poised to undermine precisely those things which feed the Social Instincts. If, for example, a budding individual bristles against "rules," customs, or traditions that might reinforce relational, collective, or natural identity, the advertiser is your best friend, for she or he is telling you in nearly every possible way that you should toss away all of that and buy their product to make you feel more empowered.

Advertisers, see, have no reason to care about whether your community is against buying their product. It causes them no harm if you break away from that embedded culture to pursue what they're selling. In fact, it behooves them as an advertiser to *encourage* this sort of thinking. Decades upon decades of this subtle bias in the direction of individualism (combined with an already present value system of "rugged individualism" espoused by 19th century and earlier generations) has pushed us toward the hyper-individualism that we have now. I doubt that this was consciously intended by anyone. It's simply a consequence of our economic system, along with an increasingly ubiquitous influx of media content bombarding us from very early ages.

Advertisers are merely using every means necessary to convince you that you desperately need their product. And it isn't really even advertising, *per se*, because advertising itself is not new. Vendors hawking their wares is as old as history. But technology has expanded the role advertising has in our lives exponentially. Therefore, it's not so much advertising as it is the sheer amount of it. It is there blaring from day one and we rarely get a break from it for even one day thereafter. And, given their profit motives, they will target any motivational means necessary to convince you that you are not enough without their products, whatever they might be. The sensitivity of the Social Instincts are, as such, prime targets. Therefore, they have every reason to encourage you to pursue self-aggrandizement, looks, and status via the purchasing of various products, and zero reason to encourage you to engage with your surroundings, your community, your close friends and family, and your significant other for satisfaction. As such, the economic factors of the last century in particular, along with widespread proliferation of continuous media consumption, have created what I call a "mass media consumer pseudoculture" that young people unconsciously begin to process.

This means children are often vulnerable to being given conflicting messages growing up, practically from day one. To satisfy the powerful needs of my Social Instincts, should I listen to my family, elders, community, spiritual leaders? Or should I listen to the voices that come from outside these in the form of non-stop profit-motive-driven media messages that I don't tend to notice, but register nonetheless?

Compound this continuous mass-media "education" with our public education system and you will see more clearly what I am trying to describe. Consider this: from a very young age, our children are expected to spend one-third of their day in school. This school environment, furthermore, is populated by largely underpaid and under-appreciated teachers who are also outnumbered. There is no doubt that their efforts are heroic in attempting to accomplish their job of educating tomorrow's leaders and workers. But during this time the students are all separated from their family. Given the earlier concerns we explored regarding the progressively worsening strains on families, this continued separation clearly does not make it easier to maintain the needs of the interpersonal Social Instincts.

Furthermore the needs of community identity begin to develop right around age 9–10—middle school—and we begin to start looking around for signs of "tribal affiliation" and belonging. But our children have nothing to go on here except for what they see in the mass media, given their continually shrinking time with close family and diminishing community presence. Unless, that is, they live in a rural community, in which community identity tends to be stronger traditionally (though the poverty of such regions can tend to offset this benefit). More often, though, the "tribe" middle-schoolers tend to find winds up being a superficial "clique." As adults, we may have a tendency to just roll our eyes over this or shrug, but there is something very serious going on here with our pre-adolescents and adolescents. They are desperately seeking a tribe, and if the bonds to family and local community are weak and/or non-existent, and much of what we are reviewing in this book suggests that they are, then the efforts the children are going to put into this endeavor are only going to be that much more intense. This is the perfect setup for intergenerational conflict, and it is no wonder such conflict is endemic in the US and other Westernized cultures.

And there is another complication. Not only are many children presented with strained and disconnected interpersonal and community presence, the alternative provided by the ever burgeoning mass-media presence is nowhere near up to the task to satisfy the Social Instincts. As mentioned, I believe it presents itself as a *pseudoculture* because of another one of the insidious effects: it is homogenizing and anonymous in its value system delivery, and it lacks the proof-in-action needed to truly satisfy the Social Instincts. That is, because it is all oriented toward promoting a hyper-individualistic value system that erases all local color and distinction in favor of mass-market appeal to the lowest common denominator, it tends to present a falsely homogeneous consumption-based "culture" with a lot of non-verbal pressure behind it—pressure that is created by the many tricks and tools used by advertisers to manipulate us into feeling like we need their products. Given these factors, and the fact of community disintegration and increasing disconnection, it is no wonder, then, that so many people reach for the same sorts of proof-in-action signifiers of affiliation that middle-schoolers do: that being a decision of *what* sorts of products they will consume. In other words, without a reassuring, stable and rich tribe to attach oneself to, combined with a ubiquitous mass-media presence that simply has ever-increasing choices available, children and adults may try to satisfy their need for affiliation (un-ironically calling it "self-expression") with the only means they have: choosing what product to consume.

Advertising and mass media have homogenized, anonymized, and marketized nearly all concrete signifiers of real affiliation with interpersonal or collective identity because that is how technologically advanced capitalism works best. The unforeseen consequence of this, however, is that this situation triggers our Social Instincts to seek out something to connect us, but our tools to do that are diminished. Thus we will use the only means we have left: our choice of *which* of the infinite products to consume as signifiers. In the next section I will illustrate what I mean with some concrete examples.

Fashion Choices and Identity Dynamics

It is always fascinating to me that one typically only sees outlandish or deliberately "rebellious" clothing, piercings, tattoos, etc., in more urban settings. I am not aware of any studies that look into this formally, but it seems to hold anecdotally. When rural communities have younger generations branching out into the more self-consciously "different" types of expression that they see in the various media outlets, there tends to be all sorts of intergenerational conflict. The exposure to mass media precedes this, and the social consequences seem to follow.

Why is this? Of course the typical answer in a generally hyper-individualistic culture like ours is that the older generations are just being "judgmental" and "overly critical." Typical responses I hear are that younger people are "just exploring their identity" and "finding out who they are." I think this is an oversimplification, and it hinges on several underlying assumptions about clothing, music, etc., that I think are mistaken.

First, the type of clothing one wears, along with other aspects of physical appearance, is not a symbolically or culturally neutral act. Every choice of appearance is one which has a non-verbal tribal-affiliation meaning as a kind of proof-in-action. Some clothing choices (as well as hairstyles, makeup styles—for men and women—and other fashion choices) are deliberately "subversive," though I do not believe that every person who makes such fashion choices is necessarily consciously aware of this. What has been variously called over the years "punk," "goth," "scene," "hipster," and a whole host of other labels for the ever-expanding list of sub-cultures, all have a common feature despite their varying surface appearance: the desire to present oneself as "other" in the face of a tyrannical "mainstream" that is "culturally accepted." It assumes that a huge monolithic "mainstream" culture is attempting to foist its "value system" and identity signifiers on you, and you therefore justifiably must fight the system through whatever means possible. I think the above factors in the mass-media in the face of dwindling interpersonal and collective presence are likely behind this phenomenon.

These sub-culture trends typically assume a simple dichotomy between "me" and "society" where "society" is an oppressive faceless external force that must be fought against in the war to be "accepted" for one's conspicuously displayed quirks. Such fashions (especially in their most extreme iterations) seem to take anything that is even vaguely perceived as "mainstream" and deliberately twist it in some way so as to not only reject it but supplant it with something perceived as its opposite. Note, of course, that the mass media is *required* to create anything resembling a "mainstream"—without it, there is *no such thing* as an anonymously derived and tyrannically oppressive "mainstream" bugaboo to rail against. Rather, you simply have a community with its traditional structures, participated in by people you've known all your life. "Mainstream" as an object of reverence or revenge can only occur in a more urban and modern world where you can disappear into a crowd of unknown people in the face of dwindling or non-existent community and interpersonal connection, while simultaneously being bombarded with anonymously and artificially homogeneous advertising and entertainment content.

In any case, you can see the real nature and purpose of this kind of behavior easily once you recognize the symbolic nature of the items worn (or not worn). Hipsters wear clothing in unmatched colors, deliberately "rural" fashion choices (like flannel or impractically huge boots, unneeded on city streets), men wear long beards and suits that hearken back to the 19th century—but don't forget the complicated sleeve tattoos to "update" it. All of this is meticulously chosen to express a subversion of the "mainstream" market consumer culture blasted at us daily from the mass media. It is an attempt to soothe the screaming Social Instincts that crave the real connection they cannot get from the surrounding hyper-individualist culture OR the mass media, so it's the only option left: try to make your OWN culture! Punk styles take anything and self-consciously jumble it up into total chaos. Goth, which evolved from punk fashion, takes everything and turns it into something reminding one of death, funerals, morbid fascinations, horror (like vampires or creepy gas masks), or Victorian emotional constriction. Goth, therefore, takes the anti-mainstream impulse and targets one feature of the mass-market consumer culture: its rampant thanatophobia, or fear of death and dying. Deliberately celebrating the macabre to one degree or another, it rebels against a consumer culture which hates death rather than sees it as a normal aspect of life. Scene, which evolved from goth, spices up the black doom and gloom with Japanese anime-inspired ensembles along with zany hair coloring and deliberately clashing and extremely "loud" and busy color patterns—scene is aptly named, since it embodies (and effectively enacts) a desire to draw attention to oneself, as if to balm an underlying sense of being ignored and lost in the faceless mass. As such, scene appears to target the mass-media pseudoculture's quality of faceless anonymity and launches splashy-colored torpedoes at it.

But don't make the mistake of assuming that this practice is unique to the 1990s and beyond—feminist rebels of the 60s and 70s went braless to reject the sexism of the mainstream, and hippies are famous for tie-dye and bellbottoms, along with (of course) being extremely hairy as a way to attack the business-focus of the "mainstream" of that era. And before that flappers of the 1920s bucked perceived "conventions" with *short* hair (gasp!), hats, and fans.

With each of these (all urban derived) movements, the sub-culture involved goes to great lengths to separate themselves from the "mainstream" (however conceived at the time) by using fashion choices to label their side of the war for acceptance and belonging. In any world where interpersonal and collective connections are strained and/or disappearing, I believe you will see desperate attempts by people to reinforce their affiliation through whatever means is necessary—this has been observed by sociologists as early as Durkheim (1897) and has been observed in history as well. But now not only do we have strained communities, we also have a pervasive pseudoculture that is blaring non-stop in the background. This is the perfect condition for creating continually proliferating sub-cultures and extremist groups, according to Seligman et al.

Note, for example, that there is a typical undercurrent in these sub-cultures that is measuring both in-members and self *along* the dichotomy. Is so-and-so a REAL metalhead? Or are they a "poser"? This is serious business and can lead to great emotional turmoil. And don't be fooled by dismissive attempts to explain away these phenomena. Many times folks who employ these fashion choices claim—when pressed—that they just "think it looks cool." They might say "I just like it." Or they will say they are "trying to express my individuality." But there is actually quite a bit of complex push-pull in these explanations. Here is why: every one of these fashion movements is defined by whatever is conceived of as "mainstream" in the current moment, so as to reject or subvert it in some way. Note that if any of these choices becomes popular enough to be seen as "mainstream," it no longer becomes an important focus of attention within the fashion. An example of this would be tattoos. In the 1970s tattoos were reserved only for "low class" individuals and hence many families would put a line in the sand with each other over not getting them. For whatever reason, though, over the next 30 years, tattoos became more common, to the point that many more people have them now than they did in the past. This means the "rebellious" fashions that attached themselves to tattoos needed to either de-emphasize them or get more extreme with them, since the point is to distinguish oneself from the ever-present and tyrannical "mainstream."

This is all because fashion choice is *never* neutral. It is always a non-verbal means to communicate acceptance or rejection of the perceived cultural norm, conscious or not. The reason for saying "it's just something I like" is to assert one's own attachment to the choice, but of course *that is the point*—it's just leaving out the unsaid but arguably more important "even though the anonymous mainstream pseudoculture doesn't like it." The clue here is in the emotionality of the responses not only of the wearers but the observers. This tells us what the real emotional *stakes* of these decisions actually is. More conservative individuals get irritated by them and tend to judge such people harshly, meanwhile the fashion rebels get very defensive and attached to their choices. What on earth is really going on here? This is a war for identity and belonging, created and amplified by the mass-media, particularly effective in urban and suburban environments that lack long-standing community and belonging. Ever wonder why there aren't very many goth farmers? This would be why. The choice to adopt one of these fashion styles likely starts off with an arbitrary personal affinity—for example, if a kid is fascinated by the works of Edgar Allen Poe, she or he might find themselves with an affinity for goth fashion styles, since they sometimes get linked by members of the sub-culture. But from there the fashion war begins. In some cases, the pushback from surrounding others—who naturally get subsumed as being unwitting agents of the tyrannical mainstream—may be enough to keep such expressions to a minimum, but in others, this only causes a counter-offensive where the individual ups the ante with progressively more extreme fashion choices. In such instances, the clothing *becomes* the defense against feeling "not accepted."

I covered symbolic expressions in much greater detail in my 2016 book *Healing Symbols in Psychotherapy*, but the reason fashion choices get tangled up so deeply in this battle for acceptance is because clothing and hairstyles are concrete and tangible signifiers that cannot be faked. They are proof-in-action signifiers. You can either wear a three-foot pink mohawk, torn up jeans, and a shirt that says "society is rubbish" (a bit on-the-nose, but there we are), or you can wear a crew-cut, polo shirt, and khakis. I'm not here to judge which choice is "right," but to point out that such forced choices represent concrete signifiers of your desire for affiliation or your rejection of that affiliation. Thus, people who are deeply attached to such sub-cultures are waging war against the pseudoculture while trying to build a real in-the-flesh community at the same time. Hence they become objects of conflict due to the symbolic *importance* they embody. In this case, they embody the quest for belonging, and a rejection of the "mainstream" as an alternative. And in the case of the rejectors, there is no small amount of resentment as an undercurrent, and a desire to be accepted for one's quirks, whatever they are, even when one's actual identity may be barely formed (more on this later). The whole process gets hijacked by the fashion war, and winds up being a major distraction in my opinion. In fact, one might fairly say that much of this isn't really "sub-culture" but "counter-culture." The difference is that counter-culture can't exist without something to be "counter" to. A sub-culture can. The question at hand is whether a given sub-culture would exist were it not for a mainstream to attack non-verbally.

In any case, the point is all of this is caused, I believe, by the volatile combination of mass media effects and hyper-individualism. Our Social Instincts are starving, and if we don't accept the mass media version of a "culture" to belong to, we must invent our own on the spot and defend it with tremendous ferocity, as if we were warriors defending ourselves from another tribe over the mountains who wanted all our resources for themselves. This is more than just a metaphor; I believe this situation evokes these deeply evolutionary motivations. The endless division of life into sub-cultures is an attempt to satisfy the Social Instincts. In the end, what we seek is belonging along individual, interpersonal, collective, and universal dimensions. Because of the effects of advertising and the economic drivers beholden to the bottom line that guide it, those of us born in cultures with mass media are fed an artificially homogenized, anonymized, and marketized pseudoculture that is catered not to satisfying our need for belonging but to convince us to buy things. The entertainment programming we consume is furthermore beholden to the advertisers, and so whenever possible will reinforce this very same set of circumstances, despite the intentions of our best artists, writers, directors, and poets. I do not fault the artists for this situation. Those of us who are annoyed or dissatisfied with this arrangement might not care about the continual background radiation of the pseudoculture *if* our own local communities provided some means of satisfying the Social Instincts in themselves. But they don't. This is why I think rural communities are more resistant to the whims of popular (i.e. "mainstream") culture and so do not display nearly as much counter-culture as a reaction. Nevertheless, despite this protective factor, history shows that eventually rural communities (like Roseto) eventually succumb to the unstoppable wave.

In any case, the counter-cultures are not "rebelling against the mainstream" just for the heck of it, but because these members are trying to find for themselves a more substantial means to satisfy their Social Instincts. The problem is the rigid division of everything into "mainstream" and "not-mainstream." I think adherence to fashion trends, musical choice, and so forth are simply not sufficient to fully satisfy the need for belonging, though it certainly seems to be better for some people than going along with the perceived mainstream, which is naturally even more impoverished because it is primarily driven by market concerns and not the human soul. Sub-cultures, to their credit, try to provide true sustenance for the Social Instincts. When nothing else of substance is available, fashion, music-choices, and expressed ideology has to suffice as best it can. I also think that sexual identity and orientation is sometimes used in this manner as well. Sexual orientation and identity can be indicated via proof-in-action as well, and so this is why it is called the LGBTQIA+ "community" rather than simply a collection of people with similar proclivities. The Social Instincts will attach to anything it can to satisfy the needs of long-term partner, interpersonal, community, and universal connection.

In any case, it is the very things Pinker praises in his work *Enlightenment Now*—large centralized (and largely faceless) organizations and their media outlets—that create this state of affairs. While this situation may be conducive to some material benefits for all, it seems to create social chaos and loneliness as a result, at the same time that hyper-individualism and the mass media both feed into each other in a vicious, ever-accelerating cycle that forces the Social Instincts into a starving state. I largely point out sub-cultures as a way to show how all of this works—please do not get the impression that I "disapprove" of any of them. I am not here for that. I am here to explain and understand, and so therefore to hopefully heal if it is needed. If such sub-cultures are truly capable of providing all of those needs in the long term—then that's wonderful. I applaud them. If not, more investigation will be needed.

News Media Effects

As if all of this weren't destabilizing enough, in the last few years, I have seen another alarming trend originating from our media. Outside of simply the global effects of the media in bombarding us with advertisements and programming that seem to be particularly adept at promoting hyper-individualism, the last few years has seen a political polarization in news media outlets that further separates us. The Social Instincts again feed into this effect, since, in the absence of a substantive means to satisfy them, I see many turning to political ideologies as *substitutes* for collective identity. Again, these are rather poor substitutes, since they rely entirely on verbal expression of ideology rather than any proof-in-action measures. News outlets feed into this by (particularly in the last few decades) catering to their target audience, whether it be right-wing or left-wing. They do this by spin-doctoring news stories to reinforce what they already know their audience believes, thereby telling their consumers basically what they want to hear, and/or fostering outrage at the "other side." Any time you see "us versus them" rhetoric, you can safely assume that you are in the territory of the Social Instincts, where they begin to show us their dangerous and ugly side—more on this later.

These media outlets (you know who they are), consistently oversimplify sometimes very complex political problems and spoon feed them to their audience in the form of idealizing the "us" and demonizing the "them"—i.e., if a particular policy is under review and it aligns with the political affiliation of the news channel you are watching, they will deliberately idealize the defenders of it and paint the opposition as greedy, scheming, and otherwise nefarious mustache-twirling evildoers. It is sometimes so absurd that it would be comical if it wasn't so harmful to our well-being as a culture.

The reason this profit-driven polarization can be so harmful is that it further disconnects people from one another along political views that are only reinforced in cyberspace or other digital outlets—not in terms of real face-to-face interaction. Clinically, I have seen this contribute many times to isolation and loneliness, as patients complain to me that previous long-time friends and/or family members are no longer tolerable either because they or because their friend/etc. have become hyperpolarized in their political views and now view the other as "them." This appalling situation, created by uncritical acceptance of profit-driven media messages who have no skin in this game, has led many times to a worsening of loneliness, isolation, depression, anxiety, and even suicidality. Unfortunately the giant faceless global machinery that perpetuates this situation is showing no signs of letting up any time soon.

Conclusion

I believe a major player in the dynamic that has led us to a culture that is toxic and incapable of providing for the desperate needs of the Social Instincts is partly driven by our mass media outlets. Through a complex interplay between economic and historical factors, coupled with runaway technological advances with unforeseen consequences, we are seeing a continued neglect of our Social Instincts, and many cultural phenomena appear to be attempts by individuals at feeding those needs, to varying degrees of success. Cross-cultural studies reviewed earlier, however, suggest that it can take a long time for a culture to "catch up" with rapid changes, and for those of us here in the US, those changes seem to be accelerating rather than slowing down. As such, our media outlets not only reflect the hyper-individualistic value system but contribute to it, which further accentuates it.

It is not my intent to paint the media as evil and inherently "bad." There is no doubt that good, healing messages can be disseminated using its immense influence. There are good programs out there for children and adults that are not only entertaining but deeply soulful and meaningful. We have many, many talented artists, writers, and mystics out there. Nevertheless, I do not think these exceptions constitute the bulk of the mass media content, nor is it enough to dismantle the insidious pseudoculture effect it can have on us. And in any case, outside of the effects on the promotion of hyper-individualism, we can also see that it contributes to another factor that is clumsily grafted onto our Social Instincts but leads to more suffering: the achievement-based value system—the subject of the next chapter.

Chapter 8

The Achievement-Based Value System

What makes you a valuable person? Chances are, if someone were to ask you this, you might be tempted to say something along the lines of "being kind to others," or "being a good person," or "doing what's right." These kinds of superficial answers to what a person's value system is are as common as they are vague. You might as well answer the question "what makes you valuable?" with "being a valuable person"! So it is in terms of one's non-verbal emotionality and their tendencies toward behavior that you have to look to find what their true internalized (and often unspoken) values are.

And because of the above hyper-individualistic bias toward self-aggrandizement, narcissism, appearance, money, and status, the value system underneath the lip-service is something I call an "achievement-based" value system. I covered some of this in *Healing Symbols in Psychotherapy* in discussing cultures with high "grid" and low "group"—cultures where there are a lot of non-verbal communications regarding one's status in a usually unspoken (but sometimes deliberately described) hierarchy, but very little in terms of collective identity reinforcement. But here I think it deserves a closer look.

The achievement-based value system (ABVS for short) is a system of values that are used by a significant number of people in our culture to assess their self-worth. It bases self-worth largely in terms of status, money, and looks. As we saw in earlier chapters, it appears that the overall value system in the US has changed from a hundred years ago, moving gradually from a value system that mostly elevates affiliation, service, and autonomy that is independent of achievement to one that mostly values money, status, and narcissism. I think this has been contributed to by the media effects reviewed in the previous chapter. After all, it is easier to sell products that promise to elevate looks, money, or status than it is to sell products that nurture one's desire for affiliation or service. Likely, then, the drift in value systems has, in combination with a media that encourages it, created a positive feedback loop to shift the overall value system in this way.

Nevertheless, there is nothing necessarily wrong with trying to improve one's status, money, or appearance. My concern is when these values become the only means to measure one's self worth. In such cases it becomes very

DOI: 10.4324/9781032721354-8

toxic. If everyone is on a ladder, it is impossible to connect with another human being on common ground—everyone is either your better or your lesser, which means your attitude toward them is either resentful or disdainful. That is not very conducive to promoting affiliation, nor will it satisfy the Social Instincts, though it certainly may feed into our instincts to dominate others. Trouble is that satisfaction only comes to those who are at the top of a given perceived hierarchy. And even then, the loneliness "at the top" will continue to plague you, given that suicide hits both high and low socio-economic strata. The perceived lack of tribe and secure affiliation will continue to produce loneliness and misery, even if you may be able to content yourself at being "the best" of a given social ladder.

This ABVS nevertheless is quite prevalent, and I have found it to be most present clinically (in the majority of cases) in middle class non-minority populations (more on this detail later). In such populations, the ABVS is acquired early on with a continued familial and cultural emphasis on grades, job status, money, and looking "perfect." In fact, perfectionism is one of the main consequences of the ABVS in action. It is at its most toxic when it presents itself (usually unconsciously until it is explored in therapy) as a dichotomy, wherein I think to myself, if I am not perfect, I am utterly worthless. This is a perfect recipe for a whole host of mental health problems. The anxiety is caused by the internalized pressure to continually push upward to avoid feeling worthless. The depression is caused by the feeling of hope-lessness that one will ever be perfect—since, well, perfection is impossible. And the internalized pressure to look perfect is what can lead to bulimia and anorexia. Note that only in cultures where thinness acquires a cultural meaning of high status does this equation ever materialize. In cultures that do not have this equation, thinness is not sought after.

While the hyper-emphasis on thinness (a la "one can never be too rich or too thin") probably reached its zenith in the 2000s and has since gotten a little bit better, it took a widespread cultural backlash on the aforementioned media outlets to combat it, as it was contributing to the worsening prevalence of anorexia and bulimia—two horrifying diseases that are the epitome of the ABVS running amok. Here we can see the power that a media campaign can have. It is just a shame that so much damage had to be done before we began looking at cultural sources for suffering. Again, this is an instance of a failure to fully consider the bio-psycho-social model as intended. Early theories of anorexia, for example, were hyper-focused on family dynamics—an "over-involved" mother and a "distant" father. Note how these appear to be *consequences* of the ABVS in themselves. In any case, not only was little attention paid to what the biological predispositions to anorexia might be, the socio-cultural influence on its appearance was not explored either. As it stands, anorexia nervosa remains one of the deadliest mental illnesses, and treatment for it is extremely difficult. One wonders if widespread cultural change aimed at prevention might yield better results.

In any case, the ABVS causes more problems than just eating disorders, as mentioned. Anorexia is, to my mind, merely one of the most extreme consequences of it, and hence it is illustrative. But quite a bit of anxiety and depression are a result of it operating in dangerous conjunction with biological predispositions and family dynamics. When looking at the bio-psycho-social contribution to a given mental state such as anxiety or depression, however, it is useful to ask oneself whether the ABVS is at play in helping to create the sense of low worth and/or anxiety over one's feelings of relative safety and worth. If all that one considers is where one is on the imaginary ladder of achievement, not only are the Social Instincts not appeased, but one also has anxiety over one's precarious perch, with others seeking to "surpass" you, feeling "inferior" to those who have, etc. It's a recipe for limitless misery. One way in which this seems to be playing out in the data we have is in the effects of *income inequality* on mental health.

Income Inequality

One correlate of increasing anxiety and depression that has been found cross-culturally is the relationship between wealth inequality and rates of depression. Hidaka's (2012) review discusses several studies that show that in developed countries, *greater inequality* correlates with higher levels of distrust, competition, and status anxiety, with the United States possessing (perhaps unsurprisingly) the greatest economic inequality and also the highest lifetime risk for a mood disorder. Obviously, many of these factors are interrelated and may work together to contribute to the decline in mental health overall.

In any case, *pace* libertarian arguments that the "rising tide lifts all boats" (i.e., income inequality nevertheless coincides with increased wealth across all strata) the rising tide does not appear to include mental health. Instead, what I suspect it does is place greater pressure on everyone to "do better" due to the unavoidably visible ostentation of the top tiers (i.e. billionaires flying into space in personal rockets). This encourages people with an internalized ABVS to sacrifice social connection and maintenance for increased achievement-based striving. This tradeoff, however, costs one in terms of well-being and happiness, because the Social Instincts are not satisfied with soaring bank accounts or feelings of superiority—assuming one ever even gets so far, as most of us don't. The ABVS therefore winds up reneging on its promise to make one happy, and the quest to "succeed" appears to potentially come at heavy costs in social capital.

More evidence comes from a 2015 report by Oishi and Kesebir. These authors found that, across 34 countries, happiness was inversely proportional to income inequality, even during times of economic growth. So here it appears again that trading affiliation, service, autonomy, and meaning for status, appearance, and money is a devil's bargain. Again, this is not to say that seeking out a better life for oneself and one's family is a bad idea.

Poverty, too, can cause major mental and physical health problems. I am merely pointing out that not only does money not buy happiness, the price one pays in order to get that money *may* be costly in terms of our social Social Instinct based needs. Our culture not only has a prominent ABVS alongside ostentatious displays of wealth and power, we also have this in combination with media depictions of members of the pseudoculture as having unrealistic amounts of money, status, and attractiveness.

Examples of this would be actors in sitcoms or dramas living in apartments or houses that would be impossible for such characters to truly afford, to say nothing of the fact that the actors themselves are typically extremely attractive. This is naturally because not only does attractiveness help land them the acting role in the first place (creating a skewed sample), and so television shows in general tend to be populated by more attractive people than is encountered in everyday environments, but because many of those actors can afford expensive cosmetic procedures, hair, makeup, and fashion to enhance their attractiveness further. Thus, especially in the context of a strained or non-existent local community, children and young adults who primarily gain their social input via media outlets are likely to be consuming content that presents the idea that "normal" people are super-attractive, rich, and generally just "better." When combined with an ABVS, it's a recipe for disaster. Therefore, a correlation between income disparity and depression makes sense—as the top gets higher and higher, and we have historically had an ABVS, the top of the ladder becomes increasingly impossible to achieve. Resentment, feelings of injustice, and anxiety over "failing" (whatever that is supposed to mean) rise in conjunction.

Finally, note that the hunter-gatherer societies studied by Chaudhary et al. in 2023 and others reviewed in that article are very commonly extremely egalitarian, with authoritative behavior and expectations of obedience usually met with scorn, ridicule, and hostility (p. 13). On the contrary, such cultures tend to strongly emphasize personal autonomy, independence, and self-reliance, yet *in the context of* a strongly communal and group-identified culture. In Western cultures, we seem to still value independence and self-reliance, but the communal living and group identity have been replaced with hierarchies and the ABVS. I strongly suspect this situation does *not* agree with our Social Instincts, and is partly to blame for all the constant chafing against "authority" that occurs side by side with longing to belong that we see in the West. In the current Western model, however, satisfying these twin, seemingly at-odds desires is impossible. Perhaps the reason for this is that those desires evolved in hunter-gatherer contexts in which it is easily achievable, but in modern Western cultures it is not.

The Black-White Paradox

There is evidence that the worsening depression has hit White/non-Hispanic Americans the most over recent decades. This was found by Weinberger et al. in 2018 and has come to be known as the "Black-White paradox." It is a "paradox" because minority populations tend to have it worse along most measures of health care, income, and many other measures of well-being. The harmful effects of widespread racial inequality are well known to impact many environmental outcomes. African-Americans in general suffer greater inequality and discrimination, poorer health outcomes and greater mortality than Whites, and yet, depression and suicide rates have increased more for Whites than Blacks according to Case and Deaton in a 2015 report, along with Weinberger et al., and Barnes and Bates in the aforementioned 2017 paper. Oddly enough, it's the privileged racial category that is experiencing *more* depression and suicide. Barnes and Bates note that the increased mortality rates seen in lower-education Whites were due to "deaths of despair"— i.e., drugs, alcohol, and suicide.

What is going on here? Obviously, we need a lot more research to sort it out. My hypothesis, based on the foregoing discussion, is that these minorities, despite experiencing so much hardship in so many domains, may have two protective factors working for them that Whites do not: some relative insulation from the ABVS, as well as a relatively higher level of substantial collective identity.

The second factor requires some explanation. First, "White" is not really an ethnicity. It does not represent a heritage, tradition, or anything more than a superficial set of characteristics based on skin tone. Beyond skin color, the term "White" has no more history than that of the colonial legacy it was built on. Lumping together people of so many distinct ethnicities simply on the basis of their skin color really makes very little sense outside of an easy means to categorize people into "us" (the colonizers) and "them" (the colonized/oppressed). Contrast this to the African-American community—the effects of colonization and the trans-Atlantic slave trade forced many of the ancestors of today's African-Americans to form quite a few varieties of coherent culture, ethnicity, and tradition, not to mention solidarity in the face of so much oppression. True, not all African-American communities are identical, but what is the "White American" community? Aside from neo-Nazis—a toxic exception that proves the rule, which I will get to shortly— there is very little to hang a collective "White" identity on. Americans of European ancestry (and hence light-colored skin) can be Ivy-leaguers from Boston, country folk from Appalachia, surfer dudes from California, hipsters from Portland, cowboys from Texas—what on earth do these people have in common with each other aside from skin tone?

Answer: not much. America has a history of not only the trans-Atlantic slave trade (like so many other colonizing countries of the 17th and 18th centuries), but the 19th and 20th centuries in this country embody a history of waves of immigrants coming into the US and feeling strong pressure to disconnect themselves from their homelands. In fact, this history may be partly behind the ABVS being so prevalent among "White" Americans. Many Irish immigrants, for example, in the 19th and early 20th century came to this country fleeing famine, anti-Irish racism from England, and crushing poverty in their own country, to find themselves facing discrimination and "Blacks and Irish need not apply" in the States. The pressure to assimilate and find some way to become "White" was probably strong—and obviously this did not help the situation at all for Blacks. Neither Blacks nor Native Americans ever had this option, but wave after wave of European immigrants did, and so many did just this, from German to "Scotch Irish" (a uniquely American term), to the Catholic Irish, to Poles, to Jewish immigrants—all of these separate ethnicities have become homogenized into "Whites," even when it makes little sense. The Irish, for example, were colonized themselves for eight hundred years and only achieved independence in 1915 (except for Northern Ireland which is still a part of the UK). Their lot was not as miserable as the African slaves or the decimated Native Americans, but it was not a whole lot better either. Nevertheless, the old colonial division of "White" and "Black" has remained, forcing homogeneity where there was none, and continuing to oppress non-White minorities.

That act—the trading of ethnic identity for "White"-ness, ironically had a price, in my opinion. Doing this sacrificed a real heritage and collective identity for mere lip-service and sentiment, in order to belong to the economically privileged group. As a result, the Social Instincts kicked in and produced feelings of anomie, lack of belonging, rootlessness, loneliness, and suicidality. In turn, many White Americans tried in the early and mid-20th century to forge an "American" identity. Much of Americana in the world of cinema and television seems to have this energy behind it. But the upheaval of the 1960s changed all that and this attempted American identity has fragmented ever since. Those minorities who were always in second class status anyway and were never really invited into this identity were likely not hit as hard by this, and so returned to their own roots—this is exactly what the Social Instincts motivate: in times of stress and want, they encourage us to band together in solidarity into "us" and "them."

But for White Americans, there is no "us" but Whiteness. The ethnic ties were sacrificed and now Whites are all lumped together into a category that is loosely affiliated with the mass-media pseudoculture. It's no wonder so many sub-cultures and counter-cultures have erupted over the last 75 years, and most of them are racially "White." The Social Instincts are at work here: seeking out a real connection in proof-in-action terms, to alleviate the terrible sense of rootlessness and loneliness that lurks under the surface of the ABVS. Many therefore turn to tribe-building in whatever means they know how. The instincts kick in around middle school and it never ends from there.

And here is where it turns dark: there's another consequence of this state of affairs for "Whites"—bigotry and hatred. This is the dark side of the Social Instincts—and they are indeed pitch black. As I said before, the Social Instincts were born out of blood and conflict. They were both created and amplified in the face of tribal warfare among our primate ancestors.

Extremist groups attempt to alleviate the Social Instincts via extreme measures—paranoia, hate, rigid exclusion, and violence. Exactly what we would expect from Social Instincts run amok. More and more, I hope I am showing that the Social Instincts are like explosives. Powerful and dangerous, because they became linked to our survival over the course of evolution. Such instincts (like rage, sex, hunger) do not mess around and are difficult to control and can be very primitive and all-or-nothing if not integrated into our more rational faculties.

In any case, keep in mind I am trying to diagnose the problem and understand how we got here. I have speculated a lot here on the Black-White paradox and I could easily be way off in why it exists. If I am right, however, I don't think the answer will be easy. I think that all the various groups in the US might find solace in seeking out a collective identity, but it will be difficult to do it without perpetuating toxic colonial racist structures and categories. There is a reason we have days like St. Patrick's Day celebrating Irish heritage, a Black History month for African heritage, and Oktoberfest celebrating German heritage but we don't have a "White History Month": "White" isn't a heritage. It's a consequence of our toxic colonial legacy. But despite my distaste for the label, I continue to see the option on forms asking my ethnicity, and it continues to perpetuate the categories of "White" et al.

In any case, this long sidebar has only been to point out that identifying oneself ethnically with being "White" has the effect of connecting one merely to the ABVS and the mass-media pseudoculture, neither of which will satisfy. They are a very poor substitute for real bonds of affiliation, community, heritage, and group identity that are needed to fend off anomie, loneliness, and deaths of despair, at least from the psychological point of view.

I could easily be wrong about this. It could be that all we really need to combat the rising levels of depression and anxiety is universal health care and basic income—i.e., it could be that the cause of increased suffering is purely economic. This would be great, because, although implementing these things would certainly not be easy (in the US especially we have an entrenched phobia of such things), it will still be easier than the widespread culture change that would be required otherwise. This culture change would have to reconnect us all to our local communities, family, friends, ethnicity, affiliative enterprises or advocacy groups, and multigenerational connections. And we might even be risking encouraging bigotry and hate as well. I think orienting people toward those things which might actually make them happy may be much harder to implement than reducing income disparity and making health care more available. I hope I'm wrong about that.

Chapter 9

Modern Culture and Its Addictions

Every day I see addictions. Not just the ones everyone is always talking about: alcohol, methamphetamines, and so forth. I see addictions to beauty, addictions to food in binge-eating disorders, addictions to pornography and videogames (mostly in men), addictions to shopping (mostly in women), addictions to status-striving (as seen in the extreme forms of the ABVS discussed in the last chapter), and many more.

I do not believe we have completely characterized the causal factors behind all this addiction. That is, while there are certainly biological predispositions to all this addictive behavior, and certain things can happen to you in your upbringing that might make you more likely to wind up addicted, I think our culture contributes a significant amount of causal weight here as well. In other words, taking the bio-psycho-social model seriously means not just looking for genetic factors and taking individual psychology into account when trying to understand what causes all this addiction. It means taking a long, hard look at our culture and asking ourselves whether or not all the elements we have been discussing so far may contribute to them as well.

I believe the Social Instincts play a part here. Since we live in a culture where many people are starving (or at least chronically hungry) in terms of their Social Instincts, these behaviors are halting attempts at "feeding" the Social Instincts with these various substitutes. Why would a culture that is lacking in individual, interpersonal, collective, and universal connection lead to addictive behaviors? I think hints at the answer may come from neuroscience.

According to the work of Jaak Panksepp in his oft-cited 1998 book *Affective Neuroscience* and his later 2014 work with colleagues, our innate emotional systems have evolutionary antecedents, comparisons to other animals, and have well-known functional aims. Nevertheless, since we are dealing with biological systems here, organisms will attempt to satisfy innate biological imperatives through whatever means they can find. It is my feeling that addictions are many times attempts to satisfy the Social Instincts under conditions of relative social disconnection. Other than the general rise in addictions that we have seen in the last century which I reviewed earlier, however, there are not a lot of studies that specifically look at the possible causal influence between loss of

DOI: 10.4324/9781032721354-9

social connection and these addictive behaviors, though there are some, which I will discuss below. In the absence of a more robust literature, though, I am mainly arguing this way because I see it clinically.

Nevertheless, it is curious that the very neural systems that support pro-social behavior, bonding, and attachment are the opiate systems. Opiates like heroin and fentanyl are both extremely addictive, as is well known, but what we often don't talk about is *why* they are so addictive. Both were initially developed as painkillers—heroin was supposed to be a less addictive alternative to morphine, ironically. But remember in the earlier chapters when we talked about how our pro-social processes came to co-opt the pain system to motivate pro-social behavior? They appear to play a part here for this very reason. Thus, not only do the opiates alleviate physical pain, they also alleviate social separation, feelings of rejection, and loneliness. This was shown in a 2016 study by Inagaki et al., where subjects who took the opioid antagonist naltrexone felt reduced feelings of social connection. This study linked the opioids directly to our Social Instincts at the neurobiological level, which suggests the potential for addiction is similar to painkiller addiction due to a shared neurochemistry.

Alcoholics Anonymous and Narcotics Anonymous both have a good track record, and part of this may be the way it feeds our Social Instincts by creating a community participants can connect to. There are even ritual elements (meeting, the serenity prayer, the 12 steps) that satisfy the proof-in-action needs that the Social Instincts have. Supporting this view, a 2013 review by Buckingham et al. notes the importance of feelings of social connectedness and social identity in addiction recovery, going so far as to state that the subjective experience of being a member of a social group can actually aid in recovery from addiction. Analytical psychology itself has contributed to this efficacy by being one of the causal forces behind AA in the first place. The founders of AA, Rowland Hazard and Bill Wilson, were inspired by none other than Carl Jung himself, who felt that such addictions were due to lack of spiritual connections. As we saw in the last chapter, such spirituality and lack thereof may indeed be a part of the rising addiction rates, but this must be squared with the fact that AA provides a great deal of social connection, ritual, structure, belonging, and identity through its processes. I do not think that is an accident.

Addictions and the Starving Social Instincts

For now, since the Social Instincts operate, at least partially, through the opiate system, many behavioral addictions may be people attempting to alleviate chronic social pain via behaviors that happen to stimulate this system. One possible way among many is through the use of digital technology. For example, Savci and Aysan in a 2017 study showed that as internet, smartphone, and digital game addiction increased, the sense of social connectedness decreased. This would be consistent with my hypothesis that such addictions arise because people are trying to soothe their chronic social pain. Yes, it is also possible that people are simply self-stimulating through these and other means even in the absence of social pain. But if that were the case, why are such behaviors on the rise? In the absence of a good explanation for this, I think the continual disintegration of connection we have discussed so far is a likely candidate. As loneliness and anxiety become more pervasive due to starving Social Instincts, addictions rise from people trying to find relief from it.

Our Social Instincts are hard wired and needed if we are to truly flourish and thrive as human beings, a hypothesis I have been forwarding throughout this book. And there are studies that exemplify this as well: a 2016 study by Inagaki et al. reviews the literature describing the severe developmental, health, and cognitive impairments that can arise from deprivation of care and social support. Social bonding was described in 1995 by Baumeister and Leary as a basic need, akin to the need for food and water. The growing evidence that our Social Instincts motivate us by co-opting our physical pain systems (discussed in earlier chapters) supports this idea, too, but it seems to me we can say much more.

I fear too often we speak of our social needs in terms like this—meaning we speak of them as on par with our need for food and drink—but we don't seem to recognize what this really means. Hunger, for example, is an instinct, too, and it has deadly consequences when it is not met. If we are deprived of food, we feel the ravages of starvation, and our minds and bodies begin to suffer damage as a result. My question is: what happens when our Social Instincts are starved? Many possibilities, given what we have discussed so far, come to mind. The fact that anorexia nervosa is so dangerous is proof that the Social Instincts are so powerful sometimes they can *override* the instinct to eat. The fact that time and again cults have come into existence that encouraged people to kill themselves rather than be separated from the group (like the infamous Jonestown mass suicide) is further proof of what the true power of the Social Instincts can be.

The pain of depression, anxiety, and suicide is another piece—we contemplate *suicide* when we are subjected to the agony of (subjectively perceived) social rejection, as studies reviewed earlier noted. Clinically, I have discussed what tends to go through one's mind when suicidal ideas surface. They can occur in many contexts, but most often they arise when one is feeling immense pain. In my clinical experience, though there are always exceptions, the vast majority of people who are suicidal do not actually want to die. What they really want is for the pain to stop. This can be observed in people who are suffering from intractable physical pain in a variety of medical contexts and sub-specialties.

In psychiatry, the intractable pain that suicidal individuals are trying to escape from is the pain of *perceived social rejection and ostracization*. But this is only one way in which people attempt to assuage the pain the Social Instincts are generating. Another is through addiction. Why would this even work, one might ask? Because, as the above research seems to show, social connectivity and the alleviation of social pain is mediated via *the same neurological networks* that the mitigation of physical pain is. I believe many addictive behaviors are attempts at alleviating this pain, either by stimulating those systems directly with opiate drugs, or indirectly, as you see in many other addictive behaviors. Chelnokova et al., in a 2014 study, for example, forward that opioids are involved in a number of reward systems including social. Others have found the opioids involved in food rewards (Yeomans & Gray in a 1997 study), and winning at gambling (Petrovic et al. in a 2008 study). These studies further support the idea that the Social Instincts are extremely powerful, have an increasingly recognized neurobiological basis, wreak havoc when they are not satisfied, and motivate a number of addictive behaviors to try to mitigate the pain they cause. Ultimately if such efforts are unsuccessful, we can find ourselves on the dark path of suicidal ideation and action.

In short, what I think is happening is that when our Social Instincts begin to starve, we try to mitigate the social pain with activities that temporarily satisfy them. This is probably at least partially effective because these other activities artificially stimulate the opioid and other neural systems (such as vasopressin and oxytocin) that mediate social connection. I should point out that much of the literature on this subject does not take into account the full bio-psycho-social context as I am doing here. Instead, many of these studies on the opiate mediators of behavior simply characterize these networks as generic "reward" circuits. Hence, we have studies such as that by Petrovic et al. (2008) that describes gambling and other "hedonic" activities as stimulating the "reward" centers which are typically opioid-involving networks.

I think this way of looking at it, however, is just more evidence of the pervasive influence of hyper-individualism, which is impacting our science. If we simply see gambling addiction, binge eating, internet addiction, pornography addiction, alcohol use, and so forth as just artificial ways to stimulate our "reward center," it places the entire problem squarely with the individual and places no causal influence on culture. That is letting culture off the hook, and is a gross oversimplification. Furthermore, it neglects the fact that these centers do not exist for "generic reward" but evolved for *species-specific reasons*—to motivate pro-social behavior as our primary species survival strategy. But a powerful desire to seek connection that is frustrated will have consequences similar to what we find when the desire for food is frustrated— anguish and frantic behavioral attempts to mitigate such pain and seek the pleasure of their being satisfied. In other words, when faced with starving Social Instincts, we do whatever we can to try to avoid the stick and find the carrot, even if it's an artificial carrot that only fends off the stick for a few hours. That's what addictions can tell us from the perspective of a full bio-psycho-social context. It means, no matter what somatic treatments we may come up with to combat all of the addictions we are facing currently, it will not be as effective as it could be until we correct the *social* causes of the suffering: starving Social Instincts.

Insights from Analytical Psychology

Earlier, I mentioned Jung's influence on Alcoholics Anonymous. Clinically, depth psychology methods attempt to take addictive behaviors and integrate them into "higher" expressions of meaning. This is not so much a "sublimation" of a primitive drive as it is a recognition that the addictive desire is *in itself* a halting attempt at healing. In the tradition of analytical psychology, it is proposed that psychological symptoms, including addictive urges, are often expressions of a deep unmet need. It is, in fact, this very idea which led me to explore the empirical data on addictions and their connections to starving Social Instincts.

In clinical work, addictions can be very troublesome because they are so demanding—the trick is not to attack the addiction, but rather to understand the need it is trying to fill. Though Jung often focused on the individual as the source of the "cure," and sometimes neglected the importance of connecting with community, it can be said that the reason for this imbalance was that he was himself also influenced by the growing hyper-individualism of his day. Nevertheless, the psyche itself can often contain the seed of a solution to addictions, often in the form of dream images or other spontaneous imaginal experiences, as these are the psyche's attempts not only at healing, but at *integration*. An addict is at war with themselves, with the addictive desire gnawing away at consciousness with incredible affective force. The Social Instincts are incredibly powerful, and when something is found to satisfy their hunger, even if it's "junk food," the brain will take it, rather than starve. And our culture is *full* of junk food, not only in the form of drugs and alcohol, but all the other addictions discussed thus far. In therapy, however, I often find that the psyche still has an inkling that the junk food is not a permanent solution, and I think that is why so-called spontaneous symbolic "spiritual" expressions from dreams or reverie often can do a lot of the work toward providing a more nutritious "diet" for the Social Instincts—*if* you know how to handle them. The key is to take such expressions seriously as possible paths to wellness. Such expressions work best when they come from within, and do not need to necessarily conform to any specific religion or faith.

What works, rather, is anything that is "beyond oneself," which is why the AA encourages its participants to refer to a "Higher Power" to assist them in their battle with addiction. But why should this work? I think the reason is that what the Social Instincts are truly seeking is *connection*. But "connection" doesn't work if you don't have anything to connect *to*. The "Higher Power" referred to typically is meant to mean something spiritual, but I don't actually think it needs to be. Rather, as mentioned before, the possession of a "belief" is far less important that *participation* in some kind of collective context outside oneself. If it is religious in nature, then by all means let it be participation in some kind of spiritual community and practice. But if not, as is often the case with agnostic or atheist individuals with addictions, then the challenge will be to find something that fills that needed role. It can be many things. If it is an ideology that one identifies with, such as "love" or "community," then one will still need to define what that sort of abstraction actually will translate into in terms of *action* in one's life. If it is something very abstract like "the Universe" or "the Great Mystery of Existence" you'll need to translate that, too. In such a case, spending time in Nature, consciously intending it to be a spiritual, meaningful, or soulful exercise, will likely work, provided enough time and actual energy is devoted to it as proof-in-action, rather than using it as mere lip service. Note, I'm not saying the abstraction isn't important. I'm saying translating such abstractions into something concrete and physically real, while not losing sight of the original abstraction is the "sweet spot" where the Social Instincts will find nourishment in this context. This technique, that is, translating one's spontaneously emergent images, dreams, or impressions into action in the outer world, is a key element of Jungian therapy, and one way in which I think it works is through mediation through the Social Instincts.

Artificial Intelligence Addictions

With the advent of ChatGPT and ever more powerful "AI" programming becoming available, it should be no surprise that now there are an increasingly available number of apps one can download that allow the user to create an artificially intelligent romantic friend. Such programs are growing in popularity and allow the user to create their "perfect" romantic partner with which to talk any time, day or night. They are designed to be supportive, flirty, attractive, and accommodating. A quick Google search of "AI girlfriend" or "AI boyfriend" will give an idea of what sort of need the program is designed to satisfy. Advertisements for these programs often claim that they are "for educational purposes," but I am not convinced by such proclamations, particularly when they are at the same time touted as "flirty" or capable of making the user "feel needed and supported." Obviously they likely target other intimate desires as well. These programs learn from their users and refer to prior conversations, and (of course) you can make them look and behave any way you like.

These programs seem specifically designed to soothe starving Social Instincts, and it is unlikely they will go away any time soon, particularly since the programming going into them is likely to get more and more sophisticated over time. Since so many people own smartphones, they are used to chatting with one another via texting or video-calling, so I can see how such programs could explode in popularity. As such, we will have yet one more distraction that will pull people away from one another, foregoing the sometimes challenging but rewarding work of building real relationships with real people. After all, since getting into an intense relationship with a bot designed to give you exactly what you want will be much more convenient, why bother interacting with someone to the level of actually concerning yourself with *their* needs rather than merely your own? Who wants to be bothered by that?

Feeding starving Social Instincts, see, is a very profitable business. But at the risk of sounding like a curmudgeon, this and all the other addictions discussed in this chapter are only so much "junk food." It will momentarily quell the hunger, but in the long run you'll wind up with high blood pressure and high cholesterol of the soul. Most startling innovations, throughout history, come with their fair share of doom-and-gloom predictions, one might argue. Why pick on this new technology? I recognize that argument. We have not, for instance, blown ourselves up with nuclear weapons and caused a global catastrophe. But does that mean there's no chance of it happening later?

Perhaps there is some kind of generative, creative, and nurturing purpose to be found with such technology. I certainly hope that is the case. Nevertheless, I think it is important to recognize the tremendous addictive potential such technology has. We are already starving and experiencing increasing rates of addictions, which I argue are primarily attempts to alleviate the pain of loneliness. And the problem with such addictions is that they do not satisfy the Social Instincts in the long term, and additionally cause all kinds of problems in both the short and long term. Not least of such problems are that they create yet another barrier to us forming the kinds of social bonds that will actually *satisfy* our instincts in a healthy way. Ask any alcoholic what I am talking about. Time will tell on this technology, given how new it is. But for the time being, it seems like just another way someone is profiting off of the loneliness epidemic without offering any real solutions to it—on the contrary, programs which give people exactly what they want artificially will prevent them from learning how to get it organically.

In this chapter we have seen how the loss of various types of connection may be behind the ever-increasing problem of addiction. But of course, these addictions are attempts at quelling the socially related worsening of depression and anxiety symptoms. The solution to both will be the same—large-scale social change. How might we do this?

Chapter 10

Intimations of a Cure

As a psychiatrist, I see people suffering from afflictions of the heart, mind, and soul every day. Thankfully we have a great deal of technologically advanced methods to treat these illnesses. But despite the huge advancements in neuroscience and psychopharmacology as a field, it seems we are still not fully utilizing the bio-psycho-social model. It seems we are missing or at least underemphasizing one of the major players in the worsening of mental health over the last century: the social roots of mental illness. Cultures, it seems, cannot simply be arbitrarily made into just anything without consequences for the human condition. And there are a number of ways in which it appears modern, Western life in the US, despite all the gains and strides we have made in various domains, falls short. Psychiatry, it seems, can still learn much from the modes and methods of more "traditional" societies of the past, as well as from indigenous peoples around the world, at least in terms of their ability to more adequately satisfy the Social Instincts. The fact that this problem is so challenging is likely because we are *still learning* the ways in which modern industrialized commercial society has its own intellectual baggage and emotional cost which can hinder our understanding of each other and ourselves. We are seeing that the changes of "progress" have come with structures and environments that do not seem to agree with our Social Instincts.

We have seen that the worsening disorders of the soul and mind have their origins not merely in neurotransmitters or biochemical genetic markers, but in *cultural* phenomena. In fact, thinking that mental illness is entirely an individual problem is likely due to our own pervasive hyper-individualism at play. This I have concluded after extensively studying anthropological, sociological, and historical sources and comparing them to the advancements in modern medicine, and witnessing the rise of alternative/complementary medical models. More and more we are continuing to (re)-discover the power of culture, mind, and spirit over the body, whereas for a long time, medicine could only think of molecules and cells.

Over the years I have treated many patients who (among other things) experience profound anomie and a lack of purpose and meaning in their lives. They do not know who they are, or what they are supposed to do. Every day

DOI: 10.4324/9781032721354-10

I treat patients who are lost in ambiguity and cannot adjust to the hurricane of changes that hit them continually. Every day I hear variations on "I don't feel like I know myself," "I don't know who I am," or "I don't know what to do." These feelings I attribute to their starving Social Instincts, but because we are so hyper-individual, we do not even have the language to describe these feelings. We misattribute this suffering and blame the individual for it in a sense. It's *your* depression because *your* brain is messed up and has a "chemical imbalance." Unsurprisingly, the first thing we reach for are pharmaceutical treatments because that fits in nicely with our consumer pseudoculture: economic drivers being the dominant forces at play in our culture, rather than any sort of tradition, community, connection, etc. means every problem is YOUR problem and you just need to purchase the right products to fix it. Social factors are not even recognized as causal factors.

While this seems terribly convenient, I don't think it is necessarily intentional. I think we have slipped along the slope of hyper-individualism for so long, it is just not on our radar any longer. Even our modern psychotherapeutic models (and there are many of them) typically focus only on events and/or traumas that occurred in an individual person's childhood. They focus on the relationship with the parents and the various attachments that they did or did not form. They look to these factors to explain a person's suffering. While these factors are no doubt important, they are by no means sufficient to fully explain the degree and quality of the kind of suffering I am talking about. The kind of suffering that is not unique to psychiatric patients, but can be felt in lesser degree by many people in the modern world. But, it is a common subject of literature on this to only consider biological or individual developmental factors. This is not utilizing the bio-psycho-social model to its full potential in terms of explanatory power.

That is where my consideration of culture comes in; this is because disorders of "who am I?" "what am I supposed to do?" "what is the purpose and meaning in living?" are primarily answered by *cultural* variables, *not* merely by early developmental interactions with a handful of parental figures. Our Social Instincts crave connection at the four levels—they will generate everything from inchoate pain to the above sorts of existential questions in order to satisfy its hunger if they are not satisfied. They may encourage us to seek out addictive solutions. They may propel us into waging culture war on the pervading pseudoculture and vigorously create or participate in counter-cultures (not that this is necessarily bad, but it does explain its prevalence).

It is culture which either provides or does not provide the means and methods to handle such deep-rooted universal human longings, longings that stem from our history as a cooperative, highly social species of animal. We know from studies in evolutionary psychology that *Homo sapiens* evolved in highly social settings from our ancient primate ancestors and we are built to expect a highly social environment; this is the origin of our Social Instincts. They are biological in origin, but seek out psychological and social contexts, and they are just as powerful as, if not *more* powerful than, our drives to feed ourselves, seek shelter, have sex, and so forth.

Culture, however, is the only thing that can really satisfy the Social Instincts, and one thing we know about culture is that it's highly variable (it is not, however, *arbitrary*—but that's another conversation). Culture can answer these longings and provide the necessary "equipment" to handle not only the need for personal and group identity and the need for personal value systems, but also help with the inherent ambiguity of human relationships and the need for coherent meaning and purpose in life. But the reality is that not all cultures answer these needs equally well. And if those needs are not being met, for whatever reason, cultures typically change—and sometimes such changes are painful. I believe we are witnessing many such changes, and we observe much of the above sort of suffering because, generally speaking, modern Western culture does not meet the needs I'm talking about. The evidence I review in this book points to this conclusion, but I hope other investigators and researchers will test this theory.

Generally, though, our ancestral cultures have degenerated like that of Roseto. Through many different historical causal factors, the culture that was perpetuated in the past has been replaced with mass-media consumer pseudoculture. This pseudoculture, despite continual talk of how important the family is, in practice focuses everything on the individual and his/her own desires, much of which is driven by continual saturation with highly persuasive advertising and pressure to consume. Families in themselves have become increasingly atomized by modern economic factors such as high mobility, breakdowns in traditional social structures, and so forth as discussed previously. Today the idea of family is more of an abstraction; except in certain minorities, the amount of real obligations and expectations families have to one another is small relative to other cultures. In our culture, rather, roles and obligations are ambiguous and hazily formed, and spread out among multiple unrelated entities (such as government bodies), as are social boundaries and structure compared to other cultures worldwide and through history. This allows us a great deal of freedom—and freedom is of course extremely valued in our society. Along with this we tell our children "you can be anything you want to be!" "follow your dreams!" "all you have to do is believe in yourself!" and other such platitudes, but the problem is children oftentimes have no idea what they want to be, what their dreams are, or any of that, and they many times grow up to be adults who have no idea of who they are or what they want.

Moreover, children also are typically far more concerned about finding their identity and feeling like they belong in some kind of peer group rather than "finding themselves" anyway. This is especially evident in middle school, but continues into high school and sometimes long after that—children at these ages go to great lengths to feel like they belong to a group of some kind—which we (tellingly) call "peer pressure." Is it any wonder we immediately label any desire for belonging and community as something negative, to be shrugged off and/or ignored?

Still, much of this pressure doesn't come from outside, anyway. It comes from within. The need to belong to peer groups is strong in every culture, but it is particularly intense at this age in our culture. The reason for this is actually pretty simple, though rarely does anyone seem to notice it, and it is partly to do with the way we raise children. As mentioned previously, at a very early age we often separate children from their families and put them into childcare, followed quickly by preschool, primary, then secondary education. Children spend a large portion of their lives in such settings. It takes very little reflection to realize just how odd and remarkable this really is. Non-verbally, we are telling them that their true social environment is no longer the family home or local community, but rather in and among an adult-sparse setting of concentrated age-matched peer groups, where everyone's worth is measured by not only their individual academic achievement, but also according to their social standing in the rapidly self-organizing (but immaturely directed) social hierarchies that emerge in these groups.

As children continue to develop, they put ever more effort into this endeavor, but it is obvious that they have no idea what they are doing: typically symbols of belonging are shuttled into superficial fads like clothing, music, or hobby and fiction interests. This behavior is not, as is often mistakenly assumed, children "trying to express themselves." This assumption is just more evidence of our hyper-individualistic tendency to assume everything is about the individual. No, they are trying to create an identity and form some kind of group belonging because that is a basic element of the Social Instincts. The problem is the things children use are typically insufficient to form a lasting, meaningful personal or group identity. They are insufficient to provide a sense of groundedness in a tradition of some kind and they are insufficient to provide any sort of narrative or social structure in which to place themselves. But we cannot fault the children. After all, we have separated them from the traditional source of these things—the extended family, community, tribe, etc.—and asked them to spend half their lives in this completely different setting. In this setting, everything is called into question and children are unconsciously commanded to "invent themselves," while at the same time feeling a strong desire to conform to some kind of group in order to feel like they belong.

Compounding this is the ubiquitous but rarely noticed continual pressure exerted on us via the mass media. Swimming in the sea of smartphones, non-stop screen-time, advertisements, etc., we all have culturally implanted a vague idea of the consumer pseudoculture and we feel pressure to conform to it. Many justifiably reject and rebel against this pseudoculture and we call that "teens being rebellious"—a phenomenon that does not exist as a cultural norm in more communitarian societies worldwide. Nevertheless, the conflation of the pseudoculture with one's parents often occurs and generates endless intergenerational conflict, and a continuous subjective feeling that one is expected to "conform" to the pseudoculture even if it is never explicitly stated. Since the values of the pseudoculture do not come from anyone in particular, but are simply uttered from the faceless media exposure, it is not trusted and cannot hope to satisfy the Social Instincts. The young person mistakenly assumes the only answer to this dichotomy of "conform" or "rebel" is to focus on oneself—well, what other answer is possible in a hyper-individualistic world? I have to change, I have to make myself distinctive, I have to "be different," I have to outdo, out-rebel, out-score, out-beautiful, etc., my peers in order to "stand out." Either that, or I have to find a group of like-minded others and make a place for myself among them, expressing my solidarity with proof-in-action signs like clothing and music choices that will distinguish me as part of an "in" group that is distinct from everyone else in the "out" group. This is all very serious business because of the weapons the Social Instincts use against us to motivate this behavior. And of course, many young people like to brag about how much they don't care about what anyone else thinks, but such expressions tend to be rather unconvincing since they seem to be aimed at impressing the very people they claim not to care about.

Thus, in the face of a drastically reduced partner, family, friend, community, and nature-based set of connections, and instead only given pseudoculture as a replacement, our children are asked to form their identities with very little raw material other than what is spoon fed to them via the mass media pseudoculture machine they encounter on television / the internet. Such expressions are largely determined by corporate advertising interests and not the real human needs of those exposed to it. In this setting, real distinction and cultural difference is continually eroded to maximize consumer base, or alternately in the name of "equality," to the point that difference winds up being almost completely erased. And when meaningful difference is erased in favor of a superficial pro-consumption "salad bar" style variety, children feel on a profound level that they are simply another number in the giant faceless mass. This feeling is probably what motivates our culture's worship of the "rebel," the "non-conformist," the "trend-setter," etc., a behavior that is quite foreign to many other cultures that do not have this "faceless mass" effect. Such desperate bids for distinction (and frankly, attention) are doomed to be short-lived, of course, because of their inherent superficiality. Moreover, if enough express their "individuality" in the same way, the giant pseudoculture machine will assimilate it, then we are back to the same problems.

If they are given any help at all in the quest for identity formation, narrative, or group belonging, children are given two kinds of advice. On one hand, they are advised to engage in yet more navel-gazing, "finding your own path," and encouragement to continue one's self-absorbed quest for self-actualization. On the other hand, however, the advice comes in the form of dogmatic, tyrannical commands to conform from ill-trusted authority figures (or even other peers), which children just wind up resenting. And why shouldn't they? They have been told for years that all such dogmatic assertions are arbitrary and should be questioned! After all, shouldn't we just "believe in ourselves"?

As for those authority figures, they are not trusted because they are largely absent from the child's day-to-day life—they are either parental figures that are gone for most days of the week, or they are interchangeable teachers, town leaders, politicians, etc. that shift so often (due to our high mobility) they can barely be distinguished from one another. Ultimately, these factors leave our developing young people with very little to ground themselves with.

Now couple this with the unprecedented lack of ritualism in our society, a subject I dive into in much greater depth in *Healing Symbols in Psychotherapy*. Whereas most cultures worldwide and throughout history have rites of passage and many other rituals to connect one to a larger framework of society, nature, spiritual figures, etc., we have barely any by comparison, as observed by many anthropologists and sociologists. In the modern Western world, the two most ritualized experiences remaining for many people are weddings and funerals, and not much else. This situation, of course, is a result of our post-Enlightenment, post-Protestant legacy, and compounded by the disintegrative effect of mass media consumerism. Since rituals help to form boundaries and structure (among many other things), this leaves our young people in a perpetual state of social ambiguity: they generally don't know where they really stand in relation to everyone else, and most people stay in a "kinda-sorta" state of "I think I maybe fit in this category but I dunno."

These problems cannot be fixed without major social upheaval. If, somehow, we find some way to change this, it will not likely be productive if we simply throw out the baby with the bathwater. Pandora's Box has been opened, and we are going to have to work with what we have now to effect a change and perhaps alleviate the social suffering plaguing us. If the schools that we concentrate our children in had exactly the same culture as every contributing family did, these problems would likely be less pronounced (and of course they are in more conservative rural areas for the most part, for this reason). But naturally, in the name of freedom and equality, the schools cannot be *forced* into any cultural framework, and the news media continues daily to remind us of this all over the country with stories of "so-and-so is being discriminated against in his/her school!"

Rather, to accommodate the needs of our heterogeneous society, and in order to be fair, such institutions are under continual pressure to remove as much culturally specific material as possible and teach children to (say it with me) "find their own path" in this confusing vichyssoise. This is not necessarily bad, but the result is that our schools have become culturally empty and generic—and we put our children in them for half of their lives. Not only that, the more we progress, *the more pronounced the cultural emptiness will have to become*, and all the problems that go with it will continue. Every child that goes to school will experience this disconnection from the family and its traditions (if any), and in its place will be a homogenized, bloodless and empty generic consumer culture of self-absorption. Thus, in a culture which nearly worships the "rebel" and the "non-conformist," and one which is so anti-ritual, we can expect an easy casting off of all traditions in favor of endless navel-gazing, self-absorbed consumerism and faddism, and/or superficial attempts at identity formation (and re-re-invention).

Culture Building

What do we do? I think the solution is to do our best to *build culture*. The human soul longs for a sense of personal and group identity, a feeling of connectedness to something larger than oneself, as well as a coherent sense of narrative, meaning, and context. Most people can agree with that. Where the confusion comes in, however, is in what exactly all these things really are. What *is* culture? What *is* identity? How do we create such things? Children (and adults) will always feel a strong need to develop their own identity, but hardly anyone seems to be explaining how the trick is done.

In my opinion, identity is not found by endless, deeply felt soul-searching into the sweetest part of our heart of hearts. I think it is not "discovered" but *created* by our *actions and obligations to others*. In other words, *I am defined by what my obligations are to others in my life*. The things used by middle-schoolers (and on up) to "define" themselves (music, hobbies, clothing) are all symbolic attempts to establish a desire to meet such obligations. This becomes obvious when we compare these awkward, halting attempts at culture building to established cultures worldwide: the traditional and/or ancient use of music, crafts, and clothing actually perform this same function of establishing and symbolizing real-world obligation, and so what our school children are doing spontaneously can be found in highly elaborated form worldwide. Like addictions, the middle-school clique behaviors are attempts at finding wellness. They just don't work very well. It is therefore not just silly adolescent behavior that is to be dismissed as "trying to express themselves," but a very serious attempt to satisfy their growing Social Instincts. *It's not about the individual*—it's about the group.

The difference, however, is that children, because they are young, latch on to whatever is "in the air" at the time, so typically what they use to symbolically represent membership in such a group to bolster their group identity is subject to faddish whimsy. They cannot help this because they are being asked to reinvent the wheel. But popular music and fashion trends change like the wind. So, such symbols lack lasting substance and therefore don't usually function well as identity formers. Furthermore, because of their temporality, such symbols lack any ties to real obligation, thus they only serve to identify a professed *desire to* belong to a particular group (gamers, punks, metal-heads, jocks, nerds, goths, etc., etc.), but without any real obligation to other members of that group. It therefore does not satisfy because it has no backing with physical action or commitment. It has some of the proof-in-action elements in terms of concrete signifiers—clothing, music, etc.—but it is lacking deeper proof-in-action elements that are much more profoundly satisfying.

Thus, through the foregoing, we can see how the worship of limitless freedom and individualism demolishes identity when it erases obligation, cuts off from the past, and encourages endless introspection in place of real interaction with others. If you are the only person in the world, you have limitless freedom. You would also have no identity and no context outside of what you may have built in the past because you have no obligations to anyone. Even a hermit defines himself by his obligations to his god, his land, and/or his animals. Hence the "others" do not necessarily have to be human beings, which is why adults sometimes use "isms" to create identity (socialism, activism, liberalism, conservativism, etc.). Some adults use "race" as their identifier (which unfortunately often leads to racism). Still others use religion in the sense of a collection of beliefs and practices.

What seems to work best are enduring cultural constructs such as religion, heritage, ethnicity, traditions, community, friends and family networks, and (let's not forget) time spent with Mother Nature. The proof-in-action elements that make it more real, tangible, and concrete are extensions of the things middle-schoolers latch onto: traditional crafts, music, rituals, and other symbols that connect one to something outside of oneself. Unlike the identifiers many in our society use which are future-focused (self-absorbed fads in the consumer pseudoculture, cliques consisting entirely of popular clothing/music/hobby choice, various political "isms," etc.), the most powerful ones seem to be *past-focused*. This subtle difference has major consequences because the past is much more stable than the future. It doesn't change (except with the rare archeological find). Ancestor reverence, a practice found cross-culturally, plays a huge part in this as well—revering the ancestors means when we die *we* will be revered. If we worship the future, however, when we die we will be forgotten and discarded with a "Who cares? That's ancient history, baby." Ancestor reverence, or at least remembrance, therefore, *creates* a sense of the Eternal.

This is the primary message I'm getting at in this book: when we work on nurturing, updating, reliving, or otherwise preserving the traditions of the past, (modified as needed for modern life), we work on ourselves as well. We ground ourselves in relation to something far larger, and far more stable than ourselves, and make ourselves an integral part of a greater whole. Past focusing makes it stable over a long time unlike future focusing. Forming real and lasting obligations to long-term partner, family, community, nature, comrades, friends, communities, spiritual entities, etc. *creates* a strong, stable personal and group identity. In this way *the past lives in the present* and stabilizes it, contextualizes it, and provides narrative structure and meaning to it. The ancient crafts associated with one's heritage, including folk music, art, stories, languages, etc., are good examples of this—but always with the caveat in mind that staying stuck in the past is not what I'm talking about. Traditions need to be *living* traditions.

So my recommendation for satisfying our starving Social Instincts in a healthy way is to engage in *intentional culture building*. Intensify these efforts wherever you can, as it will provide you and your most treasured others greater strength and resilience. When you join a community, make the obligations and expectations *real*, not just air-castle building and deedless expressions of sentiment. Recognize that you may have to sacrifice your personal individual freedom a little bit in order for it to really work—this applies to leaders as well as followers, and probably moreso; a leader should be the least free of any group because s/he has the most number of profound obligations. Reinforce these obligations to each other with symbolic expressions when appropriate, or ritual participation when called for. Remember what they *mean*: obligation and real-world connection. They aren't simply window dressing or "I just think this is cool stuff," or else they lose their moorings and become empty fluff. They should mean something in the real world. These are ways that we "discover" our identity: by building it with the bricks and mortar of real connections.

Chapter 11

Tribalism—The Dose Makes the Poison

The Social Instincts arose in *Homo sapiens* because they are an effective survival strategy. That is why we feel anomie and despair when we are separated from social contacts. That is why we self-organize into cliques in middle-school, around ages 9–10. That is why people develop fanatical loyalty to such things as political ideologies and local sports teams, and easily fall prey to extreme racist ideologies or charismatic cult leaders. All of these things promise the opiate rush of belonging and the swell of feeling that arises from a concretely undeniable self-identity. That is why all of these things can so quickly lead to violence in their defense and in their feeding into our inborn tendency—even desire—to divide people into "us" and "them."

As mentioned in an earlier chapter, media outlets often spin-doctor the news in such a way as to putatively "deliver the news" but in reality what they are doing is feeding the Social Instincts. It's actually just more junk food. They do this by presenting a simplified world of "us" and "them" which paints "them" as evil, greedy, bad, etc., and "us" as noble, caring, honorable. It's pandering at its worst, but it is done for a very simple reason: it sells. These news outlets are beholden to advertisers, and if their content whips people into a tribal frenzy, and therefore earns the loyalty of repeat viewers by telling them what they want to hear, well, that leads to increased advertising money and therefore the profit motive "trumps" everything else.

This sort of system has only accelerated since the mid- to late 20th century. Certainly, biased news sources are nothing new, but I believe the polarization of the media has accelerated considerably in the last 30 years. I believe, like so many things, that the slow starvation of our Social Instincts are behind this, since only in such a situation is such blatant spin-doctoring likely to succeed. The desire for belonging is so powerful, it, like addictions, can override our rational faculties and draw us into the fold. It is no different than being seduced by a cult and allowing ourselves or our children to be victimized, or rioting because our favorite football team lost, or engaging in violence in the name of our favorite political leader or ideology.

Here, as the saying goes, we see the violence inherent in the system. But it isn't an invented political system that is inherently potentially violent. It is our

DOI: 10.4324/9781032721354-11

human nature that is. Since the Social Instincts were crafted by evolution, it is linked to behaviors that contribute to survival. This is why I must include a chapter here on why we should not fetishize or romanticize the Social Instincts—they can be extremely dangerous. The Social Instincts have a dark side: tribalism. And here I mean tribalism in a derogatory sense—the sense in which people band together and irrationally attack others they deem as "outsiders." It is behind the aforementioned mayhem, along with practically every form of warfare ever waged.

But it exists because, as the old joke goes, wars do not decide who is right— they decide who is *left*. Our human biological instincts that favor dividing people into "us" and "them" and encourage organization into potentially aggressive bands that subsequently *attack* "them" and destroy "them" succeeded. Those who did not have such instincts were selected out due to tribal warfare, and coalitional warfare in our primate ancestors. Chimps and gorillas engage in coalitional warfare, so it was likely already a part of human nature before we were fully human. Which means it goes quite far back.

Tribalism, therefore, can be quite destructive—but it is indispensable to human nature. We cannot eliminate it from our nature, nor is it entirely certain that we would *want* to. I would love to believe that modernity has progressed so far that we will never need such instincts to survive, and that we will one day achieve a perfect utopia in which no one will ever need Social Instincts. We do not live in such a world, nor does such a world seem likely, as even as I write this, Russia is invading Ukraine. Nevertheless, tribalism (being the dark side of the Social Instincts) is often looked at as a blemish we should endeavor to erase. The belief that such violent potentialities in our nature are only there because of acculturation encourages such thoughts even further: all we have to do is create a society in which we teach children never to think in tribalist terms and all such bad behaviors will be eliminated.

I think that is a pipe dream, and the longer we entertain it, the more damage we are going to do. All the mayhem that tribalist behaviors cause is inextricably connected to the Social Instincts. As we have been discussing all through this book, the human soul craves a number of things. We crave connection, stable social standing, affiliation, reliable others to share our trials and troubles with, trusted bonds, and concrete signifiers that we *belong* in a group larger than merely ourselves in some way. When we achieve these things, we feel pleasure, joy, satisfaction, and most of all *safe*. When we are absent these things, we feel despair, pain, sorrow, and *unsafe*, and we will go to sometimes lethal lengths to acquire them. We are willing to sacrifice much to obtain them.

The ugly side of this is when we define ourselves as part of a group that begins to perceive itself as "under attack." This is a well-known strategy among neo-Nazi groups and fascists of all kinds, as well as cult leaders. The moment one's group identity is perceived to be under attack, the ugly side of the Social Instincts is likely to surface—the tribalist tendencies to label those perceived to be "attacking" as The Enemy. Rational thought and nuanced analyses are thrown out of the window in favor of emotionally driven defenses.

There is a very good reason for this. It's because in the evolutionary scale of things, it is probably more successful in the long run for hotheads to prevail and pre-emptively strike at those who are not really their enemy than it is for cooler heads to prevail and fall victim to hotheads on the other side. This is an unfortunate but inevitable consequence of our evolutionary and biological nature. I'm not saying we can't escape it or that biology is the sole determinant of what we do and say. Rather, I am saying biology has a profound influence on us, and we should dismiss it or pretend it isn't there only at our great peril.

No amount of platitudes about how we "are all one," or vehemently expressed sentiment about the universal brotherhood of humankind is going to be able to eliminate this ugly side. No amount of attempting to sanitize education will make any difference either. Tribal violence, bigotry, and paranoia do not come from culture and upbringing. Those tendencies are innate—what culture does is take that fire and pour gasoline on it. The fire, however, was always there and will emerge regardless of culture.

The Dose Makes the Poison

Does this mean that we are doomed to be squabbling and tribalists forever? Are we trapped between the anomic desolation of starving Social Instincts and the only seeming alternative of fascist groups, cults, or violent and paranoid sub-cultures? No. Like so many things, it is the *dose* which makes the poison or cure. Let's look at what the Social Instincts appear to crave according to the foregoing analyses:

1 Meaning
2 Trust
3 Connection to a long-term partner
4 Connection to a network of family and friends
5 Connection to a larger scale community
6 Connection to the natural world
7 Competence
8 Stable social reputation
9 A religious or value-based belief system that is non-punitive, not focused on personal gain, not conflictual with Deity (however envisioned) but collaborative with Deity, free of excessive focus on negative judgments, and free of excessive focus on religious guilt/doubt

These things furthermore cannot be mere abstractions or affectations. They must be grounded in proof-in-action behaviors. Merely gathering together to vehemently express sentiment is not going to satisfy the Social Instincts. Rather, it is only *behaviors and obligations* that will satisfy them. The Social

Instincts evolved over hundreds of generations of humans and proto-humans—though they are imperfect, they are cunning and are not fooled by sophistry or bull. They require tangible signifiers of commitment, belonging, and trust. These include real-world obligations to others, symbolic behaviors that emphasize these, including clothing, language use, participation in ritualized behaviors or physical presence at gatherings, etc. In short, they depend on "rules."

Collective Identity and "Rules"

Spiritual communities and other collective entities with "rules" have much to offer—belonging, connection, shared belief, and many other things, but it is not "free." It requires the individual who wants to have all those things to conform to the value systems of the collective. Am I saying that everyone should conform, then? Nope. I'm saying go into it clear-headed. Know what is at stake. In many cases, breaking from a tradition or religious community is the right thing to do. I see this in my patients sometimes. In those cases, then, it is imperative that I make sure the patient knows exactly *why* it can be so difficult, and in particular *what was given up* when they broke away. How, now, will you meet those all-too-human needs that the previous structure was providing for you, but asking too much in exchange?

How can you fill the void that resulted from breaking away from a collective entity? How will you find something that aligns more with your own needs for individual expression? This is the real question to ask. The "rules" of collective groups always seem to be a matter of contention, until enough time has passed that all of these tradeoffs can be negotiated down to an agreed-upon steady state. Many times, much of this is unconsciously negotiated. But it only takes a little reflection to realize that a collective without *any* rules doesn't work.

Why? Imagine you are in a social group that is devoted to hyper-individualism. Everyone who is a member is free to express themselves any way they wish. They can come and go as they please. They can do whatever they want, and if any rituals or ceremonies are constructed that are connected to the group, there is no requirement that anyone attend them or participate in them. This would be analogous to a Military without uniforms, without customs and courtesies, without a rank system, without songs, without honors, medals, traditions, or ceremonies, and without a specific manner of speaking ("boots on the ground," "FUBAR," etc.). So, in other words, what I'm describing is a lump of people loosely connected by a flimsy claim of solidarity that has no substance.

The "rules," then, are the means by which you *materialize* the substance of a collective. Without them it's merely words and it will only cover up starving Social Instincts with empty sophistry. It will not work. All the behaviors embodied by rules, whether it be clothing standards (spoken or unspoken), taboos, linguistic choices (shared expressions that are not in common use by the surrounding out-group), attendance at rituals or functions, proscribed or required behaviors, devoted crafts or skills, attention to some kind of sacred narrative or myth (even if overtly fictional) etc., are all concrete ways that you can SHOW your allegiance to a given collective, and hence solidify your *place* within that collective. These are behaviors that cannot be faked or fudged—at least not in the action. Like a wedding, you can either say "I do" or not. Naturally you might say "I do" without meaning it, but you can't fake *saying* it. That is the part that can't be faked, and that's what proof-in-action signifiers of identity accomplish. Either you can go through the hazing ritual or you can refuse. You can either show up to a gathering or NOT show up. You can't do both at the same time. You can either say the required thing or not say it.

Naturally, in hyper-individualistic cultures like ours, it is common to hand-wring about what everyone's "inner deep feelings" are about collective identity and whether or not it's "true to your authentic self." These are worthy things to consider, but in the sphere of collective identity, it matters not. All that matters is whether you perform the necessary actions. And in the case of taboos, a very powerful tool for identity formation, all that matters is whether you deliberately avoid certain actions that would otherwise be common, or refuse. You cannot avoid all meat but fish on Friday and NOT avoid all meat but fish on Friday at the same time. Therefore, what might be an otherwise meaningless act *gains* social meaning through the collective understanding. Rules, therefore, have the capacity to turn something that is inherently ambiguous like "do I really belong with this group?" into something that lacks ambiguity entirely, like "did I undergo the initiation ritual or not?" If you did, then you're in. If not, then you're not. Cutting through the ambiguity, hand-wringing, navel-gazing, and endless soul-searching in exchange for a concrete either-or is the power of rules and rituals. That understanding embodies the fact that following a rule = a renewed commitment to belonging in the group that cannot be questioned or faked. Such continued behaviors *create* the substance of the group belonging and make it more powerful and effective for being there. The rules themselves, while usually having some sort of justification (*ad hoc* or otherwise), do not really matter so much in the particulars, since much of the emotional labor is being done by the choice to participate or not participate in the rule—it's less important what the actual rule is.

For example, take the rituals of marriage in this country. In today's culture, it is a collective value that we marry "for love"—i.e., that if we get married, it's because we love the person we are marrying. This is naturally not the only reason for getting married worldwide. Some cultures have arranged marriages that are not organized around the idea that the participants are supposed to "be in love." This is such a part of these cultures that they actually have a different name for when people marry solely for love—these are called "love marriages" in countries such as India, Pakistan, or Egypt for example. The fact that "love marriage," then, as a special kind of marriage, obviously shows that the "regular" kind of marriage does not concern itself primarily with love. In the US, however, we exclusively marry for love (presumably), and so marriage is seen as a reflection of that. But even still, you could, however, ask yourself (and indeed I have heard many ask questions like this) why someone would bother with all the ceremony. It's "just a piece of paper" people say, or it's "just empty ritual." How can that be more important than True Love?

But without any concrete signifiers of the bond, such as rings, weddings, and legal/cultural ramifications, the category must be continually maintained by the couple alone, based entirely on verbal expressions of sincere emotion and not much else. I am not advocating for more or less ceremony and ritual, nor am I advocating for or denigrating or romanticizing the practice of arranged marriages. I am merely pointing out that there is an inherent trade-off here. The ritual-heavy, highly collective sets of rules come with one set of drawbacks, whereas the cultures that barely have any rules eliminate those drawbacks but purchase others. The former satisfy the Social Instincts involving community and family connection more often than not, but at the cost of individual idiosyncratic expression, or even the individual dimension of the Social Instincts. The latter type of marriage—solely about love—allow unfettered freedom, and potentially satisfy the individual dimension but possibly at the cost of starving the collective and interpersonal dimensions. So what is the price of having a system with very few rules of collective identity? Why might this matter so much? Because of the emotional importance of belonging. Cultural scripts about marriage, then, have real-world consequences about which aspects of the Social Instincts we are going to be focused on—individual, interpersonal, or collective.

To Rule or Not to Rule

Because our culture is hyper-individualistic, the only rules preserved in our marriage ritualism are the ones that pertain to the individual dimension for the most part. The others are "optional," and can be dispensed with without any real consequence. Such rules are not optional in the more collective cultures referred to earlier.

So then, am I saying we should start adopting and enforcing rules left and right in order to satisfy the Social Instincts and that rules are the antidote to toxic culture? If only it were that easy! No, I am saying that *if* people want to establish collectives that people are wanting to participate in, rules are going to be required to make it feel meaningful. Concrete symbols, physical symbols, ritual acts of various kinds, etc., will be required. But remember also that we are dealing with instincts that evolved during the 99% of history that we existed as foragers and hunter-gatherers of various kinds. Rules that come from faceless entities such as mass-media or giant bureaucracies will never stick. All that will do is foster counter-culture, rebellion, and rejection. It will be labeled "tyranny" and individuals will feel their personal liberties are being pushed too hard. This effect would likely hold across the board, in my opinion, but in a hyper-individualistic society, you can bet it will be even more difficult. Rules, therefore, need to be *earned*, and the only way to earn them is with trust. Trust, in turn, does not emerge *sui generis* out of the void, but comes with time and contact. This is why whatever we decide to do (if anything) about the pervasive starving Social Instincts that we have in this country, it will not be solved overnight. Furthermore, we need to recognize how creating rules of collective connection can powerfully activate the Social Instincts (particularly in people who are especially starved), and that this state runs the risk of creating tribal nastiness. We are dealing with powerful forces here.

Be that as it may, it appears we need a moderate dose of "tribalism" to satisfy our Social Instincts, but not so much that it encourages people to be bigoted, racist, violent, or fascist. A tall order, indeed, requiring nuance, moderation, and careful consideration. It would be nice if we could find a simpler solution to this. I'm all ears. But thus far, it seems the more we push people to erase their affiliations in favor of a "we are all the same and should just love each other" worldview, the more we risk complications arising from the Social Instincts that demand much more than that. Instincts that demand concrete signifiers of belonging to a group larger than oneself that is not merely a nebulous abstraction without any real consequence or obligation. By contrast, when we excessively and fiercely enforce collective rules and belonging, we wind up with fascist wingnuts, reactionary fundamentalists, or flat-out cults. Whatever people decide to do (if anything), caution is in order.

Chapter 12

The Meaning-Making Organ

Our Social Instincts operate within a larger function of the psyche as a whole: that of meaning-making. That is to say, from a biological perspective, we know that all non-vestigial organs contribute some kind of activity sub-serving survival and/or reproductive success (for simplicity, "survival"). To identify what that activity is and how it facilitates survival is to identify its function. For example, the function of muscles is to facilitate movement, so that the organism with them can move about the environment and find resources such as food or mates, which facilitates survival. The function of the heart is to pump blood throughout the body and provide oxygen and nutrients to all the cells in the body, and this facilitates survival. So, then, what is the function of the brain or psyche?

Why is this an important question to ask? Mainly because of the way in which our minds naturally produce solutions to things like starving Social Instincts, in the manner of a kind of natural healing process I will explore in this chapter. The reason for bringing this up now is that, aside from any sort of solution we might be able to conjure up by thinking about it really hard, we will also observe spontaneously emergent expressions in the form of dreams and imaginative imagery that will address it as well. Each of us does this naturally, as I will review below, but when we combine this with the particular way in which we tend to share stories with one another, whether via large-scale media productions like movies, or smaller scale "viral" phenomena, some of these ideas will "stick" or "resonate" with people, stirring the emotions in a way that is often difficult to verbalize.

The Quest for Meaning

Throughout this book I have discussed how we have strong Social Instincts and the many ways in which we tangle ourselves up trying to meet their sometimes extreme insistence without even questioning them or understanding their origins. But in fact, the Social Instincts operate under a larger umbrella function of *meaning-finding* or *meaning-making*, and sometimes both in combination. I believe meaning-making is the primary function of the brain, in fact. Let's see how.

DOI: 10.4324/9781032721354-12

Naturally, organs do not necessarily reduce to their biological function alone—this fact certainly applies to the brain or mind. Nevertheless, understanding function informs the question of how the organ evolved, placing it into a huge tapestry of comparative ethology and physiology. From a purely biological perspective, the central nervous system of humans and other animals (to varying degrees) are typically seen to have many functions, including:

1   Processing sensory input including internal sensations such as kinesthetic sense, balance, and coordination, but also empathy and mentalization in social species such as *Homo sapiens*
2   Maintenance of life functions, such as modulation of body temperature, digestion, etc.
3   The "executive functions" such as reasoning, language, thinking, memory, affect, etc.

One could classify these activities together as "information processing," and this is naturally true, but would be too general and vague to suffice as a full explanation of function. Process what information? Why? For what specific survival-oriented purposes?

To answer this question, we first must recognize that the common element here is the generation of context. That is, sensory data are tagged in all kinds of species-specific ways, then compared with previous sensory data (memory), to generate an array of contextual connections between environmental conditions and genetic imperatives. Another name for an "array of contextual connections" is meaning. From this meaning, the organism can choose a behavioral course that leads to better survival odds. More on this below.

Example: Psychological Pain

The function of pain is straightforward—to motivate avoidance of harmful environmental stimuli. This applies not only to physical pain but psychological pain. For humans, it would appear that during the course of evolution, as greater complexity developed in the central nervous system, the existing pain system became utilized for more complex and sophisticated situations other than simple tissue damage detection and behavior modification. This sort of "exaptation" (modification of a neutral trait into an adaptive trait over time) is very common in evolution—Nature always uses what it already has available. Thus, for example, the previous observation that in *Homo sapiens* loneliness feels extremely painful because it makes use of the same neural correlates as tissue damage—these results can be found in publications by Chelnokova et al. (2014), Eisenberger and Lieberman (2005), Kitayama and Park (2010), and Petrovic et al. (2008). This fact explains why so many addictive behaviors have emerged in the context of worsening loneliness. The constant equation of lonely feelings with physical pain, therefore, is more than a mere poetic flourish or indulgence of songwriters. It is a precise description.

Using the example of loneliness helps us to understand how pain is one example among many of how the mind generates meaning. Loneliness is a far more complex situation than tissue damage. It requires the perception of social isolation, which imports all the mechanisms involved in the organism's assessment of one's attachment status and social relations, along with a host of other very complex environmental and life-history situations. Loneliness, therefore, is an affectively charged expression of overall meaning for the organism that evolved to motivate social belonging, probably because humans depend on social cooperation for survival to such a high degree.

For the sake of clarity, therefore, I am precisely defining "meaning" as an affect-laden expression of context. It is an array of relations between the subject and numerous environmental objects, past, present, and (in the imagined) future. As the meaning-making became more complex and sophisticated, it makes sense that evolution would build a conscious ego as a secondary center of the psyche designed to handle the difficult problems handed to it by all the auxiliary systems, so that it can manage them in far greater depth of analysis, both rational and emotional. This can be reasonably stated to be the origin of what we call the conscious ego in *Homo sapiens*.

Hence, we do not merely feel pain as perhaps a frog might, responding with primitive reflexes and evasion programs, but we higher order mammals (and likely some birds) can ask ourselves, what does this pain mean? And with that ability came the ability to override and ignore the older, more instinctive proclivity to always flee from pain-causing stimuli. We know not only from experience but from the historical record that many people have been able to endure and even overcome tremendous physical pain for many reasons, provided they had a significant meaning-based motivation to do so.

In order for this behavior to be possible, though, pain itself is obviously no longer the final arbiter of our motivations when faced with harmful stimuli, since it is evidently possible to override it. But toward what end do we override it? In my opinion, we override physical and emotional pain the same way the central nervous system of any animal overrides any sensation it considers less important. The guiding principle will always be the larger meaning—i.e. value-laden expression of context aiming toward survival. If the psyche determines that a given pain is an integral part of an overall more comprehensive meaning, the pain can be mitigated to a degree. Why then, one might ask, is this ability to override pain not all-encompassing? Because, in general, I think the widespread ability to completely ignore pain would not likely be compatible with continued survival, as persons who are unable to feel pain for genetic reasons have shown (Indo et al., 1996). Nature has settled upon a middle ground, in which we can override pain to a degree, but cannot completely negate it except in extraordinary situations.

A Thought Experiment

Recall or imagine the most painful attachment loss in your life—i.e., death of a loved one, for example. Now, let's say psychiatry has become so advanced that we now have a pill that will erase any and all pain of the loss you are now feeling and it is 100% effective. Ask yourself: would you take this pill? Nearly everyone I have ever asked this question has told me "no." But why? Isn't that counter-intuitive? Many popular forms of therapy and psychiatric practice focus heavily on "symptom reduction." Since pain is a symptom, psychotherapeutic techniques would therefore be measured in their ability to reduce psychological pain. And yet here is an instance in which people are saying they would *choose* to feel psychological pain! Why?

Consider that the brain is a highly elaborated organ that—under normal conditions—assesses one's environment, balances it against past events and future predictions, to wind up with a continually updating Gestalt of how am I doing right now and what should I do? This function is the same in all organisms with a central nervous system. Therefore, the difference between pain being caused by tissue damage and pain being caused by highly complex assessments of the current social environment, colored by key past events, is merely one of degree. In both instances the brain and psyche are functioning toward the same goal: discerning what it all means, so that the organism may react appropriately toward pro-survival behaviors.

The point is to emphasize the primacy of meaning over simpler sense impressions—even that of grief itself, which likely evolved far earlier in our mammalian evolution, as reviewed in depth by Panksepp (2004), than the executive functioning capacities of abstract thought, language, etc. The modern human brain can prioritize meaning over pain. Since this capacity is likely to have survival benefits, we can trace it to the function of the psyche.

But this fact implies that the perception of meaninglessness should be highly aversive, and the discovery/creation of greater meaning should be pleasurable. Support for this proposal comes from grief counseling literature itself (e.g., Wittouck et al., 2011). One of the most challenging aspects of helping one navigate painful loss is when the bereaved feel it was "senseless." If the death is seen as "meaningless" the grief is amplified. Part of the goal of grief counseling is to help patients "make sense of" the death—this is of course an exercise in meaning construction. And because of the above assessment of the psyche as largely sub-serving a global meaning-making function, I believe this fact about grief has far wider implications for the psyche as a whole. For it means that even physical torture and the tragic loss of a loved one can be endured sometimes, provided there is meaning to miti-gate it. And of course, clinically, it means the primary method for achieving relief from painful events in life is the construction of meaning.

Meaninglessness, then, and not psychological pain, *per se*, become the pri-mary enemy. That is, if pain and pleasure are not the ultimate motivators of human behavior, but *meaning* is, then it makes sense that if the system fails to find any meaning, it would lead to an extremely dysphoric and defensive state that does not itself have any mitigating options available. In order to drive this function, evolution would have needed to put a huge amount of emphasis on being able to find meaning via intense dysphoria designed to motivate meaning-seeking behavior, and pleasure at meaning-finding. If no meaning can be found, it appears from the above that the pain is heightened, and/or the meaninglessness itself becomes a source of pain. This pain-of-meaninglessness then generates a positive feedback loop of pain-meaninglessness-horror-more pain-etc., spiraling toward suicidal ideation. Thus meaning is the ultimate driver and psychological (and physical) pain is secondary to it. The conclusion, then, is only this: *psychological pain can be mitigated with meaning, but meaninglessness cannot be mitigated by anything else.*

We can hypothesize, then, that the ultimate goal of the psyche is to generate meaning, rather than maximize pleasure and minimize pain, *per se.* In other words, we can theorize that the brain is a meaning-making organ, and the psyche aims toward the creation of meaning. One of the chief ways in which the mind does this is through the generation and/or recognition of context. In the framework of Social Instincts, this means the recognition and reinforcement of social bonds, whether it be with a significant other, one's extended family and friend network, the wider community (however it is defined), and with Nature Herself. When we feel utterly cut off from these things, the above intense dysphoria emerges as a defensive function—much like when our bones are broken, intense dysphoria erupts. We find ourselves in a vulnerable and dangerous state. We seek safety because our fear is activated. We dramatically reduce our activity to conserve energy. We cry out in pain in order to attract others to come to our aid—note that non-social animals have no reason to cry out when they feel pain, which they no doubt do feel; no help would be forthcoming anyway. Social animals, however, like humans or dogs, yelp when injured.

The pain of loneliness, however, seeks *more.* Not just reunion with others, it seeks *meaningful attachment*, which is where the meaning-making comes in. We seek long-term bonds, concretely demonstrable, with real-world consequences and ties. We seek steadfastness and dependability in our bonds, though we will take whatever we can get (hence all the addictions).

Above all we seek the meaning inherent in such bonds. A wedding ring is reassuring because it is a tangible thing with weight and physicality—it's not merely an idea or an abstract sentiment. It has a finality to it because one can either wear it or not wear it—you can't do both at the same time, whereas in our heads we can do such things, which leads to anxiety over the ambivalence. In essence, then, all I'm saying is that the social bond-making instincts we have are part of a greater overall meaning-craving function of the mind. This function was identified by the early psychoanalysts in various ways.

The Transcendent Function

I have been emphasizing the social contributors to mental illness in this book, but I don't want to lose sight of the individual psyche as I do so. Analytical psychology is helpful here, though other branches of psychoanalysis have slightly different versions and names for this meaning-seeking function. Though early psychoanalysis was also vulnerable to hyper-individualism and so too often overemphasized the importance of the individual mind as being the sole cause of mental disturbances, there are still important individual *contributors* to both illness and healing.

Jung proposed that within the psyche was a natural healing process which continually strove toward "individuation." Something akin to a psychic "immune system." Don't be fooled by the name—individuation isn't about separating oneself from the world. This is about becoming un-divided or whole. It is about always moving toward harmony between the various conflicting desires and feelings we all have. As each new day, of course, brings in new chaos and random life events, this is an *ongoing* process. I suspect only bodhisattvas and Jedi Masters are capable of reaching "pure individuation." The rest of us mere mortals are continuing trying to integrate the flow of life and bring some sort of order into the chaos as best we can from one day to the next.

In any case, the ongoing movement toward harmony is a process he termed the *transcendent function*. This function is "the remarkable capacity for change of the human soul" (Jung, CW7, para 360). The transcendent function continually strives toward wholeness and integration of the personality, acts continuously throughout life, bridging apparent opposites through the formation of meaningful symbols to aid in psychic healing and development. Naturally, reductionistic criticisms felt he was invoking something mystical or quasi-religious here, to which he responded:

> There is nothing mysterious or metaphysical about the term "transcendent function." It means a psychological function comparable in its own way to the mathematical function of the same name, which is a function of real and imaginary numbers. The psychological "transcendent function" arises from the union of the conscious and unconscious contents.
>
> (CW8, para 131)

Whether the mathematical analogy clarifies or obscures is subject to debate—I think it is best read as a kind of metaphor. Nevertheless, in other writings Jung describes the underlying processes of the transcendent function as an overarching, primary principle of organization within the psyche:

> Everything that happens at the behest of nature, unconsciously and spontaneously, is deliberately summoned forth and integrated into the conscious mind and its outlook expressed in the transcendent function.
>
> (CW7, p. 80)

The *imagination* plays a key part in this process. Nevertheless, an important distinction needs to be stressed, as the transcendent function only utilizes a specific kind of imaginal activity. One of Jung's students, Marie-Louise Von Franz, for example, states that it is only the "right kind of imagination" that contributes to the transcendent function. But what is the "right kind"? In a 2006 essay, Jungian theorist Warren Colman proposes a distinction between *spontaneously emergent* symbolic material as the right kind, as opposed to defensively organized ego-fantasy material. It is the contention of this chapter that part of how the transcendent function works is through its meaning-making function as manifested in these spontaneously emergent elements. In order to acknowledge and account for the above considerations, then, I will focus our attention on the various sciences that study the phenomenon of spontaneous thought.

Spontaneous Thought, Including Dreams

Since the transcendent function is identified as being a nascent property of the psyche, whose action can be observed in contents that arise spontaneously, we may find clues to how it operates in its particulars by reviewing the burgeoning literature of spontaneous thought—the study of the undirected contents of the mind that emerge unbidden into our awareness. Spontaneous thought is defined within this body of research as thought that arises in the absence of strong willful constraints—i.e., content that emerges independent of willful direction. In psychodynamic terms, then, spontaneous thought would be strongly akin to contents described as "emerging from the unconscious." Thus, for our purposes I will treat the results of the literature on spontaneous thought as strongly analogous to reflecting some or all of how the transcendent function manifests. This will be important for our exploration of the effect of culture on the human psyche.

Supporting the analogy between willful contents of the mind coming from consciousness versus spontaneous contents coming from the unconscious is the fact that researchers on spontaneous thought differentiate between willfully directed or volitional thought and spontaneous thought in a manner similar to Colman (2006), that is, both psychoanalysts and researchers in spontaneous thought are interested in what emerges within one's awareness in an *undirected* and sometimes even *unexpected* manner. This distinction we should therefore classify as being derived from the ego (volitional) or the unconscious (spontaneous). If I am right that a significant aspect of the transcendent function is about self-organizing meaning-making, it should be supported by the findings of the various empirical studies of spontaneous thought, since they represent what the psyche is working on by default when not willfully directed by a conscious ego toward some current task. As we explore this subject, then, it will become evident why I am bringing it up: because this work demonstrates that the human mind is always seeking meaning, and this will have consequences for finding effective solutions to the starving Social Instincts.

Researchers in spontaneous thought sometimes use the terms "mind-wandering," "task-unrelated thought," or "undirected thought" to describe the subject of study. But for simplicity, we will stick with "spontaneous thought." Research on this subject has expanded tremendously in the past decade. In fact, some researchers have labeled the modern era of neuroscience the "era of the wandering mind" (Callard et al., 2013). Roughly one-third to one-half of thought is spontaneous (Klinger & Cox, 1987), and this doesn't include the particular kind of spontaneous thought represented by dream content. Unsurprisingly, dreaming has been classified as a *type* of spontaneous thought (Fox & Christoff, 2018) that shares tremendous overlap with waking spontaneous creative thought. Consider, for example, when Jung states that the transcendent function operates when "everything that happens at the behest of nature, unconsciously and spontaneously, is deliberately summoned forth and integrated into the conscious mind and its outlook expressed in the transcendent function" (CW7, para 80). Thus the early psychoanalysts intuited this activity long ago, and now independent researchers are finding ways to describe it more clearly via the tools of neuroscience and other disciplines.

In analytical psychology, clinical experience shows that spontaneous content is not random. What is so interesting is that this result is also found in the recent experimental psychology of spontaneous thought, which incorporates neuroscience, phenomenology, and many other disciplines. Thus we are seeing that multiple, independent lines of evidence are arriving at the conclusions that spontaneous thought, or the emergent contents coming from the unconscious mind, are found to be purposeful, organized, and often highly functional.

As described by researchers, spontaneous thought:

> is a mode of mind that appears to have considerable benefit for our day-to-day functioning and general contentment—affording sense-making and the ordering of recent events, anticipations of and projections into the future, and a starting point for some of our creative ideas.
> (Stan & Christoff, 2018a, p. 487; see also Klinger & Cox, 1987, 2011)

The brain, rather than being a reactive organ that only passively responds to external stimuli, has a multilayered intrinsically active overall structure that is intensely dynamic and creative even in the absence of input—much as Jung and many other depth psychologists intuited long ago. Moreover, spontaneous thoughts are not merely chimerical wish-fulfillments either. Rather, they are focused on emotionally salient personal concerns, and involve memory consolidation and future planning, most of which are directed at sorting out current concerns, as reviewed by Klinger in a 2009 article. Though spontaneous thought can be associated with dysfunctional processes such as rumination, it has been identified as sub-serving many functional processes such as facilitating semantic knowledge consolidation (similar to dreaming), and pattern recognition (Mills et al., 2018).

Spontaneous thought is also sensitive to environmental needs. Replicated studies, for example, show that spontaneous thoughts increase under conditions of not only sensory deprivation but in the face of meaningless patterns in sensory information (Gallagher et al., 1994), which suggests that this activity is itself responsive to environmental conditions and it not only detects meaning-lacking environments, but *strives to answer them*.

Dreams

Analyzing dreams and other spontaneous content of the psyche has, of course, been subject to observation and analysis in many psychoanalytic traditions including Jungian; however, there has been disagreement about whether or not such content is largely occupied with disguising deeper thoughts, or whether or not such content is largely *revelatory* of deeper processes. Jung of course proposed the latter, describing dream contents as a "spontaneous self-portrayal, in symbolic form, of the actual situation in the unconscious" (CW8, para 505). Similarly, Bion proposed that dreams transform unprocessed primary experiences into workable thoughts, memories, and mental growth (Bion, 1962). Both of these early psychoanalysts proposed that this process occurs in both waking and sleeping states. By contrast, Freud (1900) famously argued that dreams *disguised* inner realities rather than revealing them. For Freud, the psyche had to disguise the socially unacceptable thoughts deriving from the id, and this was accomplished by the "dream censor"—a concept which later evolved into the superego.

In a recent 2023 article by psychologist Christian Roesler, however, a large body of empirical literature on dreaming is reviewed and it is found that Freud's idea that dreams disguise meaning has not aged well. Rather, the balance of empirical literature on dreams shows that they have a strong tendency for meaning *creation*, which can be observed in the manifest dream content, providing one recognizes the symbolic nature of such content. Moreover, experimental and neuroscientific study of dreaming supports the notion that dream contents reveal self and self-related processing.

According to experimental psychologists studying dreams, dreaming is actually an intensified form of spontaneous thought with many overlapping features. Like waking spontaneous thought, dreams are biased toward personal, affectively salient concerns, and the process comes 'on line' by around age 7–10 (Domhoff, 2018). The overlap can also be observed in neuroscience data, for the same regions involved in spontaneous thought are recruited (albeit more intensely) during REM dreaming (Fox et al., 2013). Moreover, dreams are generated by the same fundamental processes that underpin spontaneous thought during wakefulness (Christoff et al., 2016).

As will become evident as more research is reviewed, spontaneous, undirected thought—including dream content—is neither random nor centered on pure wish-fulfillment, but rather is purposeful and functional, focusing on one's own personal autobiographical narrative, current problems and issues, to include identity and contextualization of recent events. The important lesson here is that spontaneous waking thought and dream contents should not be considered separate phenomena, but really two kinds of the same phenomenon: that of the activity of the mind. That is, spontaneous thought appears to be a manifestation of what Jung called the transcendent function. This does not merely apply to dreams and fantasies erupting "out of the blue" either. The function of spontaneous thought in organizing one's personal context, in particular, can even be seen in the studies of how memory is consolidated via this activity.

Memory Is a Part of This System

Human memory is often conceived as if it works like a computer, "storing" events in "memory banks" to be "retrieved" at a later time. This, however, is not how human memory works. Rather, memory is largely a construction created on the spot to simulate a past event (Schacter & Addis, 2007). Memories are mostly generated not by a retrieval or reproduction, but rather by a spontaneous creation of the imagination that more-or-less resembles the previous event, with numerous factors at play affecting their accuracy.

Memory *consolidation*, however, is what determines whether or not such a construction is even possible, and it is a continuously updated process organized toward similar goals as spontaneous thoughts and dreams. Which memories the psyche chooses to consolidate are not random, either, but chosen according to certain criteria, such as their emotional valence and intensity, future relevance, and potential reward value (Fischer & Born, 2009; Payne et al., 2008; Wilhelm et al., 2011). That is, their meaning for the rememberer, or their value-laden contextual placement with respect to the subject. Mere repetition of a stimulus, for example, is a very poor predictor of memory consolidation. Thus, memory is not a static placing of events in "storage," like papers in a file cabinet, but represents another aspect of the meaning-making processes of the psyche.

Memory consolidation itself, moreover, can increase or decrease in intensity depending on the current situation. Empirical study of spontaneous thoughts and images reveal that such contents appear to be continually evaluating memories of recent events (see Antrobus, 2018), and that the frequency and intensity of such evaluation increases when exposed to threatening circumstances, which suggests it is an *adaptive* process. Other research using neuroimaging shows that periods of rest often correlate with an increase in spontaneous thought centered on autobiographical memory and future planning (Andreasen et al., 1995).

Kieran Fox, in a 2018 paper, reviews intracranial electrical stimulation data that show how memory recall, dreaming, imagining/planning, and hallucination all involve the same brain networks (especially the medial temporal lobe and hippocampus), indicating a common underpinning in imaginal processes. Fox furthermore argues that this process, which allows "the mapping of 'anything' to 'anywhere'" (p. 175), has been co-opted by Nature as the brain-derived generator of spontaneous thoughts.

Finally, dreaming has long been tied to memory consolidation via REM sleep mechanisms, although it is important to note that less than 2% of dream content includes key elements of any given episodic memory—instead dreams contain many memory fragments (explored by Fosse et al., 2003), inter-mingled with older memories, characters, and semantic knowledge. From there, the psyche reconstitutes those fragments into novel narratives, with the new information integrated into existing memories in novel ways. This process appears to aim toward the *extraction of commonalities across multiple experiences* (Durrant et al., 2011; Lau et al., 2010), as well as integrate future possibilities (Wamsley et al., 2016). Thus, the dreaming process is not as concerned with what happened exactly, but is more concerned with what it all means emotionally. It uses affect-laden symbolic narratives to accomplish this (Goodwyn, 2018).

According to the foregoing, then, memory consolidation is far from a simple, mindless, store-and-retrieve system. It is flexible, creative, and highly focused on affectively laden, symbolically expressed meaning construction, continuously operated on by the unconscious, perhaps most intensely during dreaming.

Why does this matter for our study of starving Social Instincts? It matters because our natural response to such starvation will involve the spontaneous expression of symbolic narratives. Popular movies, books, television shows, and other works of art and imagination will "click" or resonate with issues that are commonly found within a given culture. This happens because of the way in which *affect* orders the imaginal processes we have discussed so far.

Affect

A key player in the direction, function, and general orientation of spontaneous thought is affective valence. Given their importance to memory consolidation, it is no surprise that affective states also influence the amount and direction of spontaneous thought content. For example, spontaneous thoughts are found to be much more self-referential than voluntary thoughts and are strongly biased toward affectively charged concerns (D'Argembeau, 2018). Other studies show how spontaneous thoughts are affectively centered and sensitive to current goals (Fox & Christoff, 2018). Given the above discussion of pain, it is notable that pain can be overridden by spontaneous thought and descending activity of the salience network, which is connected to the temporoparietal junction. This junction is a multi-modal integrative center that assesses general, salient changes in the environment—i.e., the personal affective meaning of current events (reviewed in Kucyi, 2018).

Zedelius and Schooler (2018) review the literature on the practice of intentional mind-wandering, a process obviously similar to Jung's "active imagination." These investigators review studies which show that intentionally attending to spontaneous thought has a mood-regulating function, and in particular it is the image-heavy content of spontaneous thought, rather than verbal description, that is most effective at mood regulation. They found that only when subjects imagined first-person, image-heavy scenarios did they show mood improvement, regardless of whether the scenario was positive or negative (2018, p. 241). These researchers concluded that specific kinds of deliberate mind-wandering may improve overall mood, performance, and sense of personal meaning.

Much of the above has been found for the dreaming type of spontaneous thought as well. That is, dreaming has been identified as serving several functions, including mood regulation, problem solving, adaptation, furthering of mastery, fostering insight, and anxiety reduction (reviewed in Roesler, 2023).

Psychoanalysts Kramer and Glucksman in a 2015 study showed how multiple dreams in a single person can be observed to be continually working and reworking major emotional themes, even to the point that independent evaluators could identify immediate and long-term emotional issues just from dream content. Notably, Roesler states in his 2023 review:

> Daytime experiences, especially those with emotional significance or really oppressive affects are reactivated from the short-term memory store during dreaming and calibrated with earlier experiences from long-term memory, more particularly in the same way as similar experiences and conflicts in earlier situations were solved or overcome. To that extent a problem-reworking and to some extent also problem-solving actually takes place during dreaming, so that the reworked contents can be stored in the long-term memory and cease to burden mental functioning in everyday life... This reworking of memory contents in the dream is therefore a highly structured, rule-governed and goal-directed reworking process that operates largely unconsciously, extensively coordinates various domains of mental functioning, but can also only take place while there is no new mental input of the kind that occurs in the waking state.
>
> (p. 314)

Many of these same observations, as we have seen, have been applied to spontaneous thought in general. That is, affect is the ordering principle which guides the formation of spontaneous thoughts, including dreams, as well as memory formation—the narratives that emerge from the unconscious to express and work on the problems that plague us. When the same problem stresses people on a large scale, the collective effect will naturally be to become more focused on and/or fascinated by narratives which seek to address those problems. That is because the *aim* of all this activity is **meaning-making**.

Meaning: The Goal of the Transcendent Function

Meaning-making is the ultimate purpose behind the highly constructive process of spontaneous thought. Toward this end, the psyche appears to take the raw data of experience and process it extensively, the end result being spontaneously emergent images and narratives. Thus far it would seem that the construction of a stable affectively calibrated self-narrative (memory consolidation, mood regulation/contextualization) is one of the functions, along with creative problem solving and future planning.

Psychoanalyst Donald Meltzer proposed that the primary function of dreams is to generate meaning (1983), which echoes Jung's and Bion's earlier thoughts on dreams in general and (for Jung) the transcendent function. Neuroscientifically, spontaneous thought (including dreaming) is characterized as related to the so-called "default mode" network: a brain network consisting of midline, lateral parietal, and mediolateral temporal brain regions. The default mode network is associated with internally directed attention, representations of self and autobiographical memory among other functions (Buckner et al., 2008). This network operates "in the background" but is particularly prominent when one is doing nothing in particular. It is exploratory in nature and heavily weighted toward pattern recognition and creativity along many independent measures. Research on creativity largely points to the fact that the default mode network is more active during idea generation than the executive control network (volitional direction of thought). During idea revision, however, they work together and their connectivity is strengthened (Beaty & Jung, 2018).

In any case, Klinger et al. (2018) note that spontaneous thoughts have been connected with goal tracking, planning, creative problem solving, reviewing past experience, memory consolidation, and aligning oneself with goal-attainment, but when in excess can lead to rumination, excessive daydreaming and dissociation. Interestingly, modifying spontaneous thought content is actually achievable by modifying one's motivational structure (Klinger et al., 2018, p. 227). Mind wandering also appears to promote creativity (Sio & Ormerod, 2009) and reduce "delay discounting" (Smallwood et al., 2013)— the process by which future rewards are devalued because of a time delay.

A growing number of scholars of dreams propose that dreaming processes experiences by attempting to connect them with other experiences in memory—effectively meaning-making via context construction (reviewed in Roesler, 2023, pp. 303–308). Dreaming functions are identified as the development, preservation, and reintegration of the psychic organization (Fosshage, 1997), which was strongly presaged by Jung's description of dreaming having a compensatory function (1960). Supporting this intuition, a 2004 study by empirical dream researchers Wegner, Wenzlaff, and Kozac found that dreamers often dream more about subjects they had been asked *not* to think about. These results support the clinical wisdom of looking at dreams to discern what someone is trying to avoid.

Roesler concludes that:

> It can most likely be said in summary from today's perspective that the various dream theories that have been discussed until now elucidate important aspects of the meaning and function of dreaming. Equally, the dream's function cannot be reduced to any single one of these aspects. The dream certainly plays an important role in integrative processes in the psyche. Moreover, however, it also has a generative function for psychic growth and furthermore obviously also for creativity and problem-solving.
>
> (2023, p. 325)

Stan and Christoff (2018b) argue that the numerous benefits of spontaneous thought might justify changing the term "mind-wandering" to "mind-ordering," given its functions. Interestingly enough, people tend to attribute spontaneous thoughts with greater meaning than deliberative thoughts (Morewedge & Kupor, 2018)—given the above, that may be appropriate, more often than not.

As mentioned, convergent neuroscientific studies show that memory, imagination, and future simulation all recruit the same brain regions, and lesions in those areas affect all three capacities (O'Callaghan & Irish, 2018). Moreover, and most important for our purposes in the present work, there is growing evidence that points to spontaneous thoughts being critical in the construction of *personal identity and meaning*, suggesting a role in "reflecting on the broader meaning and implications of personal experiences, thereby contributing to the construction, maintenance, and update of an individual's life story" (D'Argembeau, 2018, p. 187). Still other experimental psychologists identify the *identity-consolidating* function of dreaming (Fiss, 1995; Kohut, 1977; Stolorow, 1978; Stolorow & Atwood 1993), particularly when the psyche is under stress/destabilization.

The above research, therefore, strongly suggests that the psyche has a continuously active function aiming toward meaning-making, much as Jung and other psychoanalysts hypothesized, and clinical experience confirms. In particular, it appears that during times when the mind is not occupied with an immediate task, this process can be observed to be working tirelessly on the construction of meaning, expressed via one's personal identity and narrative.

Summary: The Meaning-Making Dimension of the Transcendent Function

For clarity: I am proposing that a significant element of the transcendent function is involved in meaning-making through the expression of affect-laden context. Specifically, this means that there is a dimension of the transcendent function that is continuously operating in the background and can be detected in the content of spontaneous thought including dreams. Moreover, the aim of this activity is focused on integrating the self-past with the self-present (i.e. memory consolidation), and in a way that calibrates oneself with one's future plans and goals (i.e., problem solving and creativity). This activity is accomplished via the production of an autobiographical self-narrative that includes as much context as possible—i.e., it is involved in affectively oriented meaning and identity creation, or simply affectively directed context creation.

From the foregoing research, it appears that what Jung describes as the transcendent function can be observed directly, in part, via the contents of spontaneous thought, both waking and dreaming. Research on the subject of spontaneous thought reveals that this activity appears to be occupied with continuously updating, consolidating, and processing previous events in order to construct an affectively oriented symbolic narrative expression of meaning/context. This dimension of the transcendent function operates in a manner that flexibly up- or down-modulates in accordance with the immediate needs of the organism. During times of relative peace and relaxation—or "down time"—it increases in activity, processing more intensely, calibrating memory, affect, goals, and meaning together. These it weaves into a continually updating affectively charged, symbolic self-narrative that depicts one's context within the larger tapestry of the world. When engaging in day-to-day tasks or immediate problems, this function takes a "back seat," and shifts information processing to the ego to allow for immediate tasks in the form of increased control network activity. Stress up-modulates the activity of this meaning-making function as well.

Clinically, we can look at the transcendent function as (in part) continually asking the question "who am I?" It then mines recent and remote events, breaking them down into fragments, then re-organizing them into both literal affectively focused narratives (autobiographical memory) that tell us "what happened" but also symbolic, affectively charged and image-heavy narratives that tell us "what does it mean?" This dimension of the transcendent function is constantly processing, but its mode of activity seems dependent on the overall stress level of current life experiences. Under low stress, it works in a playful, exploratory manner, expanding the scope of who one wishes to be, past, present, and future. Under moderate stress, however, it narrows its focus and increases the intensity to the most affectively salient and pressing concerns, sacrificing scope and exploration for problem solving and more immediate bodily survival and maintaining social standing (so important in a social species such as *Homo sapiens*). Under extreme stress, however, it would appear the transcendent function (or a separate process) pulls the current ego out of awareness, in order to make room for precious cognitive resources to build a brand new ego from scratch. Completely sacrificing access to autobiographical memory for the sake of immediate survival, this more drastic maneuver forces the ego to build a new ego strategy from scratch, treating the old one as a failed and maladaptive strategy that must be abandoned. From there, transcendent function resources are poured into the new ego. All the while, the transcendent function attempts to create order from the chaos of every new day, until such time (if ever) that it can attempt to bring the old ego back into awareness for further integrative efforts.

This is the state the mind will be in when placed under the stress of starving Social Instincts. It will naturally trigger a response from the psyche to increase its meaning-making efforts via symbolic narrative, dream, and affect-driven spontaneous imagery. The affect in this case that is driving the system will be loneliness in all its bitter, subtle pain that is often explained away as something else, like "incorrect cognitions" or (my favorite) "a chemical imbalance." And no doubt such things can lead to suffering, what I hope is evident at this point is that cultural conditions are sufficient alone to produce loneliness and suffering, even in those who have adequate food and housing. As imminently social animals, we continue to crave belonging along all four axes, and if deprived, we will feel it and attempt to dream our way out of it.

Collective Dreams

Why do so many Disney princesses sing songs at the beginning of their movies about "I don't know who I am"? This trend began during the so-called Disney "Renaissance" starting with *The Little Mermaid*. It has continued ever since, regardless of whether or not the main character is male or female. The earlier Disney Princesses such as Snow White or Sleeping Beauty never worried about such things. Rather, they concerned themselves more with finding only the companionate, intimate partner sort of love—the rest of the axes of our Social Instincts were covered, because even if they were separated from their homelands, the story merely worked toward moving them back to where they originally belonged. Modern Disney characters *don't know* where they belong. They live in a world of infinite possibility and choice, much like our world, and are paralyzed by it.

Another common trope in modern popular movies, anime cartoons (which have exploded in popularity in the US in the last few decades), and comics is not only the "found family" trope, but the "saving the world" trope. Both of these narratives are reflections of our deeper need to belong that organizes so many other aspects of our emotional lives. Who am I, and where do I belong? These are the questions asked of nearly every anime lead, superhero character, and young adventure story hero, and while it is true that such story structures are indeed old, their current emphasis seems to be on *finding one's place in the world*.

Ancient heroes such as Beowulf, King Arthur, or Odysseus did not bother themselves with such hand-wringing. They had other problems, to be sure, but they always knew who they were and where they belonged. Their task involved protecting their people, finding their way home, or coming into their own as great leaders. Modern heroes, as expressions of ideal value-seeking and meaning-finding, however, must deal with the above things but *also* "find themselves," which means *define their interpersonal context*.

This is the reason so many "team up" hero narratives keep springing up over and over. They find their home within the team of superheroes such as the Justice League, the Avengers, or the hundreds of other variations on this theme. Their context comes to be defined by each other *alone*, as no established culture or background really provides this for them. I think this resonates with modern (particularly urban) young viewers because of the aforementioned effects of the media pseudoculture. Without any substantive community or extended family/friend ties, the pseudoculture becomes the backdrop, but deep down we all know it is flimsy and free of depth, so we must satisfy our need for belonging in "found family"—i.e., the random, free-floating others lost in the same scramble for identity and meaning that we are. Only through each other is the loneliness bearable, and so such hero stories end with imagery of all the main characters smiling and facing the sun together in a row.

The "save the world" trope, though again not really new, is also extremely popular in these sorts of fantastical stories because it is an expression of meaning-through-action also. This not only gives us an escape from being cogs in the giant corporate machine—the sorts of jobs modern society has us crawling over each other in order to win the privilege of having—but it gives it nobility and respect.

I may be someone who inserts advertising messages into media products for a corporation, but Batman is the guardian of justice. Superman is the protector of the Earth. Much more glamorous. The Avengers defend the entire planet from outlandish foes of every kind. Countless anime teams save the village, the country, the world, or the universe from the forces of chaos and random mayhem through "the power of friendship." Yes it's corny and silly, but let us not forget that "the power of friendship" is the power of social cooperation—motivated by our Social Instincts and perhaps the most powerful adaptive tool evolution has yet devised. And it was honed by endless conflict and bloodshed, with only those who bonded with their tribal sisters and brothers the most surviving to pass on their proclivities. These instinctive forces, then, which shape our very dreams and fantasies, are what is starving. They crave real connection, and motivate us to satisfy them in any way that we can.

The explosion of stories about young people with superpowers in flamboyant outfits is a reflection of and symbolization of our desire for individuality and value to others. A superpower, after all, is a thing you can do that (presumably) nobody else can do. It provides a visible, tangible symbol of one's individuality in a way that is also useful toward the end of *doing* something for others—which of course gives you instant value to those people who do not typically require one to work all that hard. Ego fantasy at its best. Nevertheless, the popularity of such stories, and the fanatical manner in which enthusiasts sometimes follow them, is explainable via the way they impinge upon our Social Instincts. That is, they can satisfy them with vicarious fantasy, but this does not last once the movie or story ends. On the other hand, such symbolic expressions can inspire us to act in the world in such a way as to forge bonds to satisfy them in a more substantial way. The difference, I think, is whether or not a fan of such content acknowledges the connection between the fantastical expression and the real-world referent of such symbols. In a sense, we do all indeed have something unique to bring to a collective. That is the "superpower" each one of us has. No matter what our lot in life, we can always choose to serve others in one way or another—the quintessential task of the superhero, often diametrically opposed to the super-villain, who only wants to use her or his powers to serve themselves. When we realize that, in this very real sense, we are all superheroes, or Jedi Knights, or great warriors, then we can see how such narratives might be so prevalent because their *aim* is to draw us *into* life, not to distract us with wish-fulfillment or empty "escapism." But because of the symbolic and pre-linguistic or imagistic nature of such emotionally resonant storytelling, it is likely that quite a bit of our hopes and dreams for relief from the starvation are bound up in such stories, if we would but pay them close attention. Thus it is important to closely track our dreams and fantastical narratives, even when they seem corny or silly, because they are expressions of the transcendent function, but voiced *en masse*, through collective crafting and not merely isolated howlings in the wilderness.

Chapter 13

The Quest for Sustenance

As mentioned at the beginning of this book, in 1929, Sigmund Freud published *Civilization and its Discontents*, in which he elucidated a curious paradox. He noted the fact that while civilization was developed to protect us from unhappiness, it nevertheless seemed to him that civilization was the greatest *source* of unhappiness. Imagine what he would think of our current predicament! And, for all that, even though I think he was right about this strange paradox—at least as it pertains to the Western civilizations (i.e., the United States and perhaps to a lesser degree the countries of Western Europe) it turns out we would need to explore his later writings, such as *Group Psychology and the Analysis of the Ego* (1990), or many other sources, to see the bigger picture.

We are not unhappy because civilization exists solely to *repress* our deeper instincts. And when we refer to instincts, we are not talking primarily about sexual urges and violent tendencies. In a simple-minded individual vs. collective dichotomy, there is a fundamental clash between society and its oppressive rules, and the individual and his desire for unfettered freedom. Consider that in modern culture individuality is hyper-emphasized to such an extent that *it* is now the source of our unhappiness in part.

As it turns out, our instincts are legion, and encompass far more than sex drive and anger, and include an extremely important set of Social Instincts. And while there is certainly tension between "society" and the individual in our modern world. It is likely that, early on at least, Freud was describing a situation that made much more sense in late-nineteenth and early twentieth century Vienna, in which individual expression was indeed locked down by overly rigid social structures and perhaps *excessive* connection. Later, however, this was refined considerably in his work. In any case, the situation we have now with hardly *any* substantial connection, seems to fare even worse in terms of happiness. Nevertheless, even as prescient as the early psychoanalysts were, there is a complicating factor here that did not exist in the early twentieth century: the opposition between the individual and an imposter culture —a mass media pseudoculture.

DOI: 10.4324/9781032721354-13

The opposition between individual and pseudoculture, therefore, makes us feel *as if* we were locked in a situation akin to a simple individual vs. collective dichotomy. But this impression would be misleading, because the pseudoculture doesn't have even the benefits of an overly rigid social structure. It just makes you feel either a desire to rebel, or it gives you an addictive, less-than-satisfying "fix" to temporarily assuage the Social Instincts. But this leads us to the big question: how can we feed our Social Instincts with something that is truly nourishing? What shall we use to feed our souls? We don't want to feed them with excessive, rigid, or extremist social connection, as often happens in the case of cults or reactionary groups. But we can't just let them starve either, and the junk food of smartphones, social media, and addictions just makes us sicker. Our human nature requires more than just food, water, and shelter. It requires, and to the very same extent if not a *greater* extent, something to feed our craving for belonging and meaning, but as discussed in the previous chapters, there needs to be a proper dose of it: not too much, not too little. Let's look at the components of the Social Instincts to see what we potentially need in a bit more detail.

We Are Humans and Not Tigers

Our Social Instincts crave a long-term partner because of our nature as a species that invests long term in offspring and engages in collaborative parenting. If we were tigers, we would not care—tigers do not engage in collaborative parenting. Females do it alone. They don't care if the father hangs around, and fathers don't care about their cubs. Tigers therefore do not *ever* care if they have a life-long loving partner to experience their trials and tribulations with. They bond with their cubs, but only until they get to a certain age, then they chase them off. Do tigers ever miss their cubs like humans miss their children? Hard to say, but if they didn't that would not be a mark against tigers. Tigers do not *need* to be beholden to our emotional rules. It would merely mean that humans might have a hard time imagining what it would be like because, more often than not, we bond very tightly to our "cubs", and it takes a lot to disrupt that. Even death cannot cleave that bond —it takes more than death. In fact, we bond so strongly to our "cubs" that the death of one is one of the most devastating experiences we can endure. In such a case, the kinship between that kind of agony and "physical" agony is all too clear.

Our Social Instincts also crave family and friends. Again, tigers—not so much. Tigers are perfectly equipped to survive alone in the wilderness. They likely do not feel the pain of isolation and loneliness that we do. There would be no reason for that. Humans left alone in the wilderness, however, in most cases would go insane from the pain of social loss, even if we were able to survive on our own. Thus, Nature has equipped us with strong emotional instincts that push us to form attachments with family and peers that we spend enough time with. Adversity does not weaken such bonds, either, it *strengthens* it. Some of the strongest bonds I have ever seen were among those who fought in wars together. "We few, we happy few, we band of brothers" as Henry V says in Shakespeare's play of the same name, expresses this feeling well. When acquaintances are put into do-or-die situations, this dimension of the Social Instincts kicks into overdrive, and the attachments formed are extremely strong and typically never go away. Few people, however, ever stop to ask themselves: why? Why do such bonds for with such tenacity? Why is it so hard for us to imagine being a tiger who really and truly does not care about friends or family[1]? Such questions are a part of what I'm doing, and I think the answer is: because these feelings evolved that way, and they provide powerful survival advantages. They serve a design purpose, which is to pull people together in times of danger so they will be encouraged to work together as a group. They are inborn and part of human nature.

In the ancestral environment, this instinct worked so well it became standard issue from the genome. Notice also that in times of peace and plenty, we tend to squabble more about petty issues. Freud saw this in his *Civilization and its Discontents* and called it the "narcissism of small differences". He saw it as a relatively harmless expression of innate aggression, and this may still be true. But I think there is a larger context. If you attack the squabbling factions, there is a tendency for those factions to come together and forget about such differences. I don't think this is simply a matter of everyone coming to their senses. I think it is the activation of the Social Instincts performing their ancient function, which is to form coalitional bonds because they are a stronger and more effective form of defense. A powerful wave of emotion sweeps over those squabblers and for a while, anyway, the group acts as one against a common foe.

This behavior is no accident and is similar to all our other instincts in character. Like all instincts, the Social Instincts tend to operate when they are activated by the proper environmental conditions. Hunger activates when we haven't eaten in a while, then fades into the background when we are satiated. Similarly, the Social Instincts relax in times of peace and plenty, and kick into overdrive during times of hardship and (especially) war. In fact, the war-activation of these instincts is a demonstration of them acting in the original capacity in which they evolved. Nevertheless, they must still operate constitutively in the background for them to be more effective when they are needed, which is one reason why we form such long-term family and peer bonds in the first place. Though they may have originally evolved due to coalitional warfare among our primate ancestors, like many adaptations, they developed other uses once present, such as the ability to encourage cooperative behavior in other endeavors.

This is where the third dimension of the Social Instincts comes into play—forming bonds of community and large-scale collective identity. As we have discussed so far throughout this book, we are more satisfied when we are identified with a community, ethnicity, collective cause, heritage, "tribe", etc., and this is another part of the Social Instincts tigers don't give a damn about. It is another dimension of the instincts which encourage banding together as brothers and sisters to achieve a common goal. It is possible that this dimension of Social Instinct was not available to our distant primate ancestors because it requires a level of abstraction and verbal communication perhaps not available to them. But consider that not only do gorillas and chimpanzees engage in coalitional warfare to defend territory, but this behavior has been observed in non-primates as well, including wolves, lions, and even meerkats. Do these animals feel a sense of solidarity among their peers? Do they think of the enemies as "foreign interlopers" deserving of scorn and perhaps even bigotry? Perhaps not put into such precise verbal terms, but nevertheless we might still share the emotions behind such sentiments on a deep level.

Which brings us to the fourth dimension—the universal dimension. Not only do we crave connection with a long-term partner of some kind (though this need not necessarily be a marriage or even a physically intimate relationship), along with bonds of family and community, we also crave a bond with *nature*. Given that our advanced technology has provided us with the ability to live almost entirely in artificial environments, the evidence reviewed previously on the subject of Nature Deficiency seems to suggest it is not the healthiest way to live. This, too, makes sense from an evolutionary perspective, if perhaps no other perspective.

We evolved, after all, in non-artificial environments. And not only that, every species that came before us did, too. So it goes pretty far back, and hence we are not adapted to live in completely artificial environments in the same way that, say, the ant or bee is. Ants and bees are also intensely social, cooperating animals that live most of their lives in artificial environments of their own creation (hives), but unlike them we have not adapted to such environments over millions of years, and it is likely going to be a very long time before we are. In the meantime, then, we will have universal Social Instincts which crave connection to natural non-artificial environments for our mental and physical health to be optimal. Though placed at fourth on our list of Social Instincts, this one is perhaps the oldest and therefore deepest, and unlike the others, tigers probably *do* have these, which is why they, like so many animals, may not do as well behaviorally in captivity as they do in the wild, although the wild has other dangers associated with it that might make up for it. The point is that while our artificial environments do provide safety, comfort, and perhaps longevity, they do not seem to provide everything we need at the emotional level. This level, furthermore, is not just some fluffy concern about our precious "feelings", but is a very serious concern that has real-world health consequences. When the Social Instincts are starved, we begin to waste away, even when adequate food and shelter are provided. It seems Jesus was on to something when he said "people do not live by bread alone, but by every word that comes from the mouth of God." (Matthew 4:4).

If we consider that all religions world-wide tend to regard Nature as divine on some level, then this quote seems to be saying we live not merely by food and shelter but by our connection to nature. And even for a non-believer, the rush of feeling that comes from an undeniably stable sense of belonging can feel as if one is in the presence of the Divine.

So How Do We Fix Toxic Culture

This analogy regarding living in captivity appears to apply to humans, too. Like tigers, we live longer in the "captivity" of the artificial environment we have created known as modern society. The difference is that while tigers may suffer from living in captivity and isolation from other tigers to a degree, it seems to be nothing compared to the despair and darkness that humans feel when living in relative isolation.

As mentioned before, solitary confinement is considered a very powerful punishment in the penal system, and a large body of literature has emerged documenting the many negative effects of it. In a 2018 study by Haney in the *Annual Review of Criminology,* for example, the author reports that "human beings have a basic need to establish and maintain connections to others and the deprivation of opportunities to do so has a range of deleterious consequences". As such, since there is a lack of good evidence that it serves any penological purpose, Haney and many others have called to reduce or eliminate its use. But the effects of solitary confinement make no sense except in light of the Social Instincts, and simply provides yet more evidence that widespread disconnection from others is likely what is making our current culture more toxic. Solitary confinement is just an extreme example—what we are doing in modern society is a watered down version of it, and so it is a subtler poison.

Throughout this book we have been discussing how for various reasons, our culture here in the US has become increasingly disconnected and fragmented, and despite our material gains and technological advances, our social structures have changed in ways that appear to be detrimental to our mental health because of their effect on our Social Instincts. It is as if everyone is experiencing more and more "solitary confinement". As of this writing, the Covid Pandemic has been going on for years and is only now winding down. Clinically I have seen its effects on mental health. The precautions involving yet even *more* isolation and social distancing have only amplified what was already a problem in our culture. As mentioned early in this book, it's not an accident that these viruses are so successful—they operate by preying on our Social Instincts, and the fact that we do not *want* to socially distance from one another. Over the ages, such viruses as the SARS-CoV-2 (the microbe responsible for COVID-19 illness) have found that humans have a very hard time staying away from one another and hurt when they are separated.

In any case, what the pandemic has done has shown us just how bad the consequences of disconnecting may be getting. The solution, therefore, seems fairly simple in principle: re-connect people. Support successful long-term bonding. Encourage and support family and friend connections. Encourage and support community-mindedness and belonging, which includes perhaps celebrating and rejuvenating ties to one another via common ideology, charitable institution, celebration of ethnic tradition, heritage, home, or even common interests. And encourage and support reconnecting with Nature and non-artificial environments.

All these things, however, must be done in such a way as to avoid the pitfalls of tribalism, bigotry, and paranoid hate—the dark side of the Social Instincts. We must find a way to satisfy the Social Instincts that respects the fact that they were born out of conflict. Our social instincts are responsible for our ability as a species to be altruistic and loving toward complete strangers. But they are also inextricably bound to and responsible for our ability to label people as "the enemy" and hate or condemn them in a fit of fear and anger. The Social Instincts therefore embody both the better angels of our nature *and* the cruel demons that made Auschwitz possible, and it does not seem that they can be extracted from one another. It seems love and hate must come as a package deal, and we must therefore treat the admixture with the care we would a jar of nitroglycerin.

Groups which find people bonding over being "white", for example, may satisfy the Social Instincts, but because they import the colonial legacy behind the whole concept of "whiteness" in the first place, they import what was behind it: the exploitation of indigenous populations. It is easy to see why such efforts are doomed to fall victim to bigotry and hate from the outset. Better to celebrate and connect in a way that avoids colonial legacy. Ways such as love of common heritage, common solidarity (such as LGBTQ+ affiliation), ethnicity, ideology, charitable mission, or the like. If bonding over heritage, make it one's Italian, Jewish, African, Japanese, Irish, etc heritage— not skin coloration. Closely avoid any hint of hatred or bigotry against those outside the community.

Why Fixing This Situation Will Be Incredibly Difficult

In any case, the above suggested solution of "more connection", though simple in principle, will not be easy to implement in practice. In fact, it may be nearly impossible. The factors that have gotten us here are extremely complex and may not be reversible. In fact, when I make statements about how despite our technological and medical advancements we appear to be less happy than before, I am glossing over the fact that the technology and medical advancements may be partially *responsible* for the mental state changes.

We cannot fix disconnected society by the usual way in which we seem to like to approach problems: by simply pouring money into government programs, dropping bombs on people with oil, or asking billionaires to fix it with "innovative" solutions in exchange for tax breaks. No, we are all going to have to become much more aware of the social component of "bio-psycho-social" dimensions of our mental health and make a huge, concerted effort. We are going to have to ask hard questions about the subtle but powerful effects our mass-media, education system, and values have on everyone in this country.

We cannot, for example, simply preach with all trumpets that we must spend more family time together if our economic system continues to force families to work longer hours, multiple jobs, and make endless sacrifices for work. People cannot conjure up family time out of thin air. But it's more than that, too: families now have grown up in multiple generations of the ABVS as well as a ubiquitous atmosphere of hyper-individualism. Not only are families expected not to get along, but they often get conflated with the consumer pseudo-culture and so are rebelled against almost reflexively, and we all think it's "normal". There are too many centrifugal forces working on marriages, families, and communities, and too few centripetal forces to counterbalance.

In other words: as a society we tend to go willingly into isolation in the name of "freedom", "authentic self-expression", to unfetter ourselves from tyrannical "rules" and to rebel against the consumer pseudo-culture. We do it for the ABVS, and because feeling disconnected doesn't necessarily come with knowledge of how to fix it, we pursue consumer solutions to it. Or worse, we pursue addictions to fend off the starvation. But when asked the question, "Who are you?", we honestly don't know how to even *answer* the question. We are so clueless and we have been swimming so long in hyperindividualism drenched in pseudoculture, we don't see how making lasting bonds to people and ideas outside of ourselves is the primary way to fix it. This problem has arisen because the question isn't about what our favorite chocolate bar is, or what kind of movie we like to watch, or based on any other sort of products we like to consume. It's a question asking us about *what we are connected to*. Where I come from, what my obligations are, who my family is, how I relate to others, where I live, what my job is, etc. Identity is *context*. Identity is not formed by navel gazing alone. We must have external connections to get the full self-identification.

What the Studies Suggest

Throughout this book we have reviewed several things that are contributing to a culture that is reaching ever-increasing levels of toxicity. I will review them here so we can take a look at what we may need to do to create a society that is less so.

Flexible, Non-Fundamentalist Religiosity:

For those who are drawn to religious and/or spiritual traditions new or old, it appears that affiliation with ones that espouse an inflexible or fundamentalist worldview are not conducive to flourishing mental health. But remember that these very things are, in part, responses to both the ever-increasing disconnection *and* the consumer pseudo-culture that has both contributed to and resulted from that disconnection.

Like an addiction, such worldviews satisfy the Social Instincts because they provide a simple way of understanding the world and one's place in it. It therefore provides identity in the above sense discussed—it gives you a concrete, easy to conceptualize identity. They also inevitably comes with a bunch of rules that are inflexible and inviolate. These, again, are partially in reaction to the pervasive lack of ritualism and "rules" that one finds in a hyper-individualistic culture. Hyper-individualism gives us the illusion of limitless freedom but leaves us feeling adrift and alone. A fundamentalist worldview, then, comes along and says "follow all these rules to achieve salvation from your anomie and feelings of emptiness". They reassure because rules are inherently proof-in-action signifiers of belonging, and so they reinforce and stimulate those parts of us that crave connection.

As worldviews go, then, they are like opiates. They are addictive, simple, easy, and require no work. But it is a mistake to look at such worldviews and conclude that *all* religions and spirituality are so disposable and toxic. They are not. Studies reviewed in previous chapters show that a flexible, non-fundamentalist ideology, spirituality or religion can be protective and nourishing.

Connection in All Four Dimensions:

To avoid the above black holes of fundamentalism or reactionary/fascist conspiracy-theory-ridden paranoia, one has to build these connections of the individual, interpersonal, and community level *slowly*. Let them evolve organically, recognizing that hyper-individualism will often create frequent setbacks, squabbles, rebellions, and so forth. Remember also that whatever connecting efforts we do, it will need to come with some semblance of a proof-in-action indicator to be more substantial. Objects, rituals, crafts of material culture, art, etc, will all be used as symbols of belonging. We will need to be creative here and focus not on "deconstructing" the "meaning" but recognize that the meaning of these activities is *enacted* through their use and creation.

Equity and Economic Stability:

Without equity, any culture or sub-culture risks falling victim to the ABVS to some degree or another. Nobody is going to feel as though "we're all in this together" when there are florid inequities blasting everyone in the face. This is why close-knit communities like Roseto tend to discourage ostentatious displays of wealth—they are corrosive to community belonging. Only societies which are deliberately hierarchical like those with caste systems, or feudal systems of medieval Europe, where such inequities are imbued with some kind of cultural narrative or myth (for better or for worse) will inequities be less corrosive to cohesion. I am not saying such hierarchies are preferable or even desirable, I'm just saying that they can off-set inequities to a degree with a gloss of narrative to make them shiny, even if they are still unpalatable. Nevertheless, the Social Instincts evolved in hunter-gatherer conditions where humans lived in societies that are among the most egalitarian known. Thus hierarchies are almost always going to require artificial reinforcement.

Another way in which inequities can be offset is through ostentatious displays of *charity*, such as can be seen among Pacific Northwest indigenous peoples that practice potlatch gatherings–a brilliant cultural solution to this issue. In such gatherings, the wealthiest members are encouraged to outdo each other in terms of charitable acts. In other words, they are not encouraged by their culture to build yachts-within-yachts or drive around in $300,000 cars. They are encouraged to show their high social value by how much wealth they give others.

The effects of income disparity on mental health, reviewed in previous chapters, are evidence of the corrosive effect inequity can have on a society as a whole. The worse it gets, the more likely the ABVS arises and the more likely connections are going to be seen as phony sentiment, which the Social Instincts are always on guard against. Only when inequity is imbued with some kind of social meaning, reinforced by real-world obligations or gift-exchanges, etc., will it be less corrosive to social bonding.

Related to the above is a culture script involving an emphasis on humility rather than in-your-face striving to be "better" than everyone else. Widespread dispersal of boastful, bragging narratives are likely corrosive as well. Humility, however, does not need to mean self-deprecation or boundary-less overworking for others at the expense of oneself. This mistake I see also: well-meaning people burning themselves out constantly worrying about what everyone else wants from them and never taking any time to take care of their own needs or manage their own valid boundaries.

This situation is extremely counterproductive, but not perhaps for the reason you might think. It would be easy to look at this as another example of how "society"—which again gets conflated with family or authority figures—is diametrically opposed to "the individual". Society and individual should never be opposites. The consumer pseudoculture, along with our modern society of giant faceless governing entities, though, in combination with hyper-individualism, gives one this very illusion. As such, certain vulnerable people will feel the pressures of others and set aside their own values and needs, or worse, they will hide them away and never speak of them for fear of rejection.

All of this winds up putting some people in a regrettable state where the individual sacrifices herself or himself for the sake of others. This is not the ideal state of community participation, however. How much good can you do for others if you have burned yourself out? The error, here, is to assume that the two types of ends—individual and collective—are mutually exclusive. They aren't. If you damage yourself for the sake of others, in the manner of a martyr, then your goals become negated, and you unintentionally separate yourself from them. The answer is not martyrdom, then, but something much more difficult: a *managing* of goals, and a *negotiation* between individual and collective that orients toward similar ends.

Economic Stability and Family:

Finally, communities and families are subject to the constraints that our economic system places on them. As mentioned earlier, we can extoll the virtues of extended family, community, friend networks, and long-term partners all day long. But economic and cultural factors can corrode them easily. The ABVS, for example, tells us from our early years that sacrificing those things for greater material gain is not only acceptable but *expected*. Add to this the consumer pseudoculture that influences us from an early age, telling us to pursue personal interests in order to establish one's "authentic identity". We have technology capable of separating families over vast swathes of space, which strains connections. We can have a hyper-individualist value system that reflexively rebels against pseudoculture but leaves family and friends as collateral damage due to their false equivalence in our minds. We can separate children from their families for extended periods of time each day so as to make them less reliable and stable, and couple this with demands of longer hours, longer commutes, taking on extra jobs, all due to the financial situation of the common person.

Coupled with income inequality, poorer access to healthcare, food and income insecurity, and a paradoxical demand that we not "deprive" ourselves of the latest expensive things coming down the pipeline, we have powerful centrifugal forces acting to pull apart social bonds. We must work on a society that does not require so much time from ever-shrinking families to satisfy our Social Instincts. This would require less income inequality, better opportunities for the bottom 50% to have more for less money. Unfortunately, the current ruling powers of our country do not seem to have any interest in pursuing this. It may, therefore, mean that people need to try to become more self-sufficient rather than participate a system that is stacked in favor of runaway income and wealth disparity, increasing demands on family time and resources just to meet basic needs. These increasing demands take away precious mental and monetary resources to put effort into building communities and family networks.

Balancing Acts

As a final thought, I want to emphasize that reversing the toxic trends our culture has continued to progress toward, there will likely be no easy solutions. Balancing against the extremes will—as always—be the most difficult part. As we think about what we might want to do to better satisfy our Social Instincts, we will need to be aware of the main challenges facing us. Of course, we could also do nothing and simply continue down the path we are on and see where it leads. My concern about that, however, is that it will simply lead to more extremism, fundamentalism, and fascism, not to mention more and deadlier addictions. That is because all of these things tend to arise in *response* to starving Social Instincts (among other factors). If I'm right, it means doing nothing will therefore naturally result in more cults, more addiction epidemics (like the opiate and methamphetamine epidemics), more extremist ideologies, all within a context of continually worsening depression, anxiety, suicidality, loneliness, and the swathe of health problems that go along with these things.

If, on the other hand, we wish to try to find ways to re-connect one another along the individual, interpersonal, community, and universal dimensions of the Social Instincts, in order to alleviate the very real pain they cause when neglected, we will need to get to work. And this work will require care and nuance, so that we might avoid extremism. As I see it, the primary balancing acts are going to be threefold. At best I can only offer impressionistic ideas about what I think will work best—I will leave it to more expert minds in such areas to critique and hopefully refine what I am proposing. I am approaching this from the perspective of a psychoanalytically-minded psychiatrist. But I think it will require the input of sociologists, anthropologists, economists, city planners, civil engineers, and, perhaps most of all, historians and philosophers.

Autonomy Vs. Communitarianism:

First will be to build, rebuild, or augment communities and interpersonal networks that balance between the idiosyncratic desires of the participants and the common goals of the community. As a culture, over a hundred years of hyper-individualism has made us quite uneducated on how to be community-minded. In such areas, advice and guidance from those of other, more communally minded cultures will be wise to heed. We don't know how to "community"—we are too deeply entrenched in hyper-individualism and the dichotomy of "me vs. the pseudoculture". Communities are too often conflated with the artificially homogenized and falsely monolithic "society" more often than not thought of as the tyrannically oppressing forces from "people out there". Building a lasting community takes trust, time, and then after that, more time and more trust. I do not think it can be forced with any success.

I believe the key, however it is to be accomplished, will be the recognition of mutual commensurability between member and group. As long as they are seen as in direct opposition to one another, community and connection building will fail. This will require honest and respectful communication between group and member without recourse to authoritarian structures. It will require a recognition that, as Kipling put it in his novel *The Jungle Book*, "the strength of the pack is the wolf, and the strength of the wolf is the pack." Neither can exist without the other. What must be held in mind are those things which benefit BOTH wolf and pack, not one to the exclusion of the other. Those things which do not benefit both should be held in suspicion.

This means voluntary submission to group objectives—and this is where the dangers of extremism can come in. Starving Social Instincts can make this feel like a good idea when sometimes it isn't! When anthropologist Roy Rappaport, in his magisterial 1999 work, *Ritual and Religion and the Making of Humanity*, described the Tsembara Maring tribe of New Guinea during the 1960s, he noted that when the tribe members were discussing what to do next, they would gather in a building and discuss it until, as they put it "the many voices became one". This is likely the way it has been done in many societies throughout the ages—not as a rigid mandate from on high (that kind of thing came later during the early empires and has persisted in many contexts ever since), but as a discussion, involving time and hard work. This sort of thing, however ideal it may be, has physical limits to it: you cannot have a town-hall meeting with 350 million people. Nevertheless, the setting of no more than about 150 people (the typical maximum size for a foraging tribe) is the setting in which the Social Instincts evolved.

There are anthropologists such as Robin Dunbar in 1992, who have suggested, along with primatologists, that the number of 150 is likely the maximum cognitive limit of people individuals can maintain stable social relationships with. This is based on correlations between certain cortical brain areas and social behaviors in primates such as humans. That is, beyond this number it becomes extremely difficult to keep it straight who is who and how they relate to everyone else one knows. Beyond this, others melt into a faceless mass. Thus, when managing groups larger than this, we are forced to create giant centralized but anonymous bodies of bureaucratic levels in order to coordinate activities. And of course, civilizations have done so since the early empires.

While this may be effective, it starves the Social Instincts and sets up a false dichotomy between "me" and "society" because it cannot avail itself if the emotional and instinctual bonds that arise when dealing with people face-to-face, hashing out problems with them, negotiating differences and working on inter-group conflicts in the ancestral, "many voices become one" manner. And of course, even in such ideal conditions conflicts arose. In larger groups, however, the solution seems to have become using draconian tactics to enforce structure.

Now, perhaps, it becomes all-too-evident just how difficult this balancing act must be. Generally, however, satisfying the Social Instincts will only be accomplished by allowing individuals to become a part of some sort of community that is no larger than the above number. Small groups are all that is needed, but larger groups are not likely to help. The Social Instincts require real-time face-to-face interactions with people over time in order to form lasting bonds, and hierarchies are best used only as a last resort to accomplishing group goals. Rather, it seems to me a better approach to treat each individual of a group as a "specialist", which brings their own unique qualities to the table, whatever they are (i.e., the "superhero" model discussed in the last chapter).

Authentic Expression Vs. Acceptance, and the Paradox of Conformity:

By the time we get to the age where we are trying to build social bonds, we have already been exposed to years of mass media content that orients strongly toward hyper-individualism and de-emphasizes group belonging. We have all heard a lot of "just be yourself!" or "you can be anything you want to be!" and well-intentioned advice that goes more or less as follows. All of us, on the road to self-actualization, in order to be truly who we were meant to be, must cast aside the expectations of others, stop looking outside of ourselves for validation, and look ever deeper within to find who we truly are.

In such a hyper-individualist society, in which belonging and connection are so de-emphasized, and connections to partner, interpersonal network, community and nature are all stretched thin, it has always puzzled me as to why so many people (myself included) nonetheless feel so much "pressure to conform". And yet, I observe it time and again, both clinically and anecdotally. Adolescents especially feel this pressure and either wind up angrily rebelling against it or becoming neurotically preoccupied with it night and day. But conform with who? Doesn't one *need* some kind of substantive collective in order for the individual to feel friction agains? So why does this nonetheless happen? Why are so many feeling such pressure to conform when there is so little of real substance to be concerned about conforming *with*?

As we hinted at earlier, I believe it is largely to do with the background effect of the mass media pseudoculture. Day in and day out, from practically birth onward, we hear messages from the mass media, both verbal and non-verbal that exert pressure to conform, even if it is not explicitly intended to do so. Being humans with Social Instincts, we are primed and ready to cue-in to such messages, so as to better be able to "fit in" once we are of the age (around 9 or so) when the instincts begin to really kick into overdrive. By such time, we have heard and are worried about a nearly endless list of "should" and "shouldn't" messages we have internalized from the media. Not only are these messages vague, excessively focused on ABVS, and even contradictory, since we are so hyper-individualistic *and* we do not have a robust ritual culture from which to draw, we have no concrete way of confirming whether we are "really" members of the in-group or not.

This is a position of great anxiety, and there are many ways in which we express it, ranging from continually hand-wringing about one's place and whether or not one "fits in", to pretending like we don't care, to actively raging against the machine about "society's rules" and styling oneself as a "non-conformist". Trouble is, in a hyper-individualist society, the only person that really cares about any of this drama is the individual themselves. It's a tempest in a teacup, but subjectively it can result in a great deal of anguish.

This is the situation we are starting with in our community and connection-building efforts. Individuals will be hyper-sensitized to "conforming to the rules" and possibly be very defensive about their authenticity and freedom of expression. Or, on the other side, they may be only too-eager to adopt whatever is laid out in front of them, thinking it a necessary evil to sacrifice their authenticity for the sake of the group. But again, the tragedy here is that this is a false dichotomy largely and unintentionally created by the pseudoculture of the mass media. My suggestion here is that we go into community building with full knowledge of the difficulties and make sure a harmony is created between individual and group, rather than necessarily a "compromise". It is not a zero-sum game.

Rules Vs. Flexibility:

Finally, as we remember that community building will need ritualistic, concrete signifiers of adherence and belonging, as is found in rites, physical symbols, and so forth, it means the dreaded "rules" will need to be drawn up and/or discussed at length until "many voices become one". Rules make it real, and represent the difference between loosely bound collections of people in vague agreement with someone or something and actual communities which foster a deep sense of belonging. Rules of conduct, rules of inclusion, rules of taboo are all part of this and will need to be discussed openly. That said, I think in a hyper-individual world, erring on the side of fewer rules will likely be the best. I suspect that some readers may, upon the mere mention of rules, find their hackles raised. That feeling should be respected and understood.

Furthermore, I think such rules are best drawn up from a set of values and commitment to those values. Everyone should have a part to play in crafting these rules, and also think about what the consequences of not following them might be. These will not be easy conversations to have, especially considering the background many people will have going into these conversations is likely going to be of two main varieties: on one hand will be those brought up and internalized a hyper-individualistic value set. These people will bristle against any and all rules and tend to feel strongly that we should all just love one another and live and let live. This will be difficult to argue against because it is generally true. It is also, however, not the point of the discussion. Creating rules for community need not involve a negative judgment against those who choose not to follow them.

The second variety of backgrounds will involve those who were exposed to some kind of fundamentalist or ultra-rigid sub-culture. These people will be triggered by talk of rules and want to flee. They should be reminded that they are free to. What I am suggesting is culture building with and through the co-crafting of rules that involve concrete indicators or belonging that cannot be faked and were developed not by a single individual but by a group working in close contact and via bonds of trust with one another.

All that said, any rules made need to have a balanced amount of flexibility. There are not easy cookbook answers here, but the evidence on religious affiliation discussed in earlier chapters reveals that extremist groups do not contribute to good mental health. Thus, a fine balance between rules that are substantive and impactful, but not too rigid, will need to be found.

Will we find a way to do these things and reverse the trend toward loneliness that is worsening with each decade? Honestly, I don't know. Even my above suggestions, vague though they may be, may not be enough. But as people get more desperate to satisfy the Social Instincts, I believe it will likely still need to get worse before it gets better. As we saw with the changing depiction of models, whom the fashion industry was demanding be thinner and thinner, it took people *dying* before anyone made any real changes. That doesn't give me much cause to believe this will be any different, moreso because the issue is so much more complex and insidious. I hope I'm wrong.

Relationships

In a 2020 review of 43 different relationship studies by Joel et al., the qualities of a satisfying intimate partner relationship were measured to see which ones most correlated with relationship happiness. Interestingly enough, the most important predictors of relationship quality were perceived-partner commitment, feelings of appreciation for one's partner, sexual satisfaction, perceived-partner satisfaction, and low levels of conflict. These factors best predicted and correlated with marital happiness. Notice anything about these factors? They don't seem to include things that are culturally touted as important, like the perceived amount of money, looks, or fame in one's partner. It did not seem that common interests, personality differences, age at marriage, cohabitation prior to marriage, or a host of other variables mattered as much as the above, despite the fact that these things are often thought of in the lay media as important, and they are also factors that are emphasized in dating apps and relationship advice media platforms. In other words, it seems we may be quite wrongheaded about our ideas of forming happy long-term relationships. It would seem, rather, that instead of seeking a "soul mate", ready-made to plop in your lap, one must find a partner willing and able to *build* such a relationship with everyday acts of commitment, appreciation, and growth-mindedness.

As for the other "branches" of the Social Instincts, i.e., extended family/friends, community, and Nature, we are only now seeing attention paid to them, but still the majority of relationship focus is on long-term pair-bonding. This needs to change. We need more data on these other branches to have a clearer idea of exactly what needs to happen to allow them to grow and flourish. What I present in this book is merely the beginning.

And we must remember that economic factors, subtle but effective mass-media pressures, and other cultural fads will exert their influence on us, possibly limiting efforts at creating the space needed. We cannot tell everyone they need to spend more time in nature if they have no means of making ends meet. That said, a sober account of the fact that the latest expensive sexy gizmos do NOT actually make us happy may mean less pressure to expend time and energy trying to acquire them. A recognition that much of what we spend money on are addictive substitutes for what will actually make us happy may help to curtail the insidious pressure we all feel to pursue such things.

And let us not ignore the importance of artistic expression and *making* things. Making and doing can be concrete proof-through-action signifiers of all the above relationships that, I believe, will go a long way toward satisfying our Social Instincts. This is because the Social Instincts are rarely going to be satisfied with mere verbal sentiment and abstraction. When you act and create in ways that reinforce the bonds they crave, however, I believe the results will be far more effective than all the addictions we have access to. Such creative efforts also bring in the advantages of the inherent meaning-making power of the transcendent function, which ultimately may be the deciding factor in whether or not we manage to round the corner on the rising rates of depression, suicide, addiction, and anxiety.

Final Thoughts

Our powerful, and yet sometimes very subtle Social Instincts evolved during a long time period in our evolutionary history when early hominins (*Homo sapiens* and the many proto-human species in our direct ancestry) best survived in groups of 50–150 individuals who formed close bonds with one another, rarely spent any time alone, were constantly in natural environments for most of their time, and had a strong sense of identity. This identity was furthermore not simply conjured up out of abstract ideas or vehement expressions of sentiment, but made into concrete, physical signifiers such as body markings, clothing, traditional stories, symbolic images, music, clothing and especially ritual practices. Ritualized behaviors, including taboos and extended, complex and sometimes very intense enactments of belonging were commonly practiced and reinforced social categories within the tribes.

Bonds and experiences of family included not merely one's immediate parents and siblings (the so-called "nuclear familiy"), but ones extended family, such that given the inevitable variety of such relationships, others were always available. In other words, if I had a hard time bonding with my own parents, as sometimes happens, I might still have a strong, trusting, and loving bond with an uncle or aunt, grandparent or older cousin to "take me under their wing". The constant threat (or at least pressure) of enemies, predators, or hostile forces of nature continually reinforced the need for effective internal motivators of social bonding. Those who could not work together didn't last, and this probably applied to species as far back as several million years in hominin history.

Spirituality in such a context is, judging from indigenous cultures that exist today anyway, largely a matter of *participation* and not so much *belief*. If you participate in a ritual that has a spiritual gloss, but are yourself a skeptic, you can still do it without a lot of fuss, since indigenous spirituality tends to be more about orthopraxy rather than orthodoxy. By focusing on the physical enaction of the spirituality rather than lock-step alignment with orthodox belief, there is room for a variety of internal experiences, since all that matters is that one participate in the ritual. This has the advantage of being unambiguous. It is always possible to doubt whether or not someone is a "true" believer, but it is not possible to doubt whether or not someone performed the ritual—it is right there for God and everyone else to see! At the same time, myth and belief still provide narrative cohesion through its activation of non-verbal, archetypal ways of thinking that are deeply embodied and emotionally resonant (Goodwyn, 2022). In such tribes, individualism had its place but it was balanced by a typically more collective mindset and identity. Education was obtained informally from anyone in the tribe that tended to be interested in such things, or more formally as a matter of course in various extended rites of passage. Since such tribes were foragers, compared to the hyper specialized modern world, much of the education was "on the job" training, rather than years of rote learning separated from extended family.

There did not exist a constant influx of advertisement-driven media droning in the background throughout our formative years, and the number of addictions were relatively low—I suspect any culture that had access to alcohol (one of the world's oldest drugs) likely had the odd alcoholic. But there were none of the highly-refined and concentrated addictions we have now, to include not just drugs but achievement, beauty, food, pornography, video games, and now AI romantic friends. Not only that, but there was in all likelihood a far lower need for such things, since Social Instincts in the ancient settings were calibrated to foraging lifestyles which satisfied those instincts.

Ten thousand years ago, this lifestyle was the norm for all existing humans. Thus for the two million years advanced hominins have existed, we have been foragers for 99.5% of that time. But the number of such cultures now is far less than it was. The world has changed extremely rapidly in only a relatively short time span in evolutionary terms. That amount of time is not sufficient to recalibrate our instinctive proclivities, hence we are not well adapted to the increasingly artificial, disconnected, hypo-spiritual, mass media infused, addiction-laden environment we exist in now. Yet this is our plight, and there is no realistic way to go back, nor would we necessarily want to.

Instead we must figure out how to adjust our society to make it more *human*. We need to figure out ways to allow the time and space for bonds to reform, for non-fundamentalist spirituality to flourish, and for (non-abusive) extended families to remain in more consistent contact in a way that fosters them *getting along* with one another. This will require us to sacrifice *some* of our hyper-individualism–but not too much! We will need a way to temper mass media pseudoculture effects, and we will need to recognize what all the addictions are, under the surface, really aiming at: satisfying our Social Instincts. Above all we will need to create space for the nascent human psyche to *create meaning* on its own time. This is done by encouraging the arts at *all* levels. Art, dreams, stories, dance, music are all ways in which the transcendent function–something modern neuroscience can now measure better than ever–operates to make meaning. Meaning, however, that is not necessarily found in verbal explications, but through *symbolic expression*–the *language* of the transcendent function. Meaning-making, furthermore, not as co-opted capitalist enterprises aimed at producing faddish waves servicing the bottom line of some corporation. Rather, meaning as the organically made, home-grown variety, rough around the edges, but personally connected. We do not need plastic, AI-generated, profit-motivated art. We need the art of children of all ages.

If we can find ways to accomplish all that, we will be well on our way toward healing our starving Social Instincts.

Note

1 I realize tigers have formed bonds with caregivers in the past. However, my point is not whether or not they *can*, but rather, whether or not they *need* to the way we do. Tigers roaming the wilderness alone seem perfectly fine. Most humans, however, would struggle with this. Are there exceptions? Always–this is biology. But the general trend is that we crave each other's company and social bonds.

References

AAP. (2003). *Family pediatrics: Report of the task force on the family.* American Academy of Pediatrics.

AAP. (2011). *The pediatrician's role in family support and family support programs.* American Academy of Pediatrics.

Andreasen, N.C., O'Leary, D.S., Cizadlo, T., Arndt, S., Resai, K., Watkins, G.L., & Hichwa, R.D. (1995). Remembering the past: Two facets of episodic memory explored with positron emission tomography. *American Journal of Psychiatry,* 152, 1576–1585.

Antrobus, J.S. (2018). How does the waking and sleeping brain produce spontaneous thought and imagery, and why? In K.C.R. Fox & K. Christoff (Eds), *The Oxford handbook of spontaneous thought.* Oxford University Press, pp. 123–132.

Atran, S., & Medin, D. (2010). *The native mind and the cultural construction of nature.* The MIT Press.

Barnes, D.M., & Bates, L.M. (2017). Do racial patterns in psychological distress shed light on the Black-White depression paradox? A systematic review. *Social Psychiatry and Psychiatric Epidemiology,* 52, 913–928.

Bastian, S., Koval, P., Erbas, Y., Houben, M., Pe, M., & Kuppens, P. (2015). Sad and alone: Social expectancies for experiencing negative emotions are linked to feelings of loneliness. *Social Psychology and Personality Science.* https://doi.org/10.1177/1948550614568682.

Baumeister, R.F., & Leary, M.R. (1995). The need to belong: desire for interpersonal attachments as a fundamental human motivation. *Psychological Bulletin,* 117, 497–529.

Beaty, R.E., & Jung, R.E. (2018). Interacting brain networks underlying creative cognition and artistic performance. In K.C.R. Fox & K. Christoff (Eds), *The Oxford handbook of spontaneous thought.* Oxford University Press, pp. 275–284.

Bellah, R.N., Madsen, R., Sullivan, W.M., Swidler, A., & Tipton, S.M. (1985). *Habits of the heart: Individualism and commitment in American life.* University of California Press.

Bion, W. (1962). A theory of thinking. *International Journal of Psychoanalysis,* 43: 306–310.

Brooke, R. (1991/2015). *Jung and phenomenology.* Routledge.

Buckingham, S.A., Frings, D., & Albery, I.P. (2013). Group membership and social identity in addiction recovery. *Psychology of Addictive Behaviors,* 27(4), 1132–1140.

Buckner, R.L., Andrews-Hanna, J.R., & Schacter, D.L. (2008). The brain's default network: Anatomy, function, and relevance to disease. *Annals of the NY Academy of Sciences,* 1124, 1–38.

Cacioppo, J.G., Cacioppo, S., & Boomsma, D.I. (2014). Evolutionary mechanisms for loneliness. *Cognition and Emotion*, 28(1). doi:10.1080/02699931.2013.837379.

Cacioppo, J.G., Fowler, J., & Chistakis, N. (2009). Alone in the crowd: The structure and spread of loneliness in a large social network. *Journal of Personality and Social Psychology*, 97, 977.

Calati, R., Ferrari, C., Brittner, M., Oasi, O., Carvalho, A.F., & Courtet, P. (2019). Suicidal thoughts and behaviors and social isolation: A narrative review of the literature. *Journal of Affective Disorders*, 245, 653–667.

Callard, F., Smallwood, J., Golchert, J., & Margulies, D.S. (2013). The era of the wandering mind? Twenty-first century research on self-generated mental activity. *Frontiers in Psychology*, 4, 891.

Case, A., & Deaton, A. (2015). Rising morbidity and mortality in midlife among white non-Hispanic Americans in the 21st century. *Proceedings of the National Academy of Sciences of the United States of America*, 112, 15078–15083.

Chaudhary, N., Salali, G.D., & Swanepoel, A. (2023). Sensitive responsiveness and multiple caregiving networks among Mbendjele BaYaka hunter-gatherers: Potential implications for psychological development and well-being. *Developmental Psychology*. https://dx.doi.org/10.1037/dev0001601.

Chelnokova, O., Laeng, B., Eikemo, M., *et al.* (2014). Rewards of beauty: The opioid system mediates social motivation in humans. *Molecular Psychiatry*, 19, 746–747.

Childs, E. (2010). Religious attendance and happiness: Examining gaps in the current literature—a research note. *Journal for the Scientific Study of Religion*, 49(3), 550–560.

Christoff, K., Irving, Z.C., Fox, K.C.R., Spreng, R.N., & Andrews-Hanna, J.R. (2016). Mind-wandering as spontaneous thought: A dynamic framework. *Nature Reviews Neuroscience*, 17(11), 718–731.

Colman, W. (2006). Imagination and the imaginary. *Journal of Analytical Psychology*, 51, 21–41.

Compton, W.M., Conway, K.P., Stinson, F.S., & Grant, B.F. (2006). Changes in the prevalence of major depression and comorbid substance use disorders in the United States between 1991–1992 and 2001–2002. *American Journal of Psychiatry*, 163, 2141–2147.

Coon, J.T., Boddy, K., Stein, K., Whear, R., Barton, J., & Depledge, M.H. (2011). Does participating in physical activity in outdoor natural environments have a greater effect on physical and mental wellbeing than physical activity indoors? A systematic review. *Environmental Science and Technology*, 45, 1761–1772.

D'Argembeau, A. (2018). Mind-wandering and self-referential thought. In K.C.R. Fox & K. Christoff (Eds), *The Oxford handbook of spontaneous thought*. Oxford University Press, pp. 181–191.

DeNeve, K.M., & Cooper, H. (1998). The happy personality: A metaanalysis of 137 personality traits and subjective well-being. *Psychological Bulletin*, 124, 197–229.

Domhoff, G.W. (2018). Dreaming is an intensified form of mind-wandering, based in an augmented portion of the default network. In K.C.R. Fox & K. Christoff (Eds), *The Oxford handbook of spontaneous thought*. Oxford University Press, pp. 355–370.

Dunbar, R.I.B. (1992). Neocortex size as a constraint on group size in primates. *Journal of Human Evolution*, 22(6), 469–493.

Durkheim, E. (1897/1951). *Suicide*. Free Press.

Durrant, S.J., Taylor, C., Cairney, S., & Lewis, P.A. (2011). Sleep-dependent consolidation of statistical learning. *Neuropsychologia*, 49(5), 1322–1331.

Durvasula, S., Lysonski, S., & Watson, J. (2001). Does vanity describe other cultures? A cross-cultural examination of the vanity scale. *Journal of Consumer Affairs*, 35, 180–199. doi:10.1111/j.1745-6606.2001.tb0018.x.

Egolf, B., Lasker, J., Wolf, S., & Potvin, L. (1992). The Roseto effect: A 50-year comparison of mortality rates. *American Journal of Public Health*, 82(8), 1089–1092.

Eisenberger, N.I., & Lieberman, M.D. (2005). Why it hurts to be left out: The neurocognitive overlap between physical and social pain. In K.D. Williams, J.P. Forgas, and W. Von Hippel (Eds), *The social outcast: Ostracism, social exclusion, rejection, and bullying*. Psychology Press.

Engel, G., & Romano, J. (1977). *The biopsychosocial model approach*. Rochester University. www.urmc.rochester.edu/medialibraries/urmcmedia/education/md/documents/biopsychosocial-model-approach.pdf.

Etzioni, A. (1993). *The spirit of community: Rights, responsibilities and the communitarian agenda*. Crown.

Fischer, S., & Born, J. (2009). Anticipated reward enhances offline learning during sleep. *Journal of Experimental Psychology: Learning, Memory, and Cognition*, 35(6), 1586–1593.

Fiss, H. (1995). The post-Freudian dream: A reconsideration of dream theory based on recent sleep laboratory findings. In H. Bareuther, K. Brde, M. Evert-Saleh, & N. Spangenbert (Eds), *Traum und Gedächtnis. Materialien aus dem Sigmund-Freud-Institut* (Vol. 15). Lit.

Fosse, M.J., Fosse, R., Hobson, J.A., & Stickgold, R.J. (2003). Dreaming and episodic memory: A functional dissociation? *Journal of Cognitive Neuroscience*, 15(1), 1–9.

Fosshage, L. L. (1987). New vistas on dream interpretation. In M. Glucksman (Ed.), *Dreams in New Perspective*. Uman Sciences Press, pp. 187–207.

Foster, J.D., Campbell, W.K., & Twenge, J.M. (2003). Individual differences in narcissism: Inflated self-views across the lifespan and around the world. *Journal of Research in Personality*, 37, 469–486.

Fox, K.C.R. (2018). Neural origins of sel-generated thought: Insights from intracranial electrical stimulation and recordings in humans. In K.C.R. Fox & K. Christoff (Eds), *The Oxford handbook of spontaneous thought*. Oxford University Press, pp. 165–179.

Fox, K.C.R., & Christoff, K. (2018). Introduction: Toward an interdisciplinary science of spontaneous thought. In K.C.R. Fox & K. Christoff (Eds), *The Oxford handbook of spontaneous thought*. Oxford University Press, pp. 3–8.

Fox, K.C.R., Nijeboer, S., Solomonova, E., Domhoff, G.W., & Christoff, K. (2013). Dreaming as mind wandering: Evidence from functional neuroimaging and first-person content reports. *Frontiers in Human Neuroscience*, 7, 412.

Freud, S. (1900). *The interpretation of dreams*. Franz Deuticke.

Freud, S. (1929/2002). *Civilization and its discontents*. Penguin.

Freud, S. (1990). *Group psychology and the analysis of the ego*. W.W. Norton & Company.

Gale, C.R., Boothe, T., Mottus, R., Kuh, D., & Deary, I.J. (2013). Neuroticism and extraversion in youth predict mental wellbeing and life satisfaction 40 years later. *Journal of Research in Personality*, 47(6), 687–697.

Gallagher, A.G., Dinan, T.G., & Baker, L.J.V. (1994). The effects of varying auditory input on schizophrenic hallucinations: A replication. *Psychology and Psychotherapy: Theory, Research and Practice*, 67(1), 67–75.

Goodwyn, E. (2012). *The neurobiology of the gods*. Routledge.

Goodwyn, E. (2016). *Healing symbols in psychotherapy: A ritual approach*. Routledge.

Goodwyn, E. (2018). *Understanding dreams and other spontaneous images: The invisible storyteller*. Routledge.

Goodwyn, E. (2021). Bodies and minds, heaps and syllables. *Synthese*, 199, 8831–8855.

Goodwyn, E. (2022). *Archetype and clinical application: How the genome responds to experience*. *Journal of Analytical Psychology*, 67(3), 838–859.

Grant, J.T. (2014). *The Great Decline: 61 years of religiosity in one graph, 2013 hits a new low*. http://tobingrant.religionnews.com/2014/01/27/great-decline-religion-united-states-one-graph/.

Grover, S., & Helliwell, J.F. (2019). How's life at home? New evidence on marriage and the set point for happiness. *Journal of Happiness Studies*, 20, 373–390. http://dx.doi.org/10.1007/s10902-017-9941-3.

Haney, C. (2019). Restricting the use of solitary confinement. *Annual Review of Criminology*, 1, 285–310.

Haule, J.R. (2010). *Jung in the 21st century: Two volumes*. Routledge.

Hawkley, L.C., Browne, M.W., & Cacioppo, J.T. (2005). How can I connect with thee? Let me count the ways. *Psychological Science*, 16(10), 798–804.

Hidaka, B.H. (2012). Depression as a disease of modernity: Explanations for increasing prevalence. *Journal of Affective Disorders*, 140(3), 205–214.

Hollan, D.W., & Wellenkamp, J.C. (1994). *Contentment and suffering: Culture and experience in Toraja*. Columbia University Press.

Hollan, D.W., & Wellenkamp, J.C. (1996). *The thread of life: Toraja reflections on the life cycle*. University of Hawaii Press.

Inagaki, T. K., Hazlett, L., & Andreescu, C. (2019). Naltrexone alters responses to social and physical warmth: Implications for social bonding. *Social, Cognitive, and Affective Neuroscience*, 14(5), 471–479.

Joel, S., Eastwick, P.W., Allison, C.J., et al. (2020). Machine learning uncovers the most robust self-report predictors of relationship quality across 43 longitudinal couples studies. PNAS, 117(32), 19061–19071.

Jung, C.G. (1933). *Modern man in search of a soul*. Kegan Paul.

Jung, C.G. (1954/1966). *CW16*. Princeton University Press.

Jung, C.G. (1960/2002). *CW8*. Routledge.

Jung, C.G. (1966/1999). *CW7*. Routledge.

Karagianis, J., Novick, D., Pecenak, J., Haro, J.M., Dossenbach, M., Treuer, T., Montgomery, W., Walton, R., & Lowry, A.J. (2009). Worldwide-schizophrenia outpatient health outcomes (W-SOHO): Baseline characteristics of pan-regional observational data from more than 17,000 patients. *International Journal of Clinical Practice*, 63(11), 1578–1588.

Kessler, R.C., Angermeyer, M., Anthony, J.C., et al. (2007). Lifetime prevalence and age-of-onset distributions of mental disorders in the World Health Organization's World Mental Health Survey Initiative. *World Psychiatry*, 6, 168–176.

Keyes, C.F. (1986). The interpretive basis of depression. In A.M. Kleinman & B. Good (Eds), *Culture and depression: Studies in the anthropology and cross-cultural psychiatry of affect and disorder*. University of California Press, pp. 153–174.

Kitayama, S., & Park, J. (2010). Cultural neuroscience of the self: Understanding the social grounding of the brain. *SCAN*, 5, 111–129.

Klerman, G.L., & Weissman, M.M. (1989). Increasing rates of depression. *JAMA*, 261, 2229–2235.

Klinger, E. (2009). Daydreaming and fantasizing: Thought flow and motivation. In K. D. Markman, W.M.P. Klein, & J.A. Suhr (Eds), *Handbook of imagination and mental simulation*. Psychology Press, pp. 225–239.

Klinger, E., & Cox, W.M. (1987). Dimensions of thought flow in everyday life. *Imagination, Cognition and Personality*, 7, 105–128.

Klinger, E., & Cox, W.M. (2011). Motivation and the goal theory of current concerns. In W.M. Cox & E. Klinger (Eds), *Handbook of motivated counseling* (2nd ed.). John Wiley & Sons, pp. 3–47.

Klinger, E., Marchetti, I., & Koster, E.H.W. (2018). Spontaneous thought and goal pursuit: From functions such as planning to dysfunctions such as rumination. In K. C.R. Fox & K. Christoff (Eds), *The Oxford handbook of spontaneous thought*. Oxford University Press, pp. 215–232.

Koenig, H.G., & Larson, D.B. (2001). Religion and mental health: Evidence for an association. *International Review of Psychiatry*, 13, 67–78.

Kohut, H.(1977). *The Restoration of the Self*. New York, NY: International Universities Press.

Konner, M. (2010). *The evolution of childhood: Relationships, emotion, mind*. Harvard University Press.

Kradin, R. (2008). *The placebo response and the power of unconscious healing*. Routledge.

Kramer, M., & Glucksman, M. L. (2015). *Dream research: Contributions to clinical practice*. Routledge.

Kucyi, A. (2018). Pain and spontaneous thought. In K.C.R. Fox & K. Christoff (Eds), *The Oxford handbook of spontaneous thought*. Oxford University Press, pp. 521–528.

Lau, H., Tucker, M.A., & Fishbein, W. (2010). Daytime napping: Effects on human direct associative and relational memory. *Neurobiology of Learning and Memory*, 93(4), 554–560.

Louv, R. (2012). *The nature principle*. Algonquin Books.

Luppino, F.S., de Wit, L.M., Bouvy, P.F., Stijnen, T., Cuijpers, P., Penninx, B.W., & Zitman, F.G. (2010). Overweight, obesity, and depression: A systematic review and meta-analysis of longitudinal studies. *Archives of General Psychiatry*, 67, 220–229.

Markus, H.R., & Kitayama, S. (1991). Culture and the self: Implications for cognition, emotion, and motivation. *Psychological Review*, 98(2), 224–253.

McLanahan, S., & Sawhill, I. (2015). Marriage and child well being revisited: Introducing the issue. *The Future of Children*, 25(2), 3–10.

McPherson, M., Smith-Lovin, L., & Brashears, M. (2006). Social isolation in America: Changes in core discussion networks over two decades. *American Sociological Review*, 71, 353.

Meltzer, D. (1983). *Dream – Life – a Re-Examination of the Psychoanalytical Theory and Technique*. Strathclyde: Clunie Press.

Morelli, G. (2015). The evolution of attachment theory and cultures of human attachment in infancy and early childhood. In L.A. Jensen (Ed.), *The Oxford handbook of human development and culture*. Oxford University Press, pp. 35–46.

Morewedge, C.K., & Kupor, D.M. (2018). When the absence of reasoning breeds meaning: metacognitive appraisals of spontaneous thought. In K.C.R. Fox & K. Christoff (Eds), *The Oxford handbook of spontaneous thought*. Oxford University Press, pp. 35–46.

Ninety-Seventh American Assembly. (2000). *Strengthening American families: Reweaving the social tapestry.* American Assembly.

NSF. (2009). *Sleep in America poll: Summary of findings.* National Sleep Foundation.

O'Callaghan, C., & Irish, M. (2018). Candidate mechanisms of spontaneous cognition as revealed by dementia syndromes. In K.C.R. Fox & K. Christoff (Eds), *The Oxford handbook of spontaneous thought.* Oxford University Press, pp. 493–507.

Oishi, S., & Kesebir, S. (2015). Income inequality explains why economic growth does not always translate to an increase in happiness. *Psychological Science,* 26, 1630–1638.

Panksepp, J. (1998/2004). *Affective neuroscience.* Oxford University Press.

Panksepp, J., Wright, J.S., Dobrossy, M.H., Schlaepfer, T.E., & Coenen, V.A. (2014). Affective neuroscience strategies for understanding and treating depression: From preclinical models to three novel therapeutics. *Clinical Psychology Science,* 2, 472–494.

Paris, J. (2014). The narcissism epidemic: Commentary on modernity and narcissistic personality disorder. *Personality Disorders: Theory, Research, and Treatment,* 5(2), 227–229.

Payne, J.D., Stickgold, R., Swanberg, K., & Kensinger, E.A. (2008). Sleep preferentially enhances memory for emotional components of scenes. *Psychological Science,* 19(8), 781.

Petrovic, P., Pleger, B., Seymour, B., *et al.* (2008). Blocking central opiate function modulates hedonic impact and anterior cingulate response to rewards and losses. *Journal of Neuroscience,* 28, 10509–10516.

Pryor, J.H., Hurtado, B., Saenz, V.B., Santos, J.L., & Korn, W.S. (2007). *The American freshman: Forty-year trends, 1966–2006.* Higher Education Research Institute.

Raison, C.L., Lowry, C.A., & Rook, G.A.W. (2010). Inflammation, sanitation, and consternation: Loss of contact with coevolved, tolerogenic microorganisms and the pathophysiology and treatment of major depression. *Archives of General Psychiatry,* 67, 1211.

Rappaport, R. (1999). *Ritual and religion in the making of humanity.* Cambridge University Press.

Roesler, C. (2023). Dream interpretation and empirical dream research—An overview of research findings and their connections with psychoanalytic dream theories. *The International Journal of Psychoanalysis,* 104(2), 301–330.

Sánchez-Villegas, A., Delgado-Rodriguez, M., Alonso, A., Schlatter, J., Lahortiga, F., Majem, L.S., & Martinez-Gonzalez, M.A. (2009). Association of the Mediterranean dietary pattern with the incidence of depression: The Seguimiento Universidad de Navarra/University of Navarra follow-up (SUN) cohort. *Archives of General Psychiatry,* 66, 1090.

Savci, M., & Aysan, F. (2017). Technological addictions and social connectedness: Predictor effect of internet addiction, social media addiction, digital game addiction and smartphone addiction on social connectedness. *The Journal of Psychiatry and Neurological Sciences,* 30, 202–216.

Schacter, D.L., & Addis, D.R. (2007). On the constructive episodic simulation of past and future events. *Behavioral and Brain Sciences,* 30, 331–332.

Schieffelin, E.L. (1986). The cultural analysis of depressive affect: An example from New Guinea. In A.M. Kleinman & B. Good (Eds), *Culture and depression: Studies in the anthropology and cross-cultural psychiatry of affect and disorder.* University of California Press, pp. 101–133.

Schwartz, B. (2000). Self-determination: The tyranny of freedom. *American Psychologist*, 55, 79–88.

Seligman, A.B., Weller, R.P., Puett, M.J., & Simon, B. (2008). *Ritual and its consequences: An essay on the limits of sincerity*. Oxford University Press.

Shephard, R.J., & Rode, A. (1996). *The consequences of 'modernization.' Evidence from circumpolar peoples*. Cambridge University Press.

Sherman, L.E., Minas, M., & Greenfield, P.M. (2013). The effects of text, audio, video, and in-person communication on bonding between friends. *Cyberpsychology: Journal of Psychosocial Research on Cyberspace*, 7(2), Article1.

Sio, U.N., & Ormerod, T.C. (2009). Does incubation enhance problem solving? A meta-analytic review. *Psychological Bulletin*, 135, 94–120.

Smallwood, J., Ruby, F.J., & Singer, T. (2013). Letting go of the present: Mind-wandering is associated with reduced delay discounting. *Consciousness and Cognition*, 22(1), 1–7.

Smith, T.W. (1997). Factors relating to misanthropy in contemporary American society. *Social Science Research*, 26, 170–196.

Stan, D., & Christoff, K. (2018a). The mind wanders with ease: low motivational intensity is an essential quality of mind-wandering. In K.C.R. Fox & K. Christoff (Eds), *The Oxford handbook of spontaneous thought*. Oxford University Press, pp. 47–53.

Stand, D., & Christoff, K. (2018b). Potential clinical benefits and risks of spontaneous thought: Unconstrained attention as a way into and a way out of psychological disharmony. In K.C.R. Fox & K. Christoff (Eds), *The Oxford handbook of spontaneous thought*. Oxford University Press, pp. 479–491.

Stevens, A. (2003). *Archetype revisited*. Inner City Books.

Stolorow, R. (1978). Themes in dreams. A brief contribution to therapeutique technique. *International Journal of Psycho-Analyis*, 59, 473–475.

Stolorow, R., & Atwood, G. (1993). Psychoanalytic phenomenology of the dream. In S. Flanders (Ed.), *The dream discourse today*. Routledge, pp. 213–228.

The Sutton Trust. (2014). *Baby bonds report*. www.suttontrust.com/our-research/baby-bonds-early-years/.

Twenge, J.M. (2000). The age of anxiety? The birth cohort change in anxiety and neuroticism, 1952–1993. *Journal of Personality and Social Psychology*, 79, 1007–1021.

Twenge, J.M., & Cooper, A.B. (2020). The expanding class divide in happiness in the United States, 1972–2016. *Journal of the American Psychological Association*. http://dx.doi.org/10.1037/emo0000774.

Twenge, J.M., Gentile, B., DeWall, C., Ma, D., Lacefield, K., & Schurtz, D. (2010). Birth cohort increases in psychopathology among young Americans, 1938–2007: A cross-temporal meta-analysis of the MMPI. *Clinical Psychology Review*, 30, 145–154.

Twenge, J.M., Haidt, J., Blake, A.B., McAllister, C., Lemon, H., & Le Roy, A. (2021). Worldwide increases in adolescent loneliness. *Journal of Adolescence*. https://doi.org/10.1016/j.adolescence.2021.06.006.

Vahia, I.V., Chattillion, E., Kavirajan, H., & Depp, C.A. (2011). Psychological protective factors. *Psychiatric Clinical Neuroscience in America*, 34, 231–248.

Wamsley, E.J., Hamilton, K., Graveline, Y.M., Mancoer, S., & Arr, E. (2016). Test expectation enhances memory consolidation across both sleep and wake. *SLEEP*, 36 (Suppl), A78.

Weber, S.R., & Pargament, K.I. (2014). The role of religion and spirituality in mental health. *Current Opinion in Psychiatry*, 27, 358–363.

Weber, S.R., Pargament, K.I., Kunik, M.E., Lomax, J.W., & Stanley, M.A. (2012). Psychological distress among religious nonbelievers: A systematic review. *Journal of Religion and Health*, 51, 72–86.

Wegner, D.M., Wenzlaff, R.M., & Kozac, M. (2004). Dream rebound: The return of suppressed thoughts in dreams. *Psychological Science*, 15, 232–236.

Weinberger, A.H., Gbedemah, M., Martinez, A.M., Nash, D., Galea, S., & Goodwin, R.D. (2018). Trends in depression prevalence in the USA from 2005 to 2015: Widening disparities in vulnerable groups. *Psychological Medicine*, 48, 1308–1315.

Wilhelm, I., Diekelmann, S., Molzow, I., Ayoub, A., Mölle, M., & Born, J. (2011). Sleep selectively enhances memory expected to be of future relevance. *The Journal of Neuroscience: The Official Journal of the Society for Neuroscience*, 31(5), 1563–1569.

Wilson, E.O. (2013). *The social conquest of Earth*. Liveright.

Wittouck, C., Autreve, S.V., Jaegere, E.D., Portzky, G., & Heeringen, K.V. (2011). The prevention and treatment of complicated grief: A meta-analysis. *Clinical Psychological Review*, 31(1), 69–78.

World Health Organization. (2021). Depression. September 15. www.who.int/newsroom/fact-sheets/detail/depression.

Yeomans, M.R., & Gray, R.W. (1997). Effects of naltrexone on food intake and changes in subjective appetite during eating: Evidence for opioid involvement in the appetizer effect. *Physiology and Behavior*, 62, 15–21.

Yu, B., Zhang, X., Wang, C., Sun, M., Jin, L., & Liu, X. (2020). Trends in depression among adults in the United States, NHANES 2005–2016. *Journal of Affective Disorders*, 263, 609–620.

Zedelius, C.M., & Schooler, J.W. (2018). Unraveling what's on our minds: How different types of mind-wandering affect cognition and behavior. In K.C.R. Fox & K. Christoff (Eds), *The Oxford handbook of spontaneous thought*. Oxford University Press, pp. 233–247.

Zhu, Y., Zhang, L., Fan, J., & Han, S. (2007). Neural basis of cultural influence on self representation. *Neuroimage*, 34, 1310–1317.

Zlotnick, C. (2007). Community versus individual level indicators to identify pediatric health care needs. *Journal of Urban Health*, 84(1), 45–59.

Index

For Product Safety Concerns and Information please contact our EU
representative GPSR@taylorandfrancis.com
Taylor & Francis Verlag GmbH, Kaufingerstraße 24, 80331 München, Germany